COUNSELLING SKILLS

Margaret Hough

Lecturer in Social Care and Counselling St...

Addison Wesley Longman Limited
Edinburgh House, Harlow, Essex CM20 2JE,
England

First published 1996
ISBN 0582 28738 3

Produced by Longman Singapore Publishers Pte Ltd
Printed in Singapore

Contents

5 CHALLENGE AND CHANGE

8 GROUP COMMUNICATION

Acknowledgements

Front cover: Tony Stone Images / Bruce Ayres

We are indebted to the British Association for Counselling for permission to quote from Information Sheet No. 10 and the BAC Code of Ethics and Practice for Counsellors and the European Association for Counselling for permission to quote from the EAC Information Leaflet.

The author would like to thank her husband David for the diagrams, illustrations and indexing, Sue Beesley for typing the manuscript, Barbara Eden for proof reading, and Joyce Craven for her selection of photographs.

This book is dedicated to the memory of her mother.

Introduction

This book is about counselling and helping skills and is intended for use by students who are studying introductory or foundation level counselling skills courses. It does not contain extensive reference to theory, although the model on which most of the material is based is the person-centred or Rogerian approach to counselling. The emphasis in each chapter is on identifying and describing the appropriate skills which should be used at different stages throughout the counselling process. In addition to this, the significance of the counselling relationship is underlined, and the importance of adequate professional training and supervision for counsellors is consistently highlighted.

Students who are learning counselling skills for the first time, need a substantial amount of help and support from the teachers who are involved in training them. For this reason, the practical exercises which are included in each chapter are designed to be carried out in training groups and under the guidance of experienced facilitators. Teachers and trainers know their own students well, and in counsellor training this is especially important since many of the subjects or issues raised in discussion may cause heightened emotional reactions which need to be handled with great sensitivity, tact and care. The practical exercises have been designed with these considerations in mind; so they should be appropriate for basic and foundation level training, especially when their use is well timed and supervised.

There is an increasing emphasis on the inclusion of communication skills studies on a wide variety of courses, particularly in the field of health and caring. Teachers involved in these courses will find the content of this book useful for their work as well, especially those chapters which deal with interpersonal skills and their use in a variety of care settings. There is a need, however, to make a clear distinction between professional counsellor training, and the kind of interpersonal or interactive skills courses which are now so popular. On the one hand, professional counsellor training is very specific and includes a central focus on trainee self-development and awareness – elements which are regarded as necessary for student growth and a capacity to understand other people. Communication courses are, on the other hand, usually designed for those people who wish to relate more effectively to others, at work or at home; often these courses are too short to facilitate the kind of personal development which is so important for trainee counsellors. As well as this, communication skills courses have wide application in that they are generally designed for people in diverse occupations, including teaching, nursing, social and pastoral work, occupational therapy, childcare and youth work. The point should be stressed that communication skills courses are simply different, and certainly not inferior. In future it may be that more emphasis will be placed on interpersonal skills training for everyone at work. If this happens, there may be less demand for specific counsellor training, since many of the students who apply for it now do so because they wish to enhance their interactive skills generally. In other words, it is possible that some people will, in the future, seek to learn basic counselling skills without ever wishing to become a counsellor themselves. It seems to me that this is a possibility which should be welcomed, especially if the distinction between specific counsellor training and training in the use of counselling/interpersonal skills is kept firmly in view.

One of the main objectives of this book is to help students understand the importance of good interactive and interpersonal skills in all relationships and social contexts, and for this reason a chapter specifically devoted to groupwork is included in it. The case studies which accompany each chapter – with the exception of the last – are meant to highlight the skills and concepts which were dealt with in the text. I have tried to give varied examples of good practice and to stress the point that counselling has its limitations, and is not always guaranteed to provide a successful outcome in every instance. In order to ensure client anonymity, and to uphold the principle of confidentiality, I have been careful to change all identifiable details in these case studies. Throughout the general text, the use of the personal pronoun 'she' is frequently used in relation to the counsellor, but this is for convenience only. It is certainly not based on a conviction that most counsellors are – or should be – women. In the same way, the use of the pronoun 'he' to describe many of the clients is a convenient way of avoiding semantic confusion and does not reflect in any way the gender ratio of clients who seek counselling.

COUNSELLOR TRAINING: SOME IMPORTANT COMPONENTS

CHAPTER 1

Counselling and helping

The whys and wherefores

Within the past two decades, counselling as a helping activity has grown both in popularity and general availability throughout the United Kingdom. This increase is not totally uniform across the country, however, since some areas such as cities have seen the practice of counselling burgeoning while other more remote areas are less well served in terms of training opportunities for counsellors, and access to trained counsellors by the people – or clients – who seek help. In this chapter we shall consider a range of important questions relating to counselling and its practice, and look at its evolution, antecedents, and the ways in which it differs from other helping activities.

The following is a list of questions which serve as a useful starting point for discussion. Each question will be considered individually, although many overlap or merge.

- What is counselling?
- How does counselling differ from giving advice?
- When was counselling first used?
- What are counselling skills?
- Who are the people who use these skills?
- Is counselling different from other helping activities?
- Can friends or relatives counsel?
- Why are self-development and self-awareness important elements in counsellor training?
- Why do people want to become counsellors?
- What are the qualities of a good counsellor?
- What are the aims of counselling?

WHAT IS COUNSELLING?

This is probably one of the most difficult questions of all to answer, although it is deceptively straightforward at first glance. Definitions of the word counselling are numerous and dictionary interpretations unhelpful since they tend to stress the word 'advice' which is essentially the opposite of what the therapeutic counsellor aims to give. True counselling takes places when one person enlists the help of another in order to deal more effectively with a problem or problems currently experienced. Problems in the present may well be linked to past or childhood events, or they may be related to anticipated future events which cause anxiety or worry. In either case, the person who has come for counselling – the client – has acknowledged, implicitly at least, that they have reached an impasse through which they require some assistance in order to proceed.

This last point is worth emphasizing, for even though the majority of counsellors are concerned to stress the interactive nature of counselling, and to distance themselves from the idea of counsellors as experts, the fact remains that clients – when they first come for counselling – have some expectations that the counsellor will possess the knowledge, ability and expertise which they themselves lack. In such a situation, the power balance is tilted in the counsellor's favour, and unless student counsellors fully understand this, problems can arise and abuse of position can become a real possibility. Some of these problems will be discussed in more detail in Chapter 9. For the present it needs to be stressed that even though the fundamental goal of counselling is to help clients locate and trust their own capabilities and strength, clients often do not see it like this at first, and may well expect to be told what to do by the counsellor. Clients who are emotionally upset are vulnerable and open to suggestion, and it may take some considerable time before they are in a position to identify and use their own resources fully. The British Association for Counselling includes the following in its definitions of counselling:

> 'The counsellor may set out the options open to clients and help them to follow whichever one they choose. The counsellor may help the client to examine in detail the situations or behaviour which are proving troublesome and to find a small but crucial point where it would be possible to initiate some change as a start. Whatever approach the counsellor uses . . . client autonomy is the ultimate aim: for the client to make their own choices, to make their own decisions and put them into action.'
>
> (BAC Information Sheet 10, 1990)

How can clients be helped to locate and trust their own capabilities and strength? In the first place, they may seem overwhelmed by problems and forces which they consider to be outside their own control. They may have had the experience of seeking help from friends or relatives who have been unable or unwilling to give the time and commitment needed. Trained counsellors, on the other hand, do have the time and commitment, and unlike relatives and friends they are not emotionally involved with clients' problems. In addition to this, clients are given an assurance of confidentiality in counselling, and the counsellor – who will have explored their own feelings, attitudes and prejudices in some detail during training – should be sufficiently confident and self-aware in order to become a non-judgemental and supportive presence. A range of communication skills is used by the counsellor so that the client is encouraged to speak freely, to express strong or negative emotions if they wish to, and through these processes to achieve a deeper understanding of the various issues concerning them.

In order to achieve these outcomes, the process of counselling needs a structure or framework through which the counsellor can work with the client in a coherent and systematic way. Although it is not always possible – or even desirable – to stick rigidly to a pre-determined framework, it is still essential to have one if only to act as a reference point and overall guide to the process of therapy. Perhaps the best known model is described by Egan and outlined in *The Skilled Helper* (Egan, 1990). Egan gives a systematic approach to counselling based on three main stages which are then sub-divided into further stages. These three stages are derived from a problem-solving approach to clients' problems, and they include the counsellor skills necessary to help clients deal with their problems. The stages which Egan outlines are the following:

STAGE 1   Exploration and clarification of present problems.

STAGE 2   Development of new understanding. Looking at goals and objectives.

STAGE 3   Devising and implementing plans of action. Moving forward towards a preferred scenario. (Egan, 1990)

The skills which Egan describes within these stages will be discussed in more detail throughout later chapters.

Apart from the structure or framework of counselling, there are also many theoretical approaches to it. These theoretical approaches have evolved from three principal 'schools' or orientations. These are:

- the Psychodynamic Approach
- the Behavioural Approach
- the Humanistic Approach.

THE
PSYCHODYNAMIC
APPROACH

This approach to counselling has its origins in Freudian theory. It is a model which stresses the importance of childhood experience, and seeks to establish links between past and present by drawing parallels between what has happened in childhood and what is currently happening in adult life.

THE
BEHAVIOURAL
APPROACH

This orientation is concerned with actual, observable behaviour and stems from the work of a number of psychologists who, at the beginning of the century, did experiments with animals in order to formulate and validate their theories. People's problems are seen in terms of learned behaviours which are often problematic; for example, phobias or obsessions, and the objective of therapy is to help clients 'unlearn' these patterns through a process of behaviour modification.

The Psychodynamic Approach stresses the importance of childhood experience.

THE
HUMANISTIC
APPROACH

This approach assumes that clients themselves have an intuitive know-ledge of what it is they need and want. People's problems are seen as entirely unique to them, and the most important aspect of any Humanistic therapy is to facilitate the clients' growth towards self-actualization, inte-gration and wholeness.

These three broad classifications can, in turn, be sub-divided into many different schools of therapy. Common to all of them, however, are the basic skills or tools necessary for effective counselling.

HOW DOES COUNSELLING DIFFER FROM GIVING ADVICE?

We have already seen that dictionary definitions of the word counselling are unhelpful since they tend to stress the word 'advice' and in some cases the counsellor is defined as an 'advisor' (*The Concise Oxford Dictionary of Word Origins Vol. III*). The word counsel is derived from the Latin *consilium* which translated means advice, judgement or consultation. It is obvious, therefore, that the term counselling traditionally referred to the practice of giving advice or of passing judgement. This probably explains why so many people still believe that a counsellor's main function is to fulfil the twin roles of adviser and judge. The situation is complicated even further by the fact that many people in a range of diverse occupations now describe themselves as counsellors, even though they are not involved in any form of therapeutic work in the strict sense. Thus we have colour counsellors, beauty counsellors, financial counsellors, horoscope counsellors, interior design counsellors and career counsellors – to name just a few. The intention here is not to disparage the work done by these people but simply to point out that they all give advice as part of their work. Any confusion then, on the part of the general public with regard to counselling, is easy to understand. The most important point to establish about therapeutic counselling – which refers to the help offered to clients for a range of psychological and emotional problems and is the kind of counselling we are concerned with here – is that advice is not given, at least not in a direct or explicit way. It would be naive to say that counsellors never influence their clients indirectly because, of course, they do. In fact, because the counselling relationship itself is the most important factor in therapeutic counselling, the counsellor is bound to influence the client, who after all came for help. As well as this, counsellors often encourage clients to re-assess their lives and relationships in order to clarify issues which may be problematic for them, and when this re-assessment takes place, a range of options for change may also be discussed. So even when direct advice is not given, clients are frequently influenced by the counsellor's ideas, attitudes, and even sometimes by their unexpressed views. The ways in which a counsellor's unexpressed views can be interpreted by the client will be discussed in more detail in a later chapter. In this section the intention is to look critically at the issue of advice, and to establish why it is inappropriate in therapeutic counselling. The following are some of the reasons for not giving advice in counselling.

- Very often people don't want advice. They want to be listened to and understood instead.

- The advice given may be the wrong advice.

- People seldom take advice, especially when they feel it is not right for them.

- If advice turns out to be wrong then a person who has accepted it can abdicate personal responsibility. After all, it wasn't their idea.

- Clients in counselling need to view their own abilities and experience as valuable. Any advice from a counsellor would question this basic tenet.

- Equality is vital in the counselling relationship. If advice is given by the counsellor the role of 'expert' is reinforced, and equality is denied.

- Giving advice can be offensive and intrusive, especially when the person being advised is emotionally upset and vulnerable.

- No two people have exactly the same experience in life, so any advice given is bound to say more about the adviser than it does about the person receiving it.

- Advice tends to address the superficial aspects of a problem only, so that deeper issues are often bypassed or ignored.

- Giving advice is a one-way communication system. In counselling, the client should be actively involved in the whole process.

- Advice seldom helps clients to change.

Considering all the criticisms which can be levelled against the practice of giving advice, the question needs to be asked: Why then do some clients ask for, and expect to receive, advice especially when they first come for counselling? As we have already seen, clients frequently view the counsellor as 'expert' and when this happens they need some time in order to familiarize themselves with the true nature of the relationship. In the meantime, requests for advice should always be dealt with sensitively and respectfully, and the client guided towards a more active participation in the counselling process.

The following is an example of the way clients sometimes ask for advice, and outlines the response given by the counsellor to a particular client called Patricia. Patricia, a thirty five year old woman, was concerned about the recent breakup of her marriage, and the effect it was having on her six year old son. She wanted to move house so that she could make a completely new start in life, but she was worried that the move would cause so much stress for Ian, her son. Patricia agonized at some length about the decision she was having to make. Eventually she said to the counsellor:

Client: I'm worried about another big change in his life. He's had enough already. What do you think I should do?

Counsellor: You are worried about all the recent changes in your life, and now you find yourself having to make another big decision. Perhaps we could look more closely at your own feelings and identify what you think is right for you.

Clients occasionally ask for advice when they want to sidestep the need for fundamental change in their lives. Receiving advice is much easier than embarking on – the often painful – processes of self-examination and change. Sometimes clients ask for advice when they simply want to talk, and a request for advice is seen as one way of getting started, and a means of eliciting the attention of the counsellor. Finally, most people who receive counselling do so on a voluntary basis, but there have been instances where people have been put under pressure to attend. When this happens, there is naturally resentment – quite often well hidden – on the client's part, and asking for advice is one way of playing the system. It needs to be stressed here that people should never be 'sent' for counselling. The following is an account given by one sixteen-year-old student who made an appointment to see the college counsellor.

'Well, Mrs Edwards said I should see a counsellor because she thinks I have problems. I've missed a few classes and I didn't get my last assignment in on time. I don't think there is anything wrong with me, but if counselling will help, okay. But I don't want to come every week.'

(Bruce, 1995)

The college counsellor had to spend some time with this student in order to explain to him that he, and not someone else, should decide if he needed or wanted counselling. In the end, he was quite clear that he did not want it and returned to Mrs Edwards to explain this.

HOW LONG HAS COUNSELLING BEEN IN USE?

Counselling and psychotherapy are part of a very long tradition. The words counselling and psychotherapy are sometimes used interchangeably and, in fact, it is difficult to point to precise differences between them. Differences – when they do exist – often relate to type and length of training, various theoretical orientations, and the work which the qualified practitioner chooses to do.

Most people could be forgiven for thinking that counselling (and psychotherapy) are products of the late twentieth century with no discernable background or antecedents. The proliferation of counsellors and counselling services has been so marked, especially within the past ten years, that impressions of novelty, fashion and innovation are difficult to separate from them. But people have always been concerned to help and care for each other, and this kind of mutual support has been necessary for survival. As well as this, major religions place a great emphasis on mutual support and caring. In addition, there is within the Christian tradition at least the custom and practice of confession, which apart from its spiritual significance is believed to be psychologically beneficial too.

Besides the influences stemming from religion, counselling also has its roots in psychology, psychoanalysis, and more recently in the humanistic movement. Psychoanalysis began with Sigmund Freud in the nineteenth century, while psychology – which refers to the science and study of mental life – has a long history. The word psychology was first used in the eighteenth century when it came to denote that branch of philosophy concerned with the study of the mind and its activities, including perception, introspection, reasoning and thinking (*The Oxford Comparison to the Mind*, 1987).

Contemporary humanism has generated a myriad of theoretical counselling models, including the person-centred approach of Carl Rogers, Eric Berne's transactional analysis, and Fritz Perls' Gestalt therapy.

Changing public attitudes to fitness and health generally have placed more emphasis on the responsibility of the individual for personal health and well-being. Prescribed drugs are no longer seen as the only answer to physical and psychological illness, and there is now a greater public awareness of the existence of other forms of treatment. These other forms include counselling which is increasingly regarded as helpful for emotional and psychological problems, although it is certainly not without its critics.

The British Association for Counselling (BAC) came into being in 1976, although prior to this it had been the Standing Council for the Advancement of Counselling (SCAC). Membership of the BAC is increasing all the time, and in 1994 the European Association for

Counselling (EAC) was set up in order to address the needs of different nationalities and groups in Europe and to 'assist the further development of counselling as a profession in Europe' (EAC information leaflet, 1995).

WHAT ARE COUNSELLING SKILLS?

The skills of counselling include active listening, asking questions in a helpful, non-interrogatory way, paraphrasing what clients have said in order to help them clarify their thoughts, feelings and ideas, summarizing the content of what they have said, helping them to be more specific, and helping them to focus on key areas and issues which might be especially problematic or difficult for them to deal with.

The above skills are central to the work of Gerard Egan whose three-stage model of counselling we have already referred to. Egan deals also with the skills of challenge, giving information, pointing out inconsistencies, communicating empathy throughout the whole counselling process, and helping clients to devise and implement specific plans of action (*The Skilled Helper*, 1990). Further skills used in counselling include:

- choosing appropriate settings
- opening and closing interviews
- establishing confidentiality
- timing and pacing of sessions
- establishing working relationships with clients
- use of non-verbal communication
- responding to non-verbal cues
- coping with silence
- giving feedback
- setting targets
- making referrals.

All the counselling skills mentioned in this section will be discussed in more detail in later chapters. See also Fig. 1.1.

WHO ARE THE PEOPLE WHO USE THESE SKILLS?

Apart from trained counsellors and therapists, other people in a variety of jobs use some, if not all, counselling skills as part of their work. Social workers, for example, are trained to use good listening, questioning and other basic communication skills.

Increasingly, professional people, including teachers, nurses, occupational therapists, ministers of religion and psychologists are keen to acquire counselling skills. To this end, many are now completing

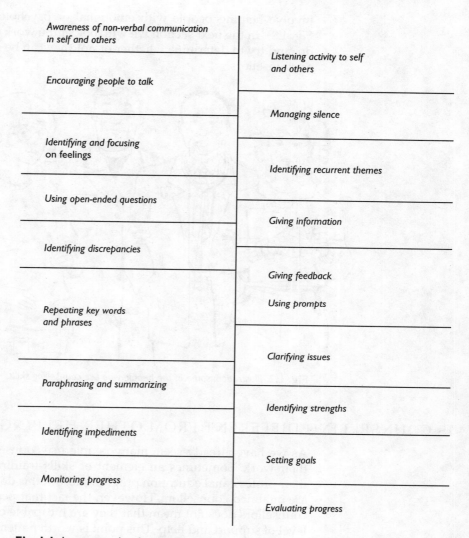

Fig. 1.1 *Interpersonal and counselling skills.*

counselling courses. Some trained counsellors work for voluntary organizations like Cruse, Samaritans or Childline, although in these instances the type of training will differ according to the needs of each client group. Other voluntary organizations also train their own counsellors. Though there is a growing trend towards standardization of counsellor training through National Vocational Qualifications throughout the country, this does not conflict with the specialisms offered by the voluntary agencies who, after all, know best what it is their counsellors need.

Probably the people who most benefit from counsellor training are the professionals like nurses, teachers and social workers who work closely with other people as part of their job, because these areas of work often involve helping people with emotional or psychological problems (see Fig. 1.2). In the next section we will look at the work which some of them do, and try to determine whether or not they can be described accurately as counsellors.

Fig. 1.2 *Illustration: some of the people who use counselling skills.*

IS COUNSELLING DIFFERENT FROM OTHER HELPING ACTIVITIES?

As we have already seen, many people use counselling skills as part of their work. Sometimes an element of skills training is included within their professional education programme, but this does not mean that they are qualified counsellors. However, the fact that people are not qualified counsellors does not mean that they are incapable of offering the highest level of support and help. This point is worth remembering in view of the fact that it is trained counsellors who are often given all the credit – and sometimes the censure – for being present in emergency situations. Counsellor training, however, is very specific to counselling, while other forms of training like social work and nursing are not. Sometimes professional people like nurses, social workers, teachers and others undertake counselling training, in which case they are entitled to call themselves qualified counsellors. When appropriate training is completed, these people can work as counsellors, but often their first professional role sets some limits to the amount of 'pure' counselling which they can do. A teacher's role, for example, includes giving advice and instruction among other things, and this is quite different from the role of a therapeutic counsellor. Why then do people already qualified in one professional area decide to pursue counselling training? The answer is that such training tends to enhance their original professional role because it improves their overall interpersonal and communication skills, and gives them a deeper understanding of themselves and others too. There is often an element of pragmatism as well, since any form of specialized training tends to upgrade a curriculum vitae and the prospects of employment or promotion besides.

CAN FRIENDS AND RELATIVES COUNSEL?

The problem with the kind of counselling offered by friends and relatives is that it often contains advice which, however well meant, is seldom helpful in the long term because people's difficulties are unique to them and cannot be resolved in superficial ways external to them. In an advice-giving situation, the person being advised is given very little chance to look below the surface of things, to engage in the process of self-examination and to determine exactly what it is they themselves want and need. As well as this, relatives and friends tend to become upset when their advice isn't taken.

Friends and relatives may also have some emotional involvement in the problem and this will inhibit their ability to listen actively. They may also want to talk about themselves, and this will certainly inhibit the process of active listening because such listening requires single-minded concentration and the capacity to set one's own preoccupations aside. Only in this way can a listener become wholly available to the other person. Friends and relatives may also become upset or disconcerted because the problems being discussed impinge on their sense of well-being or equilibrium. They may 'worry' about the person with the problem and worry can be very controlling. If someone is worried about me, then I may feel obliged to forget my own problems – or at least to pretend I have forgotten or resolved them – in order to ease the other person's distress. This should not happen in the counselling situation because the counsellor will have – in the course of training – worked through and examined all the issues within his or her own life which might provoke such a reaction, although there is always the possibility that areas of vulnerability will be activated occasionally.

Sometimes friends or relatives offer sympathy to the person who is upset, and this may be enough to help someone through a minor difficulty. Trained counsellors, on the other hand, are concerned to listen with empathy which means tuning into the client's inner world in order to appreciate fully their perceptions and feelings. The difference between sympathy and empathy is that the first tends to be superficial or even perfunctory, while the second is more difficult and requires effort and a desire to understand. These differences will be discussed at greater length in Chapter 3.

Confidentiality is assured in counselling. Even when it cannot be assured totally, the limitations to it will be discussed with the client. We shall consider the nature of confidentiality and its limitations in Chapters 2 and 9. With friends and relatives, however, the possibility of gossip is very real; even when assurances of confidentiality are given, there is a tendency – especially within families – to treat all information as communal and of interest to the group. In addition to this, families often have certain fixed ideas about the ways its members should behave, and when family rules are broken or questioned, there is always the risk that judgement will be passed and support withdrawn. Sadly, this last point highlights one of the reasons why people are also sometimes reluctant to approach ministers of religion for help. However, it should be added that it is also sometimes the case that people are inhibited by their own sense of guilt about the church, and this – like many feelings transferred from the past to the present – may bear no resemblance to current reality.

A criticism which has been levelled against professional counselling is that it seeks to usurp the traditional role of family and friends, and tends to medicalize problems, or even create them when they do not exist. This impression is sometimes reinforced when tragic events are reported by the media, and professional counsellors make themselves available to help those who need and ask for it. What tends to be overlooked here is that friends and relatives do help in these traumatic situations, but counsellors offer an extra service which – because of some of the difficulties outlined in this section – may be more appropriate for some people, especially for those who are reluctant to 'burden' family and friends with details of disturbing and painful events.

WHY ARE SELF-DEVELOPMENT AND SELF-AWARENESS IMPORTANT?

Self-development and self-awareness are important elements in counsellor training because these processes, which are often difficult and painful, enable students to understand themselves more fully. Some self-understanding is necessary for anyone who works closely with other people, but it is especially important for students who intend to work with clients in counselling. Unless students are encouraged, and given the opportunities in training, to get in touch with their own personal feelings, they will be unable to understand the wide range of emotions experienced by clients and may even confuse their own feelings with those of the client.

Identification and understanding of personal prejudices and blind spots is another important aspect of self-awareness. This can be particularly difficult for students, especially at the beginning of training. Most of us tend to ignore or overlook our shortcomings, and in fact some of our most fervently held attitudes are unquestioned anyway. But without acknowledgement of these, true humility and unpretentiousness are not possible and there is the danger that feelings of self-importance will flaw any future relationships with clients. Issues relating to the way we make moral judgements about other people and their worth also need to be discussed and recognised, and attitudes of unprejudiced objectivity fostered.

There are various ways in which students can be encouraged to engage in self-examination, and some of these will be discussed in more detail later in the chapter. In summary, some of the principal aids to self-awareness in counsellor training are the following:

- work with clients
- co-counselling with peers
- group discussion
- counselling skills training
- reading
- academic work; research
- knowledge of counselling theory
- personal counselling
- supervision
- tutorials
- residential courses
- seminars
- lectures
- written assignments
- questionnaires
- video practice
- feedback from peer group
- training in assertiveness skills
- development of the skills of critical thinking
- keeping a written record of progress and self-development (diary).

This is obviously a fairly extensive list, but all the elements outlined are essential for overall progress and development during counsellor training. Perhaps one of the most interesting and informative experiences for student counsellors is their introduction and subsequent exposure to the wide spectrum of ideas and accounts of personal experience generated by their peer group during discussions. In fact, this is one of the most important aspects of training and one which frequently takes trainee counsellors by surprise. The following impression was recounted by a student in his first year of training.

> At first it was difficult and quite threatening to mix with all the other people in the group. I was afraid I was going to make a fool of myself, or show my ignorance by asking the wrong questions or saying the wrong things. After a while though, everyone relaxed and began to enjoy the sessions. I know we all looked forward to the classes, and we all agreed that we really enjoyed the exchange of ideas from so many people from different forms of training. This was a real education in itself, this exposure to a wide range of ideas and opinions, and the sharing of experiences was like a breath of fresh air.
>
> (Sean, a student, 1995)

The point which needs to be emphasized here is that intellectual and academic ability are not enough for successful training; the process of self-examination and the need to develop self-awareness are equally important, if not more so. Interaction with other people – especially in the safe environment of the trainee situation – can help to achieve these. In addition, issues relating to sexuality – of self and others – can be discussed, while individual defence mechanisms and blind spots can be acknowledged. This acknowledgement of personal defences or weak spots does not always have to be 'confessed' or articulated openly in the group. Students may, as a result of group interaction and discussion, achieve insight about themselves at various points in training, and often these insights are so private to the individual that it would be inappropriate and unnecessary to disclose them anyway. It should, however, be added here that in specialized groupwork training there is a somewhat different emphasis on self-disclosure by participants. An intrinsic expectation of this form of training is that students will engage in significant levels of inner-directed work, including self-questioning and self-disclosure.

WHY DO PEOPLE WANT TO BECOME COUNSELLORS?

Many people want to become counsellors because they have a real desire to help others. This is especially true of those people who already work closely with others in a caring capacity – for example, nurses, social workers – and who decide to extend their range of helping abilities through counsellor training. It is obviously much easier to relate to and understand others when good interpersonal skills have been developed. Occasionally students enter training with the idea that they will eventually set up in private practice as full-time counsellors. This ambition, although sometimes realized, is often abandoned during the course of training once the difficulties and responsibilities of counselling are clearly understood. In other words, the idea of counselling as a career based solely on financial considerations comes to be seen as unrealistic, naive and even exploitative.

Perhaps the most important – and usually unacknowledged – reason which people have for becoming counsellors is that they themselves have some needs which have not been met. Unresolved problems, areas of need or even trauma may prompt a person to seek out others who also have emotional difficulties which have to be addressed. The process of dealing with one's own problems, through concentrating on the problems of others, works for some people since it serves to obscure or mask the need to look at personal issues and resolve them. Other reasons for wanting to become a counsellor might include a need to be liked by others, a need to be needed, a desire to feel important or in control, or a need for respect which is not being met in personal relationships.

Because of the reasons mentioned, it is important for student counsellors to become involved in self-development and self-awareness. Counsellors who already work with clients should receive regular supervision in order, among other things, to help them monitor their own feelings in relation to clients.

It is mainly through the processes of self-awareness and self-development that students can learn to identify and separate their own issues and problems from those of other people. A corollary of this is that once personal problems are clearly identified they can then be addressed and hopefully resolved, leaving the counsellor more 'available' to clients. This availability of the counsellor is central to good counselling practice and refers to the ability of the counsellor to be mentally, as well as physically, present for clients, so that all the attention is focused on the client's and not on the counsellor's needs.

WHAT ARE THE QUALITIES OF A GOOD COUNSELLOR?

We have already referred to the interpersonal and counselling skills which are a necessary part of counsellor training. The skills of listening, being aware of non-verbal communication in self and others, asking appropriate questions, identifying feelings, paraphrasing, summarizing and coping with silence, are just some of the areas in which counsellors need to be proficient. We shall look at these in more detail in later chapters.

In addition to the essential practical skills, however, there are other – equally important – prerequisites for counsellor effectiveness. These include what Carl Rogers referred to as the core conditions of Empathy, Respect and Congruence, which he believed to be the foremost attributes of the effective counsellor (On Becoming a Person, Rogers, 1991). These concepts will be discussed at greater length in Chapter 3, but since they represent fundamental qualities of good counselling it is relevant to say something about them here.

It is difficult to see how any counsellor could be effective without the ability to experience empathy, with clients. The word empathy refers to a particular characteristic which, when present, enables one person to understand another in a very deep sense. This can only be achieved when there is close communication between people, and when a special effort is made to stand in the other person's shoes in order to perceive things from their point of view. This is the basis of true insight and understanding.

It is also difficult to see how any counsellor could be effective without respect for clients. The term 'unconditional positive regard' is the one which Rogers frequently used in relation to respect, and the word valuing is also used in the Person-Centred approach which he describes (Client-Centred Therapy, Rogers, 1991). Respecting and valuing clients means accepting them in a totally non-judgemental way, even though their actions or value systems may be quite different to anything the counsellor has experienced. Accepting and respecting clients though would not be possible without self-development within counsellor training. Acceptance of one's own shortcoming and a willingness to work towards greater awareness need to be achieved before true acceptance of others can take place.

The third Rogerian condition of Congruence or genuineness refers to the ability of the counsellor to be a real and open person in relation to the client. This openness is based on honesty, as well as on clear verbal and non-verbal communication, but it does not mean that every thought a counsellor has should be expressed outright. Obviously only those aspects of communication which are relevant and helpful to particular clients should be expressed in this way.

Other qualities which counsellors need to have include a real interest in other people, as well as interests outside the counselling context. Very real problems can arise when counsellors invest everything of themselves in counselling so that clients come to be seen as necessary for their sense of well-being. There is the added danger that inappropriate emotional attachments to clients will be made if the counsellor's own personal life and relationships are devoid of real interest and commitment. Counsellors need to be conscious of the fact that clients, who are often emotionally vulnerable, can be exploited – even unwittingly – by counsellors whose own emotional needs are not being satisfied elsewhere. Some of these issues, which relate to Transference and Countertransference in counselling, will be discussed in Chapter 9.

It goes without saying that anyone who proposes to help others who are experiencing problems, needs to be in a position to deal effectively with any problems which arise in their own life. This does not, of course, mean that counsellors should lead perfect, problem-free lives since that would be impossible for anyone to do. What it does mean is that personal problems need to be clearly identified and coping strategies employed – including counselling therapy when necessary. Counsellors need to know how to take care of themselves before they can help others, and this taking care of self involves having basic self-esteem in the first place.

The ability to admit to mistakes, learn from them, and then engage in the often difficult process of change is another characteristic of effective counsellors. It helps to have a sense of humour, and the capacity to laugh at the contradictions and incongruities of life generally. Flexibility of thinking, creativity and problem-solving abilities are also essential; so too is the ability to relax and to enjoy cultural, artistic and other activities.

Counsellors need to be objective and unprejudiced in their attitudes, with awareness of, and respect for, diverse cultures, including their own. Acceptance of other people, regardless of their race, religion or sexual orientation, is a fundamental requirement for counselling; so too is the acceptance of people from different social groups.

Counsellors need to be clear about their own priorities and goals, and they need to understand the nature of their own ambition and how this affects their work and their relationships. A corollary of this is that balance should be the aim in relation to self and others. Overestimation of one's own importance is just as damaging as underestimation of it, for when people begin to view themselves and their contribution as indispensable, professional burnout is a real possibility.

The following is a summary of the qualities of the effective counsellor. See also Fig. 1.3 (on page 18).

- Basic self-esteem. Interest in people.
- Competence in relation to counselling skills.
- Understanding of counselling theory and the process of counselling.
- Understanding of self.
- Respect for cultural diversity, as well as respect for one's own culture.
- Acceptance of people from different racial and religious groups.
- Respect for people with a different sexual orientation.
- Ability to take care of self.
- Creativity and flexibility of thinking.
- Sense of humour.
- Enjoyment of life.
- Ability to form and to sustain relationships.
- Ability to experience and to communicate empathy.
- Ability to deal with personal problems and to ask for help when necessary.
- Capacity to learn from mistakes and to change when necessary.
- A sense of balance about one's own importance in relation to others.
- Varied cultural and artistic interests.
- Clear emotional boundaries in relation to self and clients.
- Non-judgemental in relation to others.
- Insight about personal ambition and goals.
- Possession of personal values which are not forced on others.
- Ability to be honest and genuine in relation to self and others.

WHAT ARE THE AIMS OF COUNSELLING?

Some of the aims of counselling have already been referred to within this chapter. We know, for example, that counselling is an activity which takes place when one person seeks help in order to deal with personal problems, and another person – the counsellor – gives that help. Counselling can also take place in a group setting, in which case a number of people are receiving help simultaneously not just from the counsellor, but from the interaction with other group members as well.

We have also indicated that clients are viewed in an emphatically positive way in counselling. This means that counsellors acknowledge client's own resources, strengths and capabilities in relation to problem solving. The counsellor is not therefore viewed as an expert, but as a person who

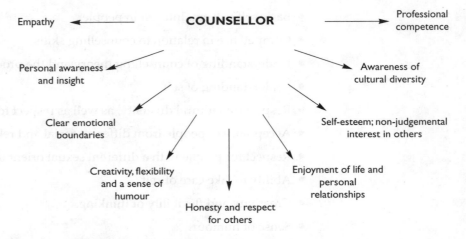

Fig. 1.3 *Qualities needed for effective counselling.*

Qualities of the effective counsellor – respect for cultural diversity and acceptance of people from different racial and religious groups.

offers help and, most importantly, is suitably trained to give it. Advice is not part of therapeutic counselling, even though clients often ask for it; the principal aim of counselling is to enable clients to identify what it is they themselves need and want. Even though clients' difficulties often impinge on – or even stem from – relationships with others, including family members and friends, it is only clients themselves who are in a position to appreciate fully the context and all the nuances of these difficulties. Counsellors serve to help clients talk through their problems in a confidential setting, to express the feelings associated with these problems, and to help them devise plans or strategies in order to resolve or cope with them.

An essential point to be made in relation to counselling aims or goals is that the ways in which counsellors help clients to identify and deal with their problems does not include trying to change them, or to make them better adjusted citizens. When clients do change through their own efforts they often find that life does become easier within their relational network and social setting, but this happens as a direct result of their own endeavour and achievements. However, since the relationship between counsellor and client is arguably the most influential element in counselling, the counsellor's values and attitudes – even when these are not stated – are bound to have some effect on the choices made by clients. This probably explains why public disquiet is sometimes expressed – often through sensational headlines – about the growth of the counselling and therapy movements. Occasionally articles appear in the press which highlight aspects of counselling which have given cause for concern. These areas of concern include the possibility of financial, emotional or even sexual exploitation of clients. The idea that people might be changed against their will by counsellors is another anxiety which is sometimes expressed. Students need to be aware of these criticisms and concerns and to understand the legitimate misgivings which prompt them. In his two books *Against Therapy* (1989) and *Final Analysis* (1992), Jeffrey Masson, the American writer and former psychoanalyst, discusses at length some of the problems which in his view are intrinsic to psychotherapy. These views are well worth reading, even though we may not entirely agree with all of them, since they are not all totally relevant to the counselling context but are more applicable to the practice of psychoanalysis or in-depth psychotherapy.

CASE STUDY: MR EVANS

The following case study is not meant to illustrate specific counselling skills, as these will be described and illustrated in subsequent chapters. It is intended to highlight some of the issues which have been dealt with in this first chapter, including the importance of suitable training for counsellors and the reasons which prompt clients to come for counselling in the first place.

Mr Evans was a sixty eight year old man whose wife was suffering from Alzheimer's disease. She was slightly younger – sixty five – and had developed the illness three years earlier, and from that time her condition had deteriorated quite rapidly. Mr Evans was taking care of his wife and, apart from intermittent spells of mild depression, he was coping very well with her at home.

The couple had moved ten years previously to the area in which they now lived. They had formed a circle of friends, some of whom were close, but their family and relatives – including two sons – lived sixty miles away. The sons visited about once a month, but both were tied up with their own family commitments and were unable to take an active part in caring for their mother. Mr Evans was reluctant to burden his sons with details about his own spells of depression, so he tended to show a cheerful and coping front whenever they visited. Neither Mr Evans nor his wife attended church, so they did not have – or look for – support at this level. A community psychiatric nurse visited them on a regular basis, and offered help and advice in relation to Mrs Evans' general care and to the medication she had been prescribed.

Mr Evans first asked for direct help for himself when he visited his doctor to ask for something for depression and sleeplessness. He had recently become more anxious and this had led to episodes of insomnia. During the visit, the doctor asked Mr Evans if he would like to talk to the counsellor who worked at the practice every weekend. Mr Evans considered this for some time and eventually decided that he needed to talk in more detail about some of the problems he was currently experiencing.

Helen, the counsellor to whom Mr Evans was referred, worked on a part-time basis each Saturday at the Health Centre. She was a psychologist who having completed her university degree had taken further training in order to obtain first a certificate and then a diploma in counselling theory. Both these qualifications had been taken at higher education level over a period of two years, and both encompassed skills as well as counselling theory.

In addition to her training, Helen had gained some experience of working with elderly people in a residential home, while attending university as a mature student. As a general practice counsellor, she worked closely as a member of the healthcare team, and received ongoing supervision for her work.

Mr Evans decided to have counselling because he wanted to talk to someone who had time to listen to him, and who would understand his current difficulties. He did not want to burden his family with all his emotional problems and stress, although he did concede later that his sons might value more information about their parent's situation generally. He arrived at this conclusion after talking at some length with Helen, over four counselling sessions in all. He also decided that he would benefit from more practical help in the home, especially with laundry and day care for his wife. Through discussion with the General Practitioner, Helen was able to highlight some of Mr Evans' needs and arrangements were made to provide assistance. It should be added here that Mr Evans was aware of these discussions between the counsellor and the doctor, since Helen had told him about them, and he was quite happy with this situation.

Like many clients, Mr Evans was helped through counselling to talk about and to experience some of the strong emotions which are often difficult to communicate to family and friends. He was also helped to see more clearly what it was he needed in terms of extra support from his family, and once this need was clearly identified he was able to communicate more openly with his sons.

Counselling certainly did not solve all his problems, but it did help to make him feel more confident about his ability to cope, and to enlist the practical and emotional help of others when needed.

KEY WORDS AND PHRASES

INTERPERSONAL SKILLS

These are the skills of listening, paying attention, asking appropriate questions, reflecting back and summarizing what has been said, being aware of body language and non-verbal cues, showing interest in others, demonstrating understanding and giving accurate feedback. Counsellors use all these skills as part of their work, and they form an important part of every training programme. However, interpersonal skills are not just peculiar to counselling but are used by people in different occupations as varied as management, business, teaching and the caring professions. As well as this, interpersonal skills courses are now widely available, and many people are keen to improve their overall interpersonal/interactive abilities. Assertiveness training is another dimension of interpersonal skills, so too is the increasing focus on group dynamics and the ways in which people function generally in relation to others.

THERAPEUTIC COUNSELLING

This refers to the kind of counselling highlighted in this chapter. Counsellors use all the interpersonal skills mentioned above, but they also form unique working relationships with clients in which there is no obvious conflict of interests. Whereas in management, for example, senior personnel may possess and use good interpersonal skills, they may also at times need to give directives, advice or even orders to subordinates. Good interpersonal skills will benefit management in the sense that overall communication will probably improve and workers will feel more valued as a result. Clients in counselling also feel valued when good interpersonal skills are used, especially when these are combined with the core conditions of Respect, Empathy and Congruence. The difference between counselling and management though is that clients in counselling are encouraged to participate as equals in the process and this equality is a fundamental prerequisite of client empowerment and autonomy. In management and business, however, production and efficiency usually take precedence over personal issues, and the concepts of autonomy and empowerment – although sometimes referred to – are seldom realized.

EXERCISES

EXERCISE I   SELF-AWARENESS

As we have already indicated in this chapter, it is important for trainee counsellors to be aware of their own thoughts, feelings, reactions or prejudices. The following is a list of situations which clients might bring to counselling. Read through the list and identify those problems which might:

a) make you feel uncomfortable
b) cause you some difficulty
c) cause you considerable difficulty.

Remember that you do not have to say how you would counsel clients with these problems since that would be impossible for you to do at such an early stage. Nor do you have to think of answers or solutions to the problems.

1 A forty five year old woman says that she has been caught shoplifting. She has done this several times, but is unable to stop herself.

2 A young mother says that she has occasionally beaten her two year old child who cries a lot and refuses to eat.

3 A middle-aged man who can't understand why his wife is so upset about his recent affair. It meant nothing to him, but she just doesn't seem to understand this.

4 A young homosexual man says that he is very lonely and is involved in casual sex. He couldn't care less about HIV or AIDS. He just wants to have a good time.

5 A woman says she wants to have an abortion because the pregnancy was unplanned.

6 A teenager says he takes drugs at weekends and regards this as a form of relaxation with friends.

7 An older man says that he sexually abused his daughter in the past. She is now receiving treatment for depression.

8 A wife says that her husband has been drinking heavily for many years. She would like to leave him, but somehow can't make the decision.

9 A teenage student says that she and some friends have bullied another girl in their class. The other girl deserves it in their opinion because she is a 'snob'.

10 A twenty five year old man is depressed and has frequently thought about suicide. He says he has nothing to live for.

11 A young man makes racist remarks about people from minority groups.

12 An older man who says that women are always complaining. In his view, they should stay at home and look after the family.

13 A man who says that he has been violent towards his wife.

14 A woman who sets out to convert everyone to her own religious beliefs. She believes it is her mission in life to do this.

15 A man who has had a drink-driving charge says that he was just unlucky to be caught.

16 A woman who works in a highly demanding and stressful job says that she has some difficulty in finding quality time for her children.

17 A man who works in a highly demanding and stressful job says that he has some difficulty in finding quality time for his children.

18 A young woman says that she doesn't see anything wrong in using her sexuality with male colleagues at work.

19 A middle-aged man says that he still accepts sums of money from his elderly mother, even though he knows that she is trying to buy his affection.

When you have identified the issues which you would find difficult to accept, discuss them with a partner. The aim here is to achieve a deeper understanding of your own responses and the ways in which these responses might inhibit your communication with clients.

EXERCISE 2 SELF-DISCLOSURE

a) Make a list of subjects which you might find difficult to discuss with other people.
b) Work with a partner and discuss the issues which you have both listed, and try to identify your reasons for choosing them.
c) When you have finished your discussion in pairs, join up with the other students in the training group and consider the main issues which have been highlighted by everyone.

The following is a list of personal topics which clients often find difficult to talk about.

> Sexual feelings
> Money problems
> Past mistakes
> Negative feelings
> Fears
> Prejudices
> Childhood
> Personal achievements
> Drinking habits
> Failed relationships

EXERCISE 3 PERSONAL SKILLS

Look at the following list of skills and abilities and indicate those which:

a) you need to improve
b) you are good at.

> Meeting strangers
> Starting conversations
> Accepting compliments
> Responding to criticism

Delegating
Caring for others
Giving encouragement
Apologizing
Expressing negative feelings
Expressing positive feelings
Asking for help
Giving compliments
Making complaints
Making decisions
Managing time
Accepting responsibility
Relaxing
Setting goals
Coping with stress
Coping with failure

In groups of three or four, discuss your findings and look at the areas which are problematic for most people.

EXERCISE 4   WORD ASSOCIATIONS

Working in groups of three or four, select a word or phrase from the following list.

Responsibility
Ambition
Friendship
Roles
Self-esteem
Confidence
Communication
Caring
Intimacy
Assertiveness
Status
Independence
Society
Social roles
Opinions
Leadership
Labels
Commitment
Intuition
Identity

Write the word you have chosen in the centre of a large piece of paper and using Fig. 1.4 as an example, make as many associations as you can think of to it. Next, select one word from the associations you have made, and repeat the process. Discuss your associations with members of the group.

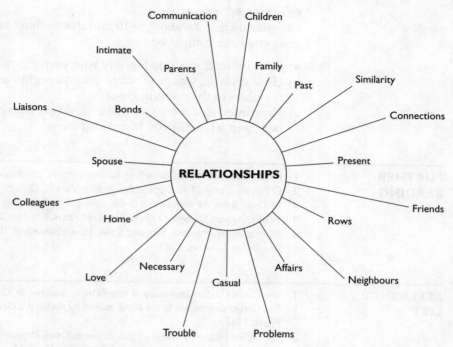

Fig. 1.4 *Relationships.*

EXERCISE 5   BRAINSTORMING

Working in groups of three or four, make a list of what you consider to be the characteristics of a good counsellor. Accept all the ideas generated by members of the group, no matter how irrelevant they may seem at first glance. One person in the group will need to act as scribe for the others. Afterwards, discuss with members of other groups the characteristics you have all listed.

EXERCISE 6   FEARS AND ANXIETIES

Work with another person and take turns to discuss the fears and anxieties which clients might experience when they first come for counselling.

a) What do clients need most?
b) What might clients find unhelpful?

EXERCISE 7   HELPFUL AND UNHELPFUL

Working alone, try to recall a time when you needed help with a personal problem.

a) What or who helped you most?
b) What or who helped you least?

Discuss your recollections with members of the class group.

EXERCISE 8   REFLECTION

On your own, take about 5–10 minutes to think about some of the exercises you have completed.

a) How difficult was it to identify your own thoughts and feelings?
b) How difficult was it to share your thoughts and feelings with other members of the training group?
c) How interested were you in the views expressed by other group members, and what did you learn from them?

FURTHER READING

1   May, Rollo, *The Art of Counselling*, Souvenir Press, London, 1992.
2   O'Farrell, Ursula, *First Steps in Counselling*, Veritas, Dublin, 1995.
3   McLeod, John, *An Introduction to Counselling*, OU Press, Buckingham, 1993.
4   Wicks, Robert J, *Helping Others*, Souvenir Press, London, 1994.
5   Munro, Anne, Manthei, Bob and Small, John, *Counselling: The Skills of Problem Solving*, Routledge, London, 1989.

REFERENCE LIST

1   *The Concise Oxford Dictionary of Word Origins* Volume III, Oxford University Press.
2   *The Oxford Companion to the Mind*, edited by Richard L Gregory, Oxford University Press, 1987.
3   *The Skilled Helper* by Gerard Egan, Brookes/Cole, Monterey CA, 1990.
4   British Association of Counselling Information Sheet No. 10.
5   *On Becoming a Person* by Carl Rogers, Constable, London, 1991.
6   *Client-Centred Therapy* by Carl Rogers, Constable, London, 1991.
7   *Against Therapy* by Jeffrey Masson, Fontana/Collins, London, 1989.
8   *Final Analysis* by Jeffrey Masson, Fontana/Collins, London, 1992.

CHAPTER 2

Forms of communication

The majority of students who come into counsellor training already possess the fundamental skills which are necessary for successful communication at work, socially and within relationships. The possession of interpersonal skills is so taken for granted by all of us that we seldom question our effectiveness. We are often taken aback to learn that it is possible – and necessary within counsellor training – to upgrade and refine these skills through repeated practice and discussions with other people.

In relation to communication, one of the first things that students need to learn is that interpersonal skills which we all use socially and in our relationships are also employed within counselling but with a different focus and with more attention to detail. In everyday communication between friends, for example, conversation tends to be unstructured and relatively unfocused, so that when one person is speaking, the other may be only half listening, or even partly involved in some other task or activity (see Fig. 2.1). There is a certain amount of shared, and sometimes superficial, understanding of what is being said between friends. Sentences are often started and left unfinished, and frequent interruptions are made, especially when conversation is animated and people are concerned to make points, to argue, or to express individual views. Friends usually know quite a lot about each other, including individual likes and dislikes, personal characteristics, strengths and weaknesses, and any other obvious problems which exist within each person's family and relationships.

During social interaction between people who are not well acquainted, conversation tends to be carried out at a superficial level, with a great deal of emphasis on making instant verbal contact which does not require any real understanding or commitment. In this way, much time may be spent in talking about the weather, the state of the economy, or even the decoration of the room in which people have come together for a particular occasion. In social situations like this, people may also be nervous, ill at ease, conscious of themselves and the impression they are making on others. Each person may be absorbed with his or her own thoughts, preoccupations or agenda, and real human contact is seldom made when interactions are constrained in this way. This is not to say that people never enjoy themselves in certain social situations because clearly many people need and like to spend at least some time communicating in this way.

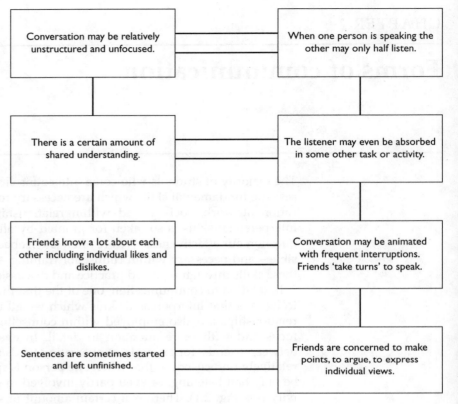

Fig. 2.1 *Communication between friends.*

In the office or workplace, another, quite different kind of communication takes place between colleagues, between employees and managers, and often between people who work in an organisation, and the members of the public who use the service provided. In these instances, conversations are frequently factual, with the stress on detail and accuracy. Information systems exist within organisations in order to ensure that efficient communication takes place at a certain level; this level does not usually include the purely personal dimension, and is certainly not concerned with any relational or emotional difficulties which employees might experience at home or at work.

Therapeutic counselling

The interactions which take place within therapeutic counselling are different from any of those mentioned above. This is because the main focus of communication in counselling is the client, and the problems which the client is experiencing. The counsellor is present in order to help the client, and does not therefore expect or need an equal share in the exchanges which take place between them (see Fig. 2.2).

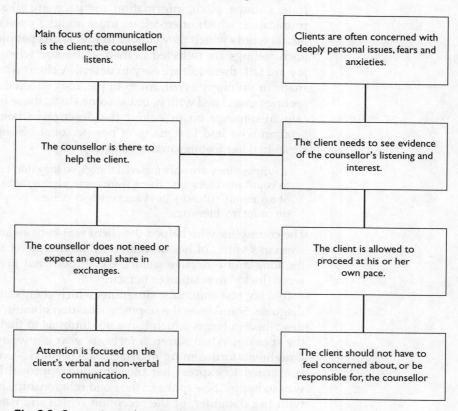

Fig. 2.2 *Communication between client and counsellor.*

An essential part of giving such help to clients is that attention needs to be directed towards all aspects of their communication, both verbal and non-verbal. Since clients are often concerned with deeply personal issues, feelings, fears and anxieties, it is often difficult for them to express everything they wish to communicate through words alone. As well as paying total attention to all aspects of a client's communication, the counsellor must also know how to respond in ways which are helpful and encouraging to them. This help and encouragement cannot be given, however, unless counsellors understand what it is that clients wish to convey through language, through gestures, through tone of voice, and all the other aspects of verbal and non-verbal exchange which we shall now consider.

VERBAL COMMUNICATION

Although the verbal component of communication is only one aspect of the exchanges which take place between people, a great deal of information can be obtained by paying attention to the manner in which things are said, as well as to the actual content of what is expressed. Voice tone, volume, pitch, information and pace, are all aspects of verbal communication which often tell us more about a person's meaning than the actual words which they choose to say. When people are unhappy or sad, such feelings are reflected in their voice, and when positive feelings like joy are felt, these too are easy to detect. A client who is describing a traumatic or unhappy event, for example, may succeed in hiding some of the feelings associated with it, but at some stage, these feelings are almost certain to impinge on or colour the description being given. An elderly woman who had lost many of her personal belongings during a flood, described her feelings in the following way:

> 'I suppose they are only material things, so they don't matter, and I feel I ought to count my blessings. There were some photographs ... (pause) ... they were of my family (silence). But I am very lucky. Some people are not so lucky, and I do count my blessings.'

The counsellor who helped the client was very aware of the sadness in the woman's voice, of her hesitation in the middle of the description and of the long and reflective silence which occurred just before she used the word 'lucky' in relation to herself.

It is not just traumatic situations which clients may try to minimize or disguise. Sometimes the opposite situation obtains, and happy events are described in terms which leave no doubt as to their true significance for the speaker. When Karen, a forty six year old woman, spoke of her only daughter's forthcoming marriage, she seemed – on the surface at least – concerned to express her pleasure and approval because her daughter was so happy. She spoke of the good relationship she had always enjoyed with her daughter, of the reception which she was helping her to plan, and of the house which her daughter and her fiancé had bought recently.

> 'It's right here, on the other side of town so it's not too far away. I'm really pleased for her. I didn't think I would feel like this when my own daughter left home, but I do.' (Laughs)

The counsellor was aware that Karen's laugh sounded slightly forced. She also observed the sad expression which momentarily clouded her face. When she had finished speaking, Karen was silent for a while until, once again, the pensive expression showed on her face. Even though she had expressed happiness about her daughter's marriage, Karen was unable to conceal – even to herself – the ambivalent feelings which she obviously had.

SILENCE

Silence is particularly significant in client communication because it is often during these periods that important associations are mentally made. Understanding is also frequently achieved when clients give themselves time to reflect in this way. What is crucial here is that the counsellor should respect the client's need for silence. In addition to this, the counsellor should be prepared to 'stay with' the client who is silent, and should resist the temptation to break it either through reassurance, observation or interpretation. Student counsellors often feel uncomfortable with these periods of silence in counselling and sometimes react against them by rushing in to fill in the 'gaps'. When this happens, clients are denied opportunities to think or reflect; they are also placed under pressure to continue at the counsellor's, rather than their own, pace. In this way also, attention is shifted away from clients, and this can have the unfortunate effect of making them feel undervalued and rushed.

One of the reasons that we find silence difficult to sustain is that we are simply not used to it in everyday life. Sound is all around us, and in many instances we are subjected to intrusive noise even when we have no wish to hear it. The fact that we have no control over the continuous music which is played in restaurants, airports and shopping areas, for example, means that we tend to be surprised – or even disconcerted – by silence when it does occur. Silence in counselling can seem intolerable for students, especially since they may associate it with feelings of personal impotence and an inability to help 'solve' a client's problems. It takes time and practice to overcome these reservations. This practice in counselling skills includes learning to pay attention to all aspects of a clients' nonverbal communication, as well as learning to listen *actively* rather than passively to everything the client says. Paradoxically, silence is often one aspect of the overall message which clients may wish to communicate, not just to a counsellor but to themselves as well.

NON-VERBAL COMMUNICATION

As we have already indicated, one way of learning to cope more effectively with silence during counselling is to actively listen to clients when they do speak so that all our attention is focused not just on what we hear, but also on the way things are said, the language used, the emotions expressed, and any hesitation, embarrassment or discrepancy. Learning to observe the client's non-verbal communication and its implications is equally important in counselling, because it is through these observations that counsellors can become aware of the underlying message or feeling which the client has been unable or afraid to put into words. A client may, for example, register very strong feeling through facial expression, posture or gestures while speaking. The face is the area of the body through which feelings are expressed most obviously, and the way in which clients use eye contact, in particular, can tell us a lot about how they are feeling. The following is a summary of the different aspects of non-verbal communication which counsellors need to be aware of.

POSTURE

A client's posture can communicate may different attitudes, including shyness, fear or discomfort; these are usually indicated when the body is drawn back or turned away from the counsellor. On the other hand, submissive behaviour or sadness is indicated when the head is bowed, shoulders drooping and eye contact is avoided. When a client keeps arms and

Positive feelings are easy to detect.

legs firmly crossed, it may mean that there is some degree of vulnerability, or fear of disclosure. Some people seek to convey dominance or status in the way they sit or stand, but counsellors should ensure that the seating arrangements between them and clients is 'equal' in the sense that chairs are of the same height and type, and are positioned correctly in relation to each other. This means that they should not be uncomfortably close – about one metre is the usual distance – and they should be placed at a slight angle so that both client and counsellor are given the opportunity to break eye contact occasionally. When people are seated directly opposite to each other there is less chance to break eye contact in this way. In addition, chairs facing each other may resemble an interview situation and while this may be appropriate in the interview context, it will probably appear too confrontational or threatening for clients in counselling.

EYE CONTACT   Too much eye contact tends to be unnerving for many people, especially when it comes to resemble a fixed stare. It takes some skill on the counsellor's part to maintain the correct degree of eye contact, especially since this depends to some extent on individual client needs, and the response which they make. Clients who feel reasonably confident and assertive will be able to maintain eye contact, while those who are frightened or vulnerable will be less able to do so. Clients may also avoid eye contact when they are depressed, or when they experience feelings of guilt, shame or abandonment.

In general, eye contact serves to indicate interest, and is associated with turn taking during verbal exchanges. We tend to look at each other for between 25 to 75 per cent of the time during conversations and this mutual exchange of gaze helps to sustain attention (*The Psychology of Interpersonal Behaviour*, Argyle, 1990). During counselling, however, this turn taking may be altered slightly because it is the client who is the recipient of most of the attention. This attention includes careful listening on the counsellor's part, and when people are listening they tend to look more at the other person than they would do while speaking (Argyle, 1990). This is why student counsellors need to learn, through practice and skills training, to adjust the amount of eye contact which they would normally give in everyday conversations.

FACIAL EXPRESSION

We have already referred to the fact that clients may register strong feelings like anger, sadness or joy through facial expression, as well as through the words which they speak. The first impressions which we get of other people are usually based on observations of the face and the expressions indicated on it. In view of this, student counsellors need to be aware of their own facial expressions and the effect these have on clients. Clients who come for counselling are often frightened, apprehensive or otherwise upset, and they will be concerned to establish just how approachable, open and accepting the counsellor is. These helping and non-judgemental attitudes are discernible in the face; so too are attitudes of boredom, impatience, lack of interest, lack of understanding and failure to make real empathic contact with clients. Our faces can convey our innermost thoughts and feelings; this is why it is virtually impossible to stimulate interest which is not truly present.

Student counsellors are often concerned about how they 'appear' to clients. This concern is frequently heightened when video practice has taken place, and sessions are viewed later in order to assess skills. It is during these viewing sessions that students become aware, perhaps for the first time, of their own non-verbal communication, including facial expression and mannerisms (Fig. 2.3). Although it is important to be aware of facial expressions and the way these affect clients, we should also remember that the counsellor's face is most likely to show the appropriate responses when real interest in the client is felt, and active listening is taking place.

GESTURES

The use of gestures is another aspect of non-verbal communication which students become acutely aware of when receiving video practice sessions. Hand gestures, in particular, often seem excessive and intrusive, and this is a problem which is sometimes associated with feeling nervous, especially at the beginning of training. There is an important analogy here between the nervousness which student counsellors experience at the beginning of training, and the nervousness which clients almost invariably feel when they first come for counselling. Anxiety, tension or agitation can serve to exaggerate a client's or counsellor's use of gesticulation, and this, in turn, can create an uneasy atmosphere which is felt by both people. Counsellors can learn, through practice, to modify their own use of gestures. They can also help clients by being open and relaxed in their

Fig. 2.3 *Illustration: during video feedback sessions.*

general demeanour. Clients will also tend to be more at ease when there are no physical barriers, like desks or tables, between them and the counsellor. This and other aspects of the physical environment are outlined at the end of this chapter.

TOUCH

Student counsellors often ask if it is ever appropriate to show warmth to clients through touch. This question inevitably sparks a great deal of animated discussion; members of the training group are usually willing to express their own views about touching, and the ways in which individuals can perceive it. Some forms of touching do not carry deep personal meaning; people shake hands frequently, for example, and are seldom disconcerted by the experience. There are occupations, like hairdressing, where touch is an integral part of the job, and clients are unlikely to object to it. Doctors touch patients, and patients accept this kind of touching in its professional context. Touch in counselling is more problematic, however, because there are clients who have experienced traumas which are directly related to inappropriate touching (for example, physical or sexual abuse) and for whom this kind of communication, however well meant, is unacceptable and perhaps even frightening. Nonetheless, a brief touch on the hand can indicate warmth and empathy for some clients, especially when it is accurately timed and genuinely felt by the counsellor. Even when clients do not object to touch, there is always a problem in relation to timing; if a counsellor touches a client too early in their relationship it may be construed as overfamiliarity. There is also the possibility that for some clients touch may indicate sexual interest on the counsellor's part, and such a response can lead to general misunderstanding about the nature of the counselling relationship.

There are also cultural differences in the amount of touch which people give and in the way others respond to it (Argyle, 1990). Perhaps one way a counsellor can judge how clients respond to touch is to take note of their reactions when handshakes are exchanged on first meeting. People who accept touch and are comfortable with it are likely to respond warmly to an initial handshake, while others who are more inhibited are less likely to show any enthusiasm. The warmth and genuineness of touch can influence the client's attitude in a very positive way, but only if it is given for the client's benefit only. Occasionally counsellors, especially those who are just beginning to work with clients, use touch as a method of reassurance – which is often inappropriate and says more about the counsellor's rather than the client's need. In other words, counsellors can use touch in a way which conveys their own distress to clients; the counsellor who feels uncomfortable with what a client is saying may want the client to get better quickly, and tactile communication may be used to signal the message 'stop'. When this happens, clients are likely to feel some guilt about 'burdening' the counsellor with their problems, and the proper focus of counselling is lost.

It should be remembered that counsellors themselves are not always totally comfortable with touch. Again, this depends on life experience and the ways in which communication has been conducted in families. In addition, there are cultural differences already mentioned: northern Europeans may be less enthusiastic than other nationalities about tactile communication, for example; and within the British culture, touch may be minimal or even absent between people who do not know each other intimately. However, touch – when it is correctly timed and sincerely motivated – can benefit clients enormously. It can convey most effectively the empathy which counsellors experience for the client.

The following are some general responses about touch and tactile communication.

- People differ in their responses to touch.

- Some forms of touch carry no personal message; for example, when a doctor examines a patient.

- Touch, if correctly timed and sincerely motivated, can help to establish a positive bond.

- Touch is particularly effective when verbal expression of feeling is difficult or impossible.

- All cultures have rules pertaining to the use of touch. These rules specify the circumstances in which touch may be used, and the parts of the body which may be touched.

- There are people whose early-life experience has made them suspicious or even fearful of touch.

- Touch is sometimes used in a sexist or patronizing way.

- Touch may also be used in a dominating or threatening way.

- Touch may invade another person's space.

- Unexpected touching can cause embarrassment.

- Touch can be supportive and reassuring.

- Touch is easily misinterpreted, especially when it is done in a clumsy or inappropriate way.

- For some people, touch offers reassurance about physical attractiveness and sexuality. This can sometimes present problems in counselling, especially if a client tries to elicit sexual responses from a counsellor. Such a situation needs to be dealt with sensitively but decisively by the counsellor concerned, and the professional nature of the counselling relationship needs to be emphasized and clarified so that the client feels accepted for 'self' alone. In other words, the client needs to feel valued without having to resort to stratagems, sexual or otherwise.

Touch can sometimes give clients 'permission' to express strong feelings which they have inhibited or suppressed for some time. When Vicky, an eighteen year old client, talked to the counsellor about her mother's death, she was obviously fighting to hold back tears. Vicky was ten years old when her mother died and nobody had talked to her about the bereavement. She had not been allowed to attend the funeral, and shortly afterwards she moved with her father to another town. While she was describing these events, Vicky stopped several times and seemed unable to proceed. During one of these pauses, the counsellor touched Vicky's hand in order to convey warmth and interest. Vicky reacted to this by pouring out all the sadness which she had been unable to express for years. Vicky expressed her sadness verbally and through crying. During a subsequent session she was able to speak with great insight about the traumatic events of her early life.

Active listening

Most of us take it for granted that our listening skills are adequate or even good. It is often quite a surprise for students, therefore, to learn that listening is an active process which requires effort and concentration, as well as the ability to set our own concerns aside – temporarily at least. During our day-to-day interactions with other people we tend to listen on a fairly superficial level, and we may even listen while doing something else. For example, we sometimes *hear* the words which other people are saying to us while we are engaged in activities like housework, watching television or driving the car. This is not active listening, however, because when we are involved in other activities we are not giving the person who is speaking undivided attention. It is important to understand that listening and hearing are not the same thing: we often *hear* the words spoken by another person without any real understanding of the overall message which that person wishes to communicate. Probably one of the reasons that listening is a poorly developed skill for many of us is that we were not taught to value it in childhood. Parents are often too preoccupied to give children total and absolute attention, and when parental listening does take place, it may be absentminded, abstracted or even oblivious to the real meaning behind the words. Children may have similar experiences at school, where teachers do not have the time to listen with undivided and exclusive attention to the experiences of each child in the group. So even though children are encouraged to listen to teachers, they may not perceive teachers themselves as models of good listening skills. It is usually only when traumatic or crisis situations occur, perhaps later in life, that people recognize the listening deficit, not just in themselves but in others as well. These traumatic or crisis triggers, especially when they affect us on a personal level, can show us how dependent we are on others to help us. Active listening, initially at least, is the most effective form of help which we can give to people who are suffering emotional upheaval or trauma in their lives.

THE SKILLS OF LISTENING

Good listening is difficult to sustain because it necessitates remaining quiet and allowing the other person to speak. This remaining quiet is especially important in counselling, because clients – who often find it difficult to come for counselling in the first place – need to know that what they say will be listened to with respect and attention. Any premature interruption by a counsellor is bound to be interpreted (correctly) by the client as intrusive, inept or lacking in interest. This failure to show interest in the client can sometimes stem from the counsellor's own preoccupation with personal issues. In other words, the client may be describing a difficulty, a behaviour or an emotion which is also problematic for the counsellor, and this can prompt the kind of interruption referred to. This last point highlights once again the importance of self-development and self-awareness in counsellor training.

Student counsellors often find it difficult to remain verbally inactive when they first start to work with clients. This desire to speak and ask questions stems partly from a wish – on the student counsellor's part – to help the client solve his problem. However, clients are unlikely to be helped in this way, for in order for them to deal with their own problems effectively, they need to be given the uninterrupted opportunity to clarify them first. This exploration and clarification of problems can only be accomplished when the client is allowed to proceed at his own pace, and it will be further facilitated if the counsellor maintains an interested and attentive, but verbally restrained, presence.

Good listening encourages clients to speak more freely since it shows respect not just for the content of what is being said, but also for the feelings and experiences behind the words. Student counsellors need to learn to listen to 'self' as well as to clients, and this listening to 'self' is an ongoing process throughout training and afterwards. Supervision promotes the process of listening to 'self' and helps students to identify and monitor their general reactions to clients. (Further aspects of supervision will be discussed in Chapter 9.) Listening to one's own reactions also takes place while a client is speaking during a counselling session. Tuning in to what a client is saying means noting every aspect of their communication, including tone of voice, posture and appearance, use of language, hesitation and any emotion discernible in what is being expressed. It also involves noting our own response to what clients convey. This assessment of both verbal and paralanguage is one of the things which makes active listening difficult to sustain in counselling. In everyday conversation much of what a speaker says and does is unconsciously noted by the listener. The counselling context is different however because what the client says and does needs to be registered by the counsellor, not just unconsciously, but at a conscious level as well.

SOME GENERAL
POINTS ABOUT
LISTENING

- When we listen carefully to people we can see things more clearly from their point of view. This is the basis of empathy.

- When we listen to people, they get the message that we are taking them and their problems seriously. This helps them to clarify and make sense of their own experiences.

- There are certain distractions which can impair our quality of listening. These include extraneous noise, interruptions, discomfort, emotions such as anger, sadness and anxiety. Thinking about other matters also inhibits good listening.

- Active listening is more than just an aural exercise. It also includes the skill of observing and receiving non-verbal messages (Egan, 1990).

- Interference to listening can also occur when the language being used is unfamiliar, or when a disability such as speech or hearing impairment is present.

- Prejudice, preconceived ideas and judgemental attitudes act as barriers to good listening.

- Mentally rehearsing our own verbal contribution will undermine listening ability. This kind of mental rehearsal often takes place when people are at meetings (see Fig. 2.4).

- Mentally trying to solve a client's problems will damage the counsellor's listening ability.

- During active listening, the listener is concerned to understand the thoughts, feelings, experiences and beliefs of the speaker. This involves intense concentration.

- Non-verbal aspects of behaviour which facilitate good listening include:
  - maintaining eye contact
  - head movements to indicate encouragement
  - mirroring the client's expressions in order to show empathy. This should be done with discretion, however, as clients often use inappropriate facial expression, for example smiling while describing painful or traumatic events.
  - adopting a warm, open posture by leaning slightly forward towards the client
  - giving appropriate verbal encouragement when natural pauses occur in the client's speech.

Fig. 2.4 *Illustration: listening at meetings.*

Communication and the counsellor

COUNSELLOR NON-VERBAL COMMUNICATION

How do clients in counselling know that counsellors really listen and pay attention to them when they are speaking? The answer to this is that clients themselves are observant and will note every aspect of the counsel-lor's non-verbal communication and general behaviour. Certain non-ver-bal responses include smiling when appropriate, using head movements to indicate interest, avoiding irritating gestures or mannerisms, giving sufficient eye contact to indicate interest, adopting an attentive and open posture, and by giving indications of encouragement which may be either verbal or non-verbal. For example, a counsellor might want to encourage a client to continue what he is saying. One way of doing this would be to give accurately timed verbal reinforcers, such as:

'Yes...'
'You felt...?'
'And so...'
'Afterwards...?'
'Ah ha...'

Another way of achieving the same effect is for counsellors to use the technique of verbal following with clients. This simply refers to the process of listening carefully to what clients say, and then making responses which logically follow on from there. In the following example a client is referring to her husband's depression:

Client: When I came in from work yesterday, he was sitting in the dark by the window, all on his own. It made *me* depressed to see him.
Counsellor: You became depressed too...

It is important to keep these responses to a minimum, and to wait for a natural pause before making them. Verbal following is similar to para-phrasing, which will be discussed in the next chapter.

It should be remembered that while knowledge of our own non-verbal responses is essential for counsellors, excessive preoccupation with it can be counterproductive and may lead to behaviour which seems inauthen-tic or forced. Student counsellors need to learn to use their own bodies 'instinctively' (Egan, 1990), but this instinctive use of communication can only be achieved when students have sufficient confidence to be them-selves in relation to clients.

THE COUNSELLOR'S USE OF LANGUAGE

The counsellor's use of language is an important issue in counselling. Clients need to know that they are being spoken to as equals, and to this end counsellors should avoid using jargon which is, by its nature, exclu-sive. This is especially important at the beginning when a client and coun-sellor first meet because it is during this initial contact that rapport should be established. Clients may also ask for information about the counsel-lor's training or theoretical approach and this too should be given in clear, explicit terms without use of jargon. Counsellors should also be careful to avoid the use of sexist language, disparaging terms or labelling when they speak to clients. These language pitfalls may seem too obvious to actually state, but people sometimes resort to the use of certain terms through habit and lack of conscious awareness. In this way it is possible to fall into the trap of labelling people according to certain conditions; for example, 'Is he an alcoholic? Depressive? Manipulative?' and so on. Awareness of colloquial and informal language is also important for counsellors; so too is familiarity with and acceptance of the words and terminology commonly used to describe sexual behaviour.

PRACTICAL ASPECTS OF COMMUNICATION

There are certain practical aspects of counselling which need to be addressed in the general context of communication. Student counsellors have to learn how to greet clients when they first meet; they need to know how to ensure privacy and comfort, how to establish time constraints and contracts, how to talk about confidentiality, and whether it is appropriate to take notes during or after sessions. Some of these issues will be discussed in more detail in later chapters (for example, confidentiality in Chapter 9), but the following are some general points in relation to practical aspects of counselling.

- The client should receive a warm and friendly greeting from the counsellor. This will include shaking hands, giving good eye contact and using the client's name. The counsellor should also introduce herself by name, and indicate a chair in which the client can sit. The following is an example of the kind of verbal exchange which might take place:

  Counsellor: Hello, Mrs Edwards? Please come in. My name is Karen Woods.
  Client: (*hesitates nervously*) Hello. I don't really know how to start now that I'm here.
  Counsellor: It is difficult to get started sometimes. Perhaps you could tell me why you decided to come. We have an hour together to talk about it.

- Clients need to be seen in privacy and in a comfortable environment.

- Clients need to know the time of appointments, the length of sessions, and how often they should attend.

- Client and counsellor need to form a contract which should cover all aspects of the counselling agreement.

- The client needs to know how he can be helped, and what efforts he will need to expend in order to help himself.

- Issues relating to confidentiality should be discussed, along with any issues of boundaries.

- Depending on the setting in which a counsellor works, notes may need to be taken after sessions. A truly client-centred approach would dictate that clients are informed about these notes and why they are needed. Taking notes during sessions can have the effect of switching attention from the client to the paperwork. Note-taking activity also tends to disrupt client concentration and trust.

- Clients should not be stopped abruptly at the end of sessions, but should be given some information in advance that a certain amount of time remains. For this reason, it is a good idea to make sure that there is a clock in the counselling room, positioned in a way which makes it visible to both counsellor and client. The counsellor should avoid looking at her watch because this is nearly always obvious to clients, no matter how surreptitiously it is done.

- The room in which clients are seen should be free from interruptions. If necessary, a 'Do Not Disturb' sign should be placed on the door. It is preferable to have no telephone in the room, but if there is one arrangements should be made to redirect calls until sessions are over.

- Furniture should be arranged in a comfortable, user-friendly way, with no obvious barriers like tables or desks between client and counsellor. It is useful, however, to have a small table nearby with a box of tissues for use by clients who become emotionally upset or tearful.

- It is also useful to keep a diary close by in which to arrange future appointments.

CASE STUDY: KEIR

Keir was nineteen years of age, and had been involved in a car accident with her father and brother two years before she came for counselling. She made an appointment to see a counsellor at the university she was attending because although she had been treated by her doctor immediately after the accident, she had never really been able to talk in depth to anyone about it.

The factors which prompted Keir to seek counselling included loss of confidence, some difficulty in concentrating and vague feelings of anxiety which were not linked to anything specific. She did not immediately connect these factors with the accident two years previously, but later on she started to associate many of her current problems with the earlier trauma.

When Keir arrived for her first appointment, Steve, the counsellor, greeted her warmly and took her to one of the counselling rooms in the student services department. It was comfortably furnished with armchairs and a small coffee table, and was situated in a quiet area of the building where there were no extraneous noises, no telephone, and little possibility of interruption or distraction.

Steve introduced himself to Keir, and told her that they had fifty minutes to talk together. He also assured her that their conversation would be confidential, although he did refer to the fact that he often discussed his work, in general terms, with a supervisor. He added that he did not use clients' names during these discussions. Keir was interested in the details given by Steve, and she seemed to be reassured by his openness. However, not all clients would be able to absorb this amount of information so early in a first encounter. This inability to absorb details is linked to the fact that clients are often emotionally distressed when they come for counselling. Later on though, they do need to be given the necessary factual information.

Keir talked to Steve and he listened to her carefully. He noticed that she described her current problems quite fluently and without obvious difficulty, but when she touched on the subject of her accident there were clear indications of distress and anxiety. This distress and anxiety was visible in her non-verbal communication and in the tone of her voice, which was faltering and tearful at times. Then she paused and was silent for a while, as if mentally picturing the accident all over again. Steve waited until he sensed that she wanted him to speak to her.

STEVE: So this was a very frightening experience for you. You still remember it vividly.

KEIR: It was terrible. I couldn't talk to my brother or to Dad about it. They had their own problems to sort out.

STEVE: You had to keep it all to yourself. And now you feel you need to talk about it.

KEIR: Yes. It's such a relief to talk to someone who doesn't get uptight about it.

STEVE: To someone who wasn't involved.

At the end of their exchange Steve used the technique of *verbal following* which had the effect of demonstrating his interest and attention to Keir. This, in turn, gave her the encouragement to continue with the necessary task of exploring and clarifying her thoughts and feelings. Keir remembered how she had argued with her brother just before the accident in which he had been seriously injured. Afterwards she was filled with self-blame and self-condemnation and the doctor had said she was suffering from *Post Traumatic Stress Disorder*. He gave her treatment in the form of medication for this, but she had never received help for the frequent psychological problems she had suffered since that time. Keir was adamant that she did not want to take any more medication; she wanted to understand her reaction to the accident, and she asked Steve if it would be possible to see him over a period of time in order to talk through her problems.

Throughout this and subsequent counselling sessions with Keir, Steve used the skills of *Active listening, Paraphrasing, Summarizing, Asking questions* and *Reflecting* back both feelings and content. The practice of these skills will be shown in future case studies in the following chapters.

Steve made a contract with Keir and agreed to meet her for six counselling sessions initially. During these meetings she was able to explore her reactions to the accident two years earlier.

'Post Traumatic Stress Disorder' describes a pattern of reactions which occur following a traumatic event. These reactions include irritability, inability to concentrate on work, emotional numbness, and difficulty in relating to other people. Perhaps the most common reaction is the re-experiencing – either through flashbacks or nightmares – of the original trauma. Guilt, anger and depression are also common, especially when survivors blame themselves for what happened. These problems tend to occur immediately after the event, but they can be delayed for quite long periods of time.

Keir had not experienced flashbacks or nightmares, but she did suffer from self-blame and self-condemnation. Many of the problems relating to Post Traumatic Stress Disorder are alleviated through adequate expression of painful emotions and through the support of friends and professional help (Lowe, 1994).

Since Keir had not been able to talk to either family or friends about her reactions, counselling did help her work through some of the painful emotions and feelings she had experienced.

KEY WORDS AND PHRASES

PARALINGUISTIC OR PARALANGUAGE

The words paralinguistic and paralanguage refer to the various aspects of speech which are present in addition to the actual words spoken. These extra aspects of speech can convey deep emotion and meaning much more powerfully than words. They include tone of voice, rhythm, volume, timing, accent, pitch, silence, stressing of words and phrases, hesitation and speech errors. Someone who says 'I am very happy' for example, means something quite different when the word 'am' is stressed. Thus 'I *am* very happy' tends to indicate a determination to be happy, perhaps against all odds.

NON-VERBAL COMMUNICATION

Non-linguistic aspects of behaviour are commonly referred to as non-verbal communication. Non-linguistic behaviours include gestures, gaze, posture, body movements, body space, appearance, contact or touch and facial expression. Certain aspects of paralanguage are also included under the heading of 'non-verbal communication'. These include some of those features already referred to, such as timing, emphasis and stress on certain words or phrases.

Non-verbal communication is also a powerful medium for conveying emotions and when non-verbal and linguistic messages are in conflict it is the non-verbal communication which carries greater weight (Argyle, 1983).

The ways we present ourselves to others through dress, hairstyle, makeup and adornment also transmits very powerful messages about how we would view ourselves and how we would like to be viewed by others. Rituals such as handshaking and greeting behaviour also serve to communicate messages which are not included in any of the words spoken.

EXERCISES

EXERCISE I   LISTENING WITHOUT INTERRUPTION

Work with a partner for about five minutes. One person should speak about a topical subject of choice, while the other person listens. The task for the listener is to avoid interrupting the speaker, while at the same time giving non-verbal signals of interest and encouragement. Afterwards, discuss the exercise, paying special attention to any difficulties experienced by the listener.

EXERCISE 2   HOMEWORK ASSIGNMENT

This is a homework exercise which can be completed and discussed in the next training session. Spend some time observing the way other people around you communicate. What are the factors which contribute to good communication and what are the factors which discourage it?

EXERCISE 3   NON-VERBAL COMMUNICATION AND EMOTIONS
Working in groups of three or four, brainstorm a list of all those aspects of non-verbal behaviour which might indicate the following emotions:

- sadness
- anger
- agitation
- euphoria
- despair
- happiness

EXERCISE 4   TOUCHING
Working in groups of three or four, consider the following questions:

a) When is touch appropriate?
b) When is touch inappropriate?

One way of doing this is to write the word TOUCH in the centre of a large page, and then list all your associations to it. Afterwards, discuss your findings with other members of the training group.

EXERCISE 5   GREETING CLIENTS
Working in pairs, make a list of verbal greetings which counsellors might use to convey warmth to clients at the beginning of a session. For example:

'My name is Karen. How can I help you Mrs Brown?'

EXERCISE 6   LISTENING TO SELF AND OTHERS
Work in pairs with one person acting as speaker, the other as listener. The speaker should talk for about five minutes on any subject of choice, while the listener concentrates on the speaker's use of words, tone of voice, posture and gestures.

Afterwards, discuss the exercise, concentrating on any significant aspects of the interaction which were helpful or problematic, for either speaker or listener. For example:

A: How did the speaker experience the listener's attention?
B: Was it easy or difficult for the listener to monitor mentally the significant aspects of the speaker's communication?

EXERCISE 7   SILENCE
This is a group exercise which should be carried over a period of about ten minutes. Everyone in the group is instructed to be totally silent for the specified time. Participants are asked beforehand to monitor their own thought processes during the time, and to take mental note of any extraneous noise or interference which they experience. Afterwards, discuss the exercise with the group as a whole.

EXERCISE 8   PERSONAL COMMUNICATION

Working individually complete the following sentences:

'My best communication skill is ...'
'I would like to communicate with ...'
'I would find it difficult to communicate with ...'
'Communication to me means ...'
'I talk best to people when ...'
'I listen best when ...'
'The things which interfere with my listening ability are ...'
'I can't really speak when other people ...'
'The best conditions for communication are ...'
'Things which improve listening ability are ...'

FURTHER READING

1 Argyle, Michael, *The Psychology of Interpersonal Behaviour*, Penguin, London, 1983.
2 Culley, Sue, *Interactive Counselling Skills in Action*, Sage, London, 1991.
3 O'Farrell, Ursula, *First Steps in Counselling*, Veritas, Dublin, 1995.
4 Nelson Jones, Richard, *Practical Counselling and Helping Skills*, Cassell, London, 1989.
5 Nelson Jones, Richard, *Human Relationship Skills*, Cassell, London, 1991.
6 Munro, Anne, Manthei, Bob and Small, John, *Counselling: The Skills of Problem Solving*, Routledge, London, 1989.
7 Wicks, Robert J, *Helping Others*, Souvenir Press, London, 1994.
8 Oliver, Robert W, *Psychology and Health Care*, Balliére Tindall, London, 1993.

REFERENCE LIST

1 *The Psychology of Interpersonal Behaviour* by Michael Argyle, Penguin, London, 1983.
2 *Bodily Communication* by Michael Argyle, Methuen, London, 1975.
3 *The Skilled Helper* by Gerard Egan, Brookes/Cole, Monterey CA, 1990.
4 *COMMUNICATE – A Communicator's Skills: Guide for Healthcare Workers* by Philip Burnard, Edward Arnold, London, 1992.
5 *Social Skills in Interpersonal Communication* by Owen Hargie, Christine Saunders and David Dickson, Routledge, London, 1995.
6 *EYE TO EYE – How People Interact* by Dr Peter Mars, Guild, London, 1988.
7 'Post Traumatic Stress Disorder' by F Lowe in *Nervous Breakdown* edited by C Kean, Mercier, Dublin, 1994.

CHAPTER 3

Responding to clients

In this chapter we shall consider the ways in which counsellors attempt to see things from what Carl Rogers described as the client's 'internal frame of reference' (*Client-Centred Therapy*, Rogers, 1991). We shall also look at what he defined as the opposite or 'external frame of reference' (Rogers, 1991) and examine the ways in which these two perspectives differ from each other, in terms of their characteristics and distinguishing qualities.

The importance of establishing emotional rapport with clients in counselling will also be discussed, and the significance of the actual relationship between counsellor and client will be considered. In addition, the following counselling skills and qualities will be examined in this chapter:

- Reflecting
- Paraphrasing
- Summarizing
- Encouraging people to talk
- Focusing on client's feelings
- Conveying empathy
- Conveying respect
- Conveying attitudes of sincerity and openness with clients.

Reflecting

Perhaps the most helpful way to highlight the role of reflection and paraphrasing in interpersonal exchanges is to indicate their use in dialogue form. Dialogue takes place between people in many different contexts: socially, at work, with friends and among family members. According to its context, the form of dialogue used can vary enormously. One person may be concerned to elicit information from another person, in which case the conversation which takes place will reflect this. Doctors and nurses may, for example, communicate with patients in this way, especially when case histories are being taken. However, doctors and nurses may communicate with patients in other ways too, particularly when there is less pressure on them to elicit factual information. A nurse could, for example, talk to patients about their personal concerns, although this kind of interaction requires sufficient time, and some degree of training in interpersonal skills. When factual information only is required from an interaction, there is little opportunity to establish an emotional link between two people. The following dialogue is an example of this kind of exchange – this time between a general practitioner and an elderly man with a chest infection.

Patient: I've had a cold this two weeks past. Now it's gone down to my chest.
Doctor: When did you feel it in your chest?
Patient: About three days ago.
Doctor: What about breathing? Any pain? Any cough?
Patient: Well no, no pain. Cough in the mornings, and a bit breathless. I'm a bit fed up and depressed with it.
Doctor: (*writing*) No pain. Early morning cough and a bit breathless. Any sputum?
Patient: Coughing up, you mean? No.
Doctor: Anything else?
Patient: Not much appetite. Oh, and headaches too.
Doctor: Have you taken anything?
Patient: Nothing, except a drink of hot whisky at night.
Doctor: Just take off your coat and I'll examine your chest.

The doctor conducting this interview was concerned to make a professional diagnosis of the man's condition. For this reason, the interaction between patient and doctor was based on a series of questions which the doctor needed to ask. In response to each question, the patient gave factual answers which referred to his physical condition. On one occasion, however, he does mention a feeling of being 'fed up and depressed', but the doctor in his summary of symptoms fails to record this. As a result of this failure to respond, no emotional link is established between patient and doctor, and although the man's physical condition will be treated – probably successfully – his low spirits and depression have not been acknowledged. It is quite likely, though, that successful treatment of the patient's physical symptoms will also restore his emotional health; and if this is the case, then the communication which has taken place between doctor and patient will be concluded in a satisfactory way.

In contrast to the interaction just described, there is another more empathic way of responding to people which is specifically designed to establish emotional rapport between helper and client. The concept of *Reflection of feeling* is one which Carl Rogers refers to (Rogers, 1991) in connection with this form of empathic communication. The following dialogue should illustrate some aspects of *reflection* as it is used in conversation between two people.

Mrs Williams is a seventy five year old woman who attends a day centre three days per week. She is visited there by an occupational therapist (OT) who wants to assess her overall circumstances at home.

MRS WILLIAMS: I'm alright at taking care of myself, except for the stairs and the bath. I've always been independent and tried to do for myself.

OT: You've valued your independence and your ability to cope.

MRS WILLIAMS: ... Yes I have ... I go slowly ... don't do things too fast. Getting in and out of the bath is a problem though.

OT: Although you manage well most of the time, there are some areas you might need help with ...

MRS WILLIAMS: I don't like to ask for help, but sometimes it is frustrating when you are on your own.

OT: Being alone has its drawbacks for you ... not getting help when you need it.

MRS WILLIAMS: It's not just the help ... it's lonely at times as well, especially since my daughter moved to Aberdeen. She used to visit me often.

OT: So your daughter moving away means that you have less company now ... and that makes it harder to cope alone.

MRS WILLIAMS: It does .... Yes, it does make it harder to cope, and I don't like to trouble other people with my problems. Everybody has their own problems.

OT: You don't feel you can ask other people for help, when they might need help themselves.

MRS WILLIAMS: That's it ...

OT: People need help at different times. It's alright to ask for it, especially when it's available for you.

MRS WILLIAMS: (nodding) ... Yes ... I remember when Mrs Taylor was getting on, they fitted her up with a stair lift ... rails and gadgets in the kitchen too if I recall ... There probably are some things that would help me.

Sarah, the occupational therapist who conducted this interview, wanted to convey interest and warmth in the responses which she gave to her client. As well as conveying interest and warmth, she also wanted to understand fully what it was that Mrs Williams was experiencing at that time. In order to achieve all these aims, Sarah made a point of listening carefully for the emotional content of Mrs Williams' replies. Both the *emotional* and the circumstantial elements of the client's responses were, in fact, closely linked in this case.

Mrs Williams states that she has always been independent and capable of coping alone. Behind the actual words which she speaks there are clear messages of self-reliance, freedom and autonomy. In the response which Sarah gives her, these messages are picked up and acknowledged, and this reflection and acknowledgement encourages Mrs Williams to describe her home conditions in greater detail.

Throughout her exchange with Mrs Williams, Sarah is concerned to stay *within the client's internal frame of reference*. To do this, she needs to keep herself in the background as much as possible, and she needs to confine herself to those responses which will enable Mrs Williams to look more closely at her own circumstances and needs. At one point in the conversation, however, Sarah does offer a direct view of her own when she assures Mrs Williams that it is alright for people to ask for help when they need it. But the expression of this view occurs towards the latter part of the interview, and is expressed only when Sarah is convinced that her client is ready to receive it.

In the interaction with her client, Sarah was using good interpersonal skills, including the skills of *reflecting* both the content and meaning of Mrs Williams' words. By responding in this way, Sarah showed that she accepted the client's view of her own situation. Another way of looking at this kind of response is to say that it *validates* the truth, accuracy and importance of the client's viewpoint. When it is done correctly, reflection should state clearly what it is the client is conveying about her situation, her problems and her emotional reactions to these. The client who senses that her viewpoint is accurately perceived by the helper, will then feel valued and understood, and more importantly will feel encouraged to explore in greater depth all the issues concerning her situation. By clearly communicating a willingness to listen and understand, the helper enables the client to speak openly about significant – and often previously unacknowledged – feelings, difficulties and needs. Reflection shows that the helper is paying close attention to the client, and is actively listening, not just to the words but to the meanings behind the words as well (see Fig. 3.1).

This use of active listening helps to make clients more aware of their experiences, thoughts and feelings, and should encourage them to become more courageous in their exploration and assessment of these.

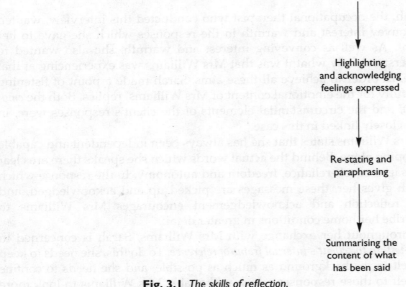

THE SKILLS OF REFLECTION INCLUDE

Highlighting
and acknowledging
feelings expressed

Re-stating and
paraphrasing

Summarising the
content of what
has been said

Fig. 3.1 *The skills of reflection.*

Paraphrasing

Paraphrasing is one aspect of reflection; in fact, the words reflection and paraphrasing are often used interchangeably by helpers and counsellors. Strictly speaking, however, they are slightly different because the term paraphrasing refers to the process of re-wording the *content* of what a client has said; whereas the term *reflection of feeling* means restating the kernel or essence of what a client has said, in a way which focuses more on the *feelings* behind the words.

In counselling, the emphasis is on both content and feelings. The counsellor's task is to reflect these back to the client in a way which conveys empathy and understanding. It is not enough, therefore, to simply 'echo' a client's words verbatim since this would become monotonous, tiresome and boring – quite apart from the fact that it would also be meaningless and unhelpful for clients. Literal *re-statement* of key words can be helpful in some instances, and can be used to prompt clients when a specific or important issue needs to be looked at in more detail. The following is an example of re-statement used in this way:

Client: I know I eat more when I'm depressed.
Counsellor: Depressed . . .
Client: Yes, really down. Eating helps to fill up the empty space inside me.

By using one word which the client has already used (depressed) the counsellor is successful in encouraging the client to explore her feelings about food, and her need to use it in certain ways.

This re-statement of key words and phrases is often most helpful at the beginning of counselling when a client may experience some difficulty in getting started. The following client experienced this kind of difficulty, and the counsellor used *re-statement* in order to help him clarify what it was he wanted to say.

Client: It's difficult to say how she has changed . . .
Counsellor: To say *how* she has changed . . .
Client: Yes. It seems to have changed her attitude to the children . . .

Through repetition of the last part of the client's sentence and through focusing on his use of the word 'how' the counsellor helped the client to find the best way of describing his experiences. Even though this kind of 'echoing' response is effective at certain times in counselling, it can, nevertheless, be overdone. When it is overdone, there are clear indications of poor listening on the counsellor's part. Real *active listening* always tunes into the emotional as well as the factual content of what clients say. Sensitive reflection of client responses, therefore, involves good listening and paraphrasing skills, and the ability to convey understanding of both content and feeling back to the client.

Steven was thirty four years of age and had been referred for counselling because he was depressed after the break up of his marriage. He had been married for ten years, but had quarrelled frequently with his wife during that time. In spite of their often acrimonious disagreements, Steven still loved his wife and deeply regretted their separation. However, she was adamant that she wanted a divorce, and Steven felt he had no alternative but to acquiesce. His main concern was that he and Lisa (his wife) should do the best for their children.

STEVEN: Lisa brought the subject up again on Saturday...you know...about us, the divorce. Well, we had a row as usual. The way I feel at the moment, I can't possibly make a decision about it.

COUNSELLOR: You find it difficult to think clearly about your relationship with Lisa at the moment, and this leads to more tension between you...

STEVEN: Yes, things seen to go from bad to worse. The more she talks about it, the more I get depressed. I just don't want to do it...

COUNSELLOR: To make the decision?

STEVEN: No. Well...yes, I know I have to come to a decision some time. If I don't, Lisa will go ahead anyway. But I need to have some say in what's happening because of Rosie and Bethan [the children].

COUNSELLOR: So, on one level, you know you need to talk to Lisa about this since she might set things in motion herself anyway.

STEVEN: Yes... (pause)

COUNSELLOR: And you feel you need to have some influence on events because of the children...

STEVEN: I am absolutely determined to have my say in that...And there are all the other practical aspects that I need to have a say in as well. But I feel so tired and depressed by it all...the very thought of it makes me tired.

COUNSELLOR: The prospect of the divorce, and everything it involves, is emotionally draining for you. It's hard for you to get to grips with it...

STEVEN: Perhaps if we could talk about it without having a row, I wouldn't get so down about it.

COUNSELLOR: So approaching the discussions in a calmer way would help you to feel more in control...and capable of sorting out the practical issues involved.

STEVEN: I know it would...if we could just do it.

COUNSELLOR: You, at least, know a calmer approach would help...which is a step to doing it.

By listening carefully to what Steven said, and by focusing on his words and his feelings, the counsellor was then able to frame appropriate reflective responses. These reflective responses were – in the main – paraphrases of what Steven said, but they were worded in a slightly different way and they stressed the affective or emotional element of his statements. Steven appeared to find this helpful since it enabled him to move to a point in the discussion where he could see what he needed to do in order to feel more in control of his situation.

The counsellor was concerned to avoid asking questions, although one of the responses (To make the decision?) is made in question form. Some of the problems associated with asking questions will be discussed in the next chapter. In the context of reflection and paraphrasing, however, the point should be made that direct questions seldom help clients to feel understood or to clarify the issues which concern them.

Summarizing

Summarizing is an interpersonal skill which is used by people in a variety of occupations. Teachers frequently use summaries in order to review subject areas which they have already covered, while interviewers, doctors, healthcare workers and members of the legal profession routinely abridge the information they have been given as a way of considering it and highlighting salient points.

Summarizing is also used in counselling and is especially helpful as a 'bridging response' (Egan, 1990). In Chapter 1 we looked at the three-stage model of counselling which Egan formulated as a structure or framework for the counselling process. One way of linking these three stages is through the use of summarizing.

Summarizing can also be used to provide a link between counselling sessions. In this respect, it is particularly effective when carried out at the end of one session and the beginning of the next.

When using summarizing, the counsellor's task is to paraphrase and reflect a series of statements which the client has made in the course of a session, or at various stages throughout a session. Clients seldom talk in a totally structured way, and when they are emotionally upset – as they often are – their statements may seem disjointed, unconnected and lacking in overall coherence. Summarizing, therefore, requires discipline and – once again – active listening on the part of the counsellor. When it is done accurately, summarizing gives clients the opportunity to review what they have said and through the process of review to identify and abstract those areas of concern which are most important to them at a given time. Summarizing is a skill which is of benefit to counsellors as well, since it enables them to monitor their own listening and understanding. It is not always possible to memorize and retain every aspect of a client's story, but when summarizing is used by the counsellor the client is given the opportunity to add details which may have been overlooked or under-emphasized. This process helps to ensure that both client and counsellor are 'together' throughout sessions.

Summarizing – like reflection and paraphrasing – lets clients see that their experiences, emotions and thinking have been acknowledged and validated by the counsellor. Any inconsistencies in what clients say can also be highlighted during an accurate summary. Counsellors need to be sensitive, however, in the way they identify clients' inconsistencies or contradictions. One way of avoiding insensitive or judgemental statements in a summary is to stay conscientiously within the client's *internal frame of reference.* What may seem like a contradiction to the counsellor, may have a totally different meaning for the client.

Summarizing in counselling is valuable because it necessitates three important things (see also Fig. 3.2):

- understanding of what has been said

- accurate selection of key elements and themes

- verbal expression of these key elements and themes in a clear, straightforward and empathic way.

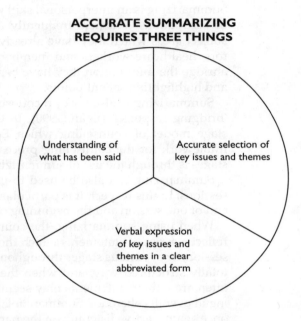

**ACCURATE SUMMARIZING
REQUIRES THREE THINGS**

Understanding of what has been said

Accurate selection of key issues and themes

Verbal expression of key issues and themes in a clear abbreviated form

Fig. 3.2 *Accurate summarizing.*

Summarizing, therefore, is more than simply cutting down the number of words which the client has used. To summarize well, it is necessary to grasp the client's line of thought and expression of feeling, and then to select the core message or messages from this. Logical links should be established between the various ideas, thoughts and feelings expressed, and all this needs to be achieved in the counsellor's own words. It is not enough to repeat what the client has said, in abbreviated form, although it would be unrealistic to expect that appropriate synonyms could be found to match the client's every word. The sequence of a story or account is also important, and to complete an accurate summary counsellors need to remember the order of events. The timing of a summary is crucial in counselling, since any premature interruption of a client's narrative may inhibit or embarrass him. Clients should be given the opportunity to correct any mistakes in a summary, and when summarizing is used to close a session, both client and counsellor need to agree that it is accurate.

The following is an example of how summarizing can be used at the end of a counselling session.

Corinna was referred for counselling by her general practitioner and gave the following account of her situation and problems. She had just moved with her husband and baby to a house in the country. Before this, they had lived in town. The move to the country caused her some anxiety, since she didn't like being so far away from her family and friends. She also found it difficult to make new friends in her rural setting, and the isolation and loneliness had led to bouts of depression. Just recently, she found herself reluctant to do the shopping, and the housework and cooking had become burdensome as well.

Her husband, whose new job included promotion, was keen to entertain his colleagues and business contacts to occasional meals at home, but Corinna felt unable to agree to this. In addition, she did not feel that she should have to be involved, especially since she had a small baby to care for and felt herself totally drained of energy at times. Her husband was sympathetic to some extent, but Corinna did not really believe that he understood her position. When she went to her GP with symptoms of fatigue, anxiety and mild agoraphobia, he asked her if she would like to be referred for counselling. She agreed to this.

The counsellor (Anna) listened to Corinna throughout the first session and made the proper responses to her. At the end of the counselling session, Anna gave the following summary:

'Since we're coming towards the end of the session, let's put together what you have told me so far. You started by saying that you have just moved with your family to the area, and the change has been fairly traumatic for you. You have developed some health problems, and find it lonely being away from relatives and friends. Now your husband wants you to entertain, and that just seems like the last straw, especially when you have the baby to care for and you feel so tired. Your husband is supportive, but not totally understanding. You feel that things might be better if you could communicate more. Does what I have said so far seem about right?'

The client (Corinna) responded to this by stressing her anxiety at the thought of entertaining her husband's colleagues. Clients often select one aspect of a summary for further discussion, and this helps to focus attention on the areas which are most problematic for them. An accurate summary gives both counsellor and client the opportunity to select or prioritize issues in this way. In addition, clients may add something else to the summary – something which perhaps they had forgotten to mention in their original account.

Internal and external frames of reference

When counsellors respond to clients through the use of reflecting, paraphrasing and summarizing skills, they need to do so – if they are to be effective – from what Rogers describes as the client's *internal frame of reference* (Rogers, 1991). This term was mentioned at the beginning of the chapter, and refers to the client's individual experience of himself, his circumstances and his world. The ability to understand a client's internal view of things requires a special effort on the counsellor's part, along with discipline, active listening and a willingness to lay one's own preconceived ideas aside.

EMPATHY

Empathy is at the very centre of this kind of counsellor/client experience. However, Carl Rogers points out that a client's inner world is not the same thing as 'emotional identification' with the client (Rogers, 1991). In other words, it is not necessary or desirable for a counsellor actually to experience the emotions which a client experiences, but it is necessary to apprehend, appreciate and understand them. A counsellor who becomes overwhelmed by the client's strong emotions is unable to sustain the proper balance of the relationship – which should, after all, be geared to helping the client.

Reference was made in Chapter 1 to the fact that sympathy and empathy are different because sympathy tends to be superficial, and fairly easy to demonstrate, while empathy requires effort and a genuine desire to understand. To some extent, sympathy involves feeling sorry for the other person, and may even encompass such emotions as compassion and kindness as well. Quite often, sympathy includes a willingness to offer assistance or practical help if this is needed. Sympathy, therefore, has a very important part to play in human interaction and when it is appropriately given among family and friends, its effects are usually positive. Sympathy cards and letters are often sent to people who have been bereaved, for example, and this expression of sympathy has the effect of conveying support for, and recognition of, the emotional trauma which another person has experienced. Conventional expressions of sympathy from friends, relatives and neighbours are an integral part of a cohesive and caring social network, and in this respect they are valuable and necessary. When people experience suffering, whether through bereavement, loss or other trauma, they need to know that their fellow human beings are aware of what has happened. This awareness is appropriately expressed through sympathy.

Perhaps one of the most important points to make about it is that sympathy almost invariably derives from an *external frame of reference*. Another way of putting this is to say that a person expressing sympathy can do so without any real understanding of what another has experienced. Sympathy can stem from a superficial or outside view of another person's suffering, but it makes no attempt to achieve real insight into the true nature or quality of that suffering. When we approach someone else's experience from an external frame of reference, we tend to categorize it, and impose our own views upon it. This tendency to make another's experience conform to our way of thinking is limited and distorting, and has the added disadvantage of producing a one-dimensional view of the actual experience itself. The following example should illustrate this last point:

Mrs Rankin had nursed her ill husband for many years. He suffered from a progressive illness which meant that his condition deteriorated quite rapidly in the year before his death. Mrs Rankin was forty six when her husband died, and although she had loved him she felt some measure of relief when the long period of nursing was over. Alongside the experience of relief, there were also feelings of guilt and remorse. She had been impatient and cross with her husband at times. He had been a difficult man in many ways, and now that he was gone Mrs Rankin felt free to pursue her own interests – most of which she had abandoned during the course of her husband's illness. In addition to this, she was able to take up with old friends and acquaintances and generally socialize more.

A conventional and sympathetic response to Mrs Rankin's experience would almost certainly focus exclusively on her loss. Other important aspects of her situation might not be acknowledged partly because they may not have been communicated to friends, neighbours or acquaintances anyway. On the other hand, traditional attitudes to bereavement and loss have tended to assume that such experiences are wholly distressing. But events which are ostensibly tragic, can also be positive in some respects. In Mrs Rankin's case, there are many complex aspects of her experience which certainly could be described as positive. This is not to say that she is unlikely to suffer emotionally as a result of her husband's death; she might well suffer more than another bereaved person whose marriage was idyllic – if it is ever possible to describe any marriage in this way. The point to be made here is that we can never really know the exact nature of someone else's experience, nor can we assume that certain events are either intrinsically negative or positive. The only way we can attempt to share another person's experience is through the development and practice of empathy. When empathy is present in a relationship – as it should be in counselling – then the person receiving help will know that all the unique features and complexities of their situation are accepted, valued and understood.

Empathy therefore, unlike sympathy, is concerned with understanding the client's individual and unique view of things. Another way of putting this is to say that empathy is what makes it possible for counsellors to imagine and appreciate the client's *internal frame of reference*.

It is not enough, however, for counsellors to simply experience empathy without the means or the ability to communicate it effectively to clients. Empathy is a two-way process, and clients need to know that it is present in the counselling relationship. The ability to use a range of counselling skills well is a fundamental prerequisite for the counsellor who wishes to establish and convey empathy to clients. A summary of the skills and personal attributes needed to do this includes:

- interest in the client and in the client's experiences

- the ability to understand and use the client's language

- the ability to reflect back feelings expressed by the client

- understanding of why clients experience certain feelings

- the ability to establish emotional rapport with the client through the use of active listening, and careful attention to the nuances behind the client's words

- accurate paraphrasing and summarizing of the essential elements of the client's story
- sensitive and well-timed use of questions in counselling
- sufficient self-restraint and patience to allow clients to proceed at their own pace
- the capacity to identify with clients without becoming emotionally engulfed by their problems
- the ability to use non-verbal cues and prompts which will encourage clients to talk through their problems
- the ability to make clients feel valued and worthwhile
- the ability to make clients feel confident and motivated.

In addition to the skills and characteristics already mentioned, counsellors need to be capable of and willing to use their own personal experiences as reference points for deeper understanding of clients. This does not mean that personal reminiscences should be shared with clients during sessions, since this would be inappropriate in therapeutic counselling. Nor does it imply that counsellors should concentrate on mentally comparing their own experiences with those of clients during sessions. What it does mean is that counsellors can utilize the knowledge and experience which they have gained throughout life in order to refine and develop their capacity to empathize with clients. Student counsellors frequently ask if it is possible to 'practise' empathy, and the answer to this is yes. We can practise empathy by, first of all, identifying our own experiences, and this can be accomplished through self-awareness exercises in training. We can continue to practise by sharing our experiences with others in training. Students can also learn to observe their own use of empathy in communication with others, and they can – over a period of time – increase their use of empathic responses.

CONVEYING WARMTH

Warmth is the second of Rogers three core conditions and is sometimes referred to as acceptance, unconditional positive regard or caring. It is obviously much easier for clients – or for anyone – to discuss sensitive, personal or intimate issues when the person they are talking to is clearly showing attitudes of warmth and acceptance. Acceptance implies a non-judgemental approach by counsellors. This important attribute has already been referred to in previous chapters, especially in connection with counsellor self-development and awareness.

Another significant aspect of warmth and acceptance is that, when these are present, clients are more likely to gain confidence in themselves, and in their own ability to cope. The feeling that someone else cares for and values us, prompts a sense of confidence almost immediately. This can, in turn, lead to greater courage and self-assurance in tackling problems.

Acceptance of clients does not imply that the counsellor needs to approve of everything they say and do. Once again this raises the issue of counsellor self-awareness, and the importance of being able to separate our own views and opinions from those of the client. A client's views, experiences and behaviour may be at variance with the counsellor's own value system, but the client − as a person − is entitled to acceptance and positive regard, especially when he has placed his trust in the counsellor and made himself vulnerable in the process.

Counsellors need to believe in their clients' rights to autonomy and self-governance. When this belief is present, the temptation to exert pressure − subtle or otherwise − on clients will be absent in the counselling situation. Understanding of human nature and the myriad problems which people can experience is a fundamental requirement for people who wish to work in a helping capacity with others.

Warmth and acceptance are especially important when client and counsellor first meet. In Chapter 1 we referred to Egan's three-stage model of counselling, and described the first stage as a time when clients are encouraged to explore and clarify their problems. This exploration and clarification cannot take place, however, unless the client feels accepted and valued as a person. Some of the skills already outlined can help to establish and demonstrate these attitudes of acceptance and caring. Active listening and sensitive reflection are particularly effective, but the personality of the counsellor is important too. It is not always the case that counsellors and clients automatically like each other, and there are occasions when emotional links are never established at all. In Carl Rogers' view, it is the client's perception of the counselling relationship which will determine the course of therapy (Rogers, 1991). Another way of putting this is to say that the client needs to feel comfortable and at ease with the counsellor before any progress can be made. Rogers makes the further important point that the way in which clients perceive the counselling relationship is, to a large extent, influenced by previous expectations and preconceived ideas gained from interactions with people in the past (Rogers, 1991). Clients who have been criticized habitually by parents in childhood, may well expect the same approach by a counsellor. Counsellors therefore face the task of conveying warmth and acceptance in a way which is 'unconditional' and has no strings attached.

When respect, acceptance and warmth are present in counselling, clients are more likely to accept themselves. This should, in turn, enhance their self-esteem, and enhanced self-esteem will go a long way in helping them to cope with change. Attitudes of respect and acceptance are crucial when challenging skills are used by the counsellor, because challenge is always difficult for clients. These skills of challenge are described in Chapter 5.

Another significant aspect of caring for clients is that it is indicated not only in the attitudes expressed by the counsellor to the client, but also in the actual environment in which sessions take place. A cold and uninviting room, for example, will certainly inhibit the development of trust and the ability – on the client's part – to engage in the difficult task of self-disclosure. Hargie et al. (1995) point out that a bare room with harsh lighting and poor furnishing is reminiscent of an interrogation centre. Clients do perceive all these things, which are registered firmly at unconscious or conscious levels.

It is worth mentioning here that the counsellor's appearance and style of dress will also make an impression on clients. Although it would be inappropriate to suggest that counsellors should dress in a special or prescribed way, they need to remember to show respect for clients – and for themselves – by paying some attention to details of dress and grooming. Counsellor respect for, and acceptance of, self go hand in hand with respect for others.

GENUINENESS

Genuineness is a quality which counsellors should possess if they are to be effective in their work with clients. Other words which describe this quality include honesty, congruence, sincerity and authenticity. It goes without saying that honesty with 'self' is necessary before honesty with others can be achieved. Student counsellors need to be aware of the fact that all of us are capable of self-deception, at least occasionally. If we deceive ourselves, then clients will perceive us as incongruent or false, and ultimately incapable of receiving their trust.

When counsellors are honest and open in their communication with clients, an atmosphere of trust is established and this atmosphere is helpful in stimulating clients to become more honest and open in turn. It is possible, therefore, for the counsellor to act as a 'model' of openness for the client, and through this modelling to enhance the client's capacity to engage in the often painful process of self-disclosure. One of the problems which student counsellors experience, however, is that they sometimes find it difficult to master a range of counselling skills without becoming artificial or unnatural in their use of them. In other words, student counsellors may find it hard to be congruent when they are preoccupied with saying and doing the right thing in a purely technical sense. Spontaneity and openness tend to be lost at the beginning of training, but they do return once the focus on skills is diminished, and some measure of competence achieved.

Discussions about counsellor genuineness almost invariably stimulate controversy among student counsellors in training. This is because the idea of honesty or openness is often taken to mean uninhibited frankness with clients. It has to be emphasized that uninhibited counsellor frankness is inappropriate, since its effect would be to strengthen the client's defences against self-disclosure. The true meaning of counsellor genuineness is that empathy and unconditional positive regard for the client are real and not spurious. When empathy and positive regard are truly present, then the counsellor will be open, honest and natural in a totally unfeigned way. The client's experience of this congruence or genuineness should help him to see that such attitudes are helpful in a relationship, and this may encourage him to become more honest in his own relationships as well.

Counsellors who are openly responsive to clients have no need to hide behind a professional façade or to pretend. They treat their clients as equals and acknowledge their potential abilities to deal effectively with their own problems. A counsellor who lacks awareness of her own limitations and who fails to identify any covert feelings of superiority, will only succeed in alienating clients who will quickly see through her self-deception and vanity, and rightly reject them.

In order to 'be' themselves, counsellors need to 'know' themselves. When this self-knowledge is present, the ability to be genuine in relation to clients will also be present. An appropriate and genuine response is always a 'natural' response which is prompted by a real concern to help the client. When congruence is present, there is a consistency between what the counsellor feels, and the way she speaks and acts. The following is an example of how congruence might look in practice.

The client, Lydia, had attended several counselling sessions and had talked at length about the stress she was under. She did not like her job and was having some difficulties at home.

CLIENT: At times I have absolutely no energy. I feel totally drained. You have heard me say this before... You must be bored by it...

COUNSELLOR: No... I'm not bored by it. But I know you have said it several times before, so it seems to be an area that you need to look at more closely.

CLIENT: I know my family get fed up listening to me. They just switch off now.

COUNSELLOR: I won't switch off. I'm listening to you...

CLIENT: It started really... about two months ago...

The client went on to tell her story in detail. This involved lengthy ruminations about many aspects of her work and family life. At one stage, she referred again to the possibility that this might all be too much for the counsellor.

CLIENT: Everything seemed to just build up... this must seem like a real catalogue of problems...

COUNSELLOR: It does seem that there are a lot of problem areas for you at the moment. Maybe we could draw together the main threads of what you have just said...

At this point, the counsellor summarized what Lydia had said throughout the interview. Her responses to the client were made in an open and genuine way, and her concern overall was to stay within the client's frame of reference.

| CASE STUDY: PAULINE | Pauline was forty five and had spent most of her married life at home looking after her two children. She had made a conscious decision to do this, but now |

that the children were grown up she wanted to continue the education she had cut short in order to settle down and have a family.

Pauline took up a healthcare course at college, in the hope that this would help her get into university to study nursing. At first her husband, Martin, was supportive and enthusiastic about her work, but after a while he became critical and impatient, especially when she spent long periods studying alone in her room. Her son and daughter had been supportive too, but they made little effort to pull their weight in the home. At a time when she needed practical help as well as encouragement, Pauline found that her family's expectations of her had not changed in the least since she started the course. In fact, they seemed to believe that she should fulfil her original role of cook, housekeeper and carer, while simultaneously pursuing a full-time, demanding course at college. The strain of all this was beginning to show on her relationships generally, and Pauline felt that her college work was beginning to suffer as well. She decided to seek counselling because, she said, it was available in her area, and nobody else seemed 'willing to listen' to her anyway.

When she first came to see the counsellor, Pauline spent some time describing her position at home.

PAULINE: Sometimes I get into a real panic about housework...there's the shopping at weekends too, the ironing and the planning the meals for the week.

COUNSELLOR: There's so much for you to do in a limited amount of time...

PAULINE: It seems endless. Quite apart from the fact that I'm exhausted, I get so upset inside. I feel that I'm doing everything on my own.

COUNSELLOR: You feel angry and isolated as well as being tired...

PAULINE: Yes...not angry with anyone in particular...more angry with myself for not being more organized.

COUNSELLOR: So in a sense you blame yourself because there is so much to do, and you alone can't do it...

PAULINE: That's right. I suppose it is unrealistic...

COUNSELLOR: Unrealistic to expect so much of yourself?

PAULINE: Yes. My problem is that I can't tell the others what I want without sounding as if I'm complaining.

COUNSELLOR: And yet there might be some grounds for complaint...

PAULINE: (laughs) You can say that again. I suppose I know what I should do really...

COUNSELLOR: You are aware of what it is you need to do...it's just putting it into action.

PAULINE: It's gathering up the courage to make them all sit down and talk to me seriously.

COUNSELLOR: So the first step is making the decision to do it. And for that you need some courage...

PAULINE: There is another thing though that stops me...apart from the courage aspect.

COUNSELLOR: Something else that is a worry to you...

PAULINE: Well, it's my husband. He loses his temper and shouts when I try to explain how I feel.

COUNSELLOR: And that adds to your overall stress...

PAULINE: He just can't seem to cope with emotional issues...

COUNSELLOR: So you do most of the housework and the others don't help you. Then you feel resentful and blame yourself that you don't cope. You would like to discuss it with the family but your husband loses his temper and that puts an end to the conversation...

During this exchange with Pauline, the counsellor used the skills of paraphrasing and reflection of feeling. She summed up the content of what had been said by the client in the course of the session. Afterwards, the counsellor continued to listen to Pauline, and to talk to her about other aspects of her problems at home.

KEY WORDS AND PHRASES

AGORAPHOBIA

The condition Agoraphobia was referred to in one of the case studies given in Chapter 3. The word describes an anxiety state which is characterized by a strong fear of being away from home and among strangers. People who suffer from this, and they are usually women, tend to seek help only when they are almost totally housebound.

Fear of social situations, travelling, shopping and crowds are also characteristic of the condition. Eventually, life for the sufferer becomes totally disrupted and circumscribed. Agoraphobia tends to occur in late adolescence or around the age of thirty (McGoldrick, 1994). It produces a range of physical symptoms including dizziness, sweating, racing pulse and difficulty in breathing. People who suffer from agoraphobia often experience panic attacks as well, and there is usually a history of stress or stressful events. Feelings of hopelessness and guilt often accompany and compound the other symptoms.

Behavioural methods of therapy are frequently used to help deal with agoraphobic problems. Counsellors who are trained in the behavioural approach often use the technique of *systematic desensitization* to help clients overcome the phobia.

SELF-ACTUALIZATION

Self-actualization is a concept which is central to the person-centred approach of Carl Rogers. According to Rogers, people have an innate desire and tendency to grow, to develop, and to move towards integration and wholeness (Rogers, 1991). This desire to reach maximum potential is not achieved without some difficulty on the individual's part. Movement towards growth and wholeness involves effort, courage and often a great deal of suffering. Nevertheless the impetus to move forward and improve is present in everyone, and even when the tendency seems to be absent – as it may be in a variety of circumstances – its potential is there and can be re-activated when the right conditions prevail. People work towards self-actualization in a number of ways: they may look for it in education, in relationships, or through religion or spiritual experience. Occasionally people need help – through counselling –

in order to continue their search for meaning. This kind of help is usually sought when emotional upheaval or traumatic events have occurred in a person's life.

EXERCISES

EXERCISE 1   WORDS AND METAPHORS

The purpose of this exercise is to help to identify a range of words or metaphors which clients might use in order to describe their experiences. For example, a client who has been deceived by someone, might describe his feelings in the following way:

'I was *stunned*. I felt I had been *stabbed in the back*.'

Working in pairs, make a list of words or phrases which you think clients might use to describe their experiences of:

a) relief
b) suspicion
c) disappointment
d) rejection
e) incredulity

EXERCISE 2   PARAPHRASING

Working individually, write a paraphrase of the following, concentrating on the content of what has been said.

Client: My handbag was stolen while I was shopping in town today. It's just the last straw for me. Yesterday we had a gas leak and had to get someone out to fix it. Everything seems to happen all at once.

When you have completed the first paraphrase, write another one, this time reflecting back both content and feeling.

EXERCISE 3   WAYS OF COMMUNICATING

Working in groups of two or three, draw up a list of people who work in a caring capacity with others; for example, doctors, social workers. Discuss the ways in which these people usually communicate with their patients or clients. Is their aim to:

• establish emotional rapport?

• elicit information?

• understand feelings?

• convey empathy?

• convey information?

Suggest ways in which health and caring workers could improve their overall communication skills.

EXERCISE 4   SUMMARY

Working individually, read the following hypothetical account given by a client who has come to talk to you about his problems. Write a *summary* of what he has said, in a way which could be reflected back to him. Afterwards, discuss your summary with other members of the training group.

'I really can't stand my boss. He is the kind of man you would tend to stay clear of if you could. Since he came to work at the firm, the atmosphere has changed completely. There is no feeling of security at work any more, and everyone is at everyone else's throat. It's a terrible atmosphere. The stress levels are really high, and more and more tend to be taking off sick. I've had to go to the doctor to get something to help me sleep. He gave me some tablets to take for two weeks, but he said I need to get to grips with the cause of all this stress. That's why my wife suggested I should talk to someone about it, and I'm certainly willing to do that if it will help. Mind you, I'm not the one with the problem. He's the one with all the problems if you ask me. When Jeff – that's my colleague – asked if we could expand the work we were doing at our end, he wouldn't even listen. He seems to think nobody can be trusted but himself and he won't delegate. Mike, our previous boss who has just left, was a great guy. He was the kind of person who inspired you and gave you some confidence. When he left, everyone was upset. Now I don't feel it's worth making an effort at work any more. It just seems so thankless and unappreciated.'

EXERCISE 5   SYMPATHY AND EMPATHY

Working in groups of two or three, take two large sheets of paper and write the words 'sympathy' and 'empathy' on them. Now write whatever associations come to mind in connection with these two words. Join the larger training group and discuss your findings.

EXERCISE 6   SHOWING ACCEPTANCE

Working individually, think of at least one occasion in your life when you experienced warmth and acceptance from someone you had just met.

a) How did that person demonstrate these qualities?
b) How did this warmth and acceptance influence your attitude towards that person?

Try to remember another occasion when these qualities were lacking in someone you had just met. How was this indicated in their general attitude and behaviour?

Write down your observations, and then discuss them within the training group.

EXERCISE 7   INTERNAL AND EXTERNAL FRAMES OF REFERENCE

Working with a partner, read through the following responses given to clients. Then discuss the responses which you think are given from an internal frame of reference, and those which you think are given from an external frame of reference.

1 Client: My wife left me a year ago. She just took her clothes and left without saying a word. I was devastated.

Counsellor: (a) That must have been terrible . . .
         (b) She must have given some indication of her plans.
         (c) So the discovery that she had gone was a total shock for you.

2 Client: I wish I could be a different kind of person. At the moment, I just feel useless. If only I had the nerve to put an end to it all . . .

Counsellor: (a) Life is difficult at times and people go through these phases.
         (b) At the moment things seem so bleak to you that you don't see the point of going on . . .
         (c) How long have you felt this way?

3 Client: I just can't seem to please my parents. Everything I do is wrong. They criticize my friends, my clothes and my taste in music.

Counsellor: (a) Parent sometimes seem over-critical when they are really trying to help.
         (b) So they find fault with the things that are of value to you.
         (c) Getting it right for parents is an impossible task.

4 Client: When I was a child I didn't do well at school. Deep down I know I had ability, but to everyone else I was stupid. I think that's why I started to cause trouble.

Counsellor: (a) You were a capable child who got labelled as stupid, and you rebelled against that.
         (b) The trouble you refer to . . . tell me more about this.
         (c) You may have seemed stupid to others because you were a troublemaker.

5 Client: I wash my hands all the time. If I'm going through a period of stress, the washing becomes more frequent.

Counsellor: (a) You say you wash all the time, and yet you also say it becomes more frequent.
         (b) Stress can make any problem worse.
         (c) The stressful times are the worst for you . . .

In these exchanges, the responses which convey most empathy, and are nearest to the client's internal frame of reference, are:

1: **answer C**
2: **answer B**
3: **answer B**
4: **answer A**
5: **answer C**

EXERCISE 8

In order to use the skills of paraphrasing and summarizing well, student counsellors need to have a varied vocabulary and the ability to select appropriate words to reflect the feelings which clients express. Working individually, look at the following client responses and try to think of as many words as possible which could be used to reflect back the feelings which might be present.

1 'I don't want to go back there. It's not the place for me.'

2 'My little girl was three when I had to go into hospital and leave her.'

3 'When I went to Canada, it was my first experience of leaving home.'

4 'My marriage to Ian broke up a year ago. He was my first real love.'

5 'I work hard to support my family. Sometimes that means not seeing them for weeks on end.'

6 'We had a good time at the party. Then afterwards we got the bad news.'

7 'My reasons for helping were well meant. I wasn't to know that he didn't value my help.'

8 'I used to drink heavily, but stopped when the doctor said I was slowly killing myself.'

9 'Some nights I don't sleep at all. I lie awake, toss and turn, and the time goes very slowly.'

10 'It was a job I really wanted. When someone else got it, I kept on applying for others, though I didn't put so much effort into these applications.'

FURTHER READING

1 Egan, Gerard, *The Skilled Helper*, Brookes/Cole, Monterey CA, 1990.
2 Mearns, Dave and Thorne, Brian, *Person Centred Counselling in Action,* Sage, London, 1989.
3 Culley, Sue, *Interactive Counselling Steps in Action*, Sage, London, 1991.
4 O'Farrell, Ursula, *First Steps in Counselling*, Veritas, Dublin, 1995.
5 Murgatroyd, Stephen, *Counselling and Helping*, The British Psychological Society, London, 1988.
6 Rogers, Carl, *Client-Centred Therapy*, Constable, London, 1991.

REFERENCE LIST

1 *Client-Centred Therapy*, by Carl Rogers, Constable, London, 1991.
2 *The Skilled Helper* by Gerard Egan, Brookes/Cole, Monterey CA, 1990.
3 *Social Skills in Interpersonal Communication* by Owen Hargie, Christine Saunders and David Dickson, Routledge, London, 1995.
4 'Phobias' by M McGoldrick in *Nervous Breakdown* edited by C Kean, Mercier, Dublin, 1994.
5 *On Becoming a Counsellor* by Eugene Kennedy, Gill and Macmillan, New York, 1977.

CHAPTER 4

Asking questions and helping clients to look at issues

We have already seen that the counselling process is much more than just an ordinary exchange of information between two people; it involves a wide repertoire of skills, one of the most important of which is questioning. A useful starting point when considering questions is to look at the ways we employ them in everyday exchanges, as well as the purposes for which we use them. In the main we ask questions in order to elicit information from others, and we may do this out of simple curiosity or in order to get to know other people more fully. A summary of the principal reasons for asking questions would include the following:

- to elicit information
- to satisfy curiosity
- to show interest
- to encourage further conversation
- to facilitate understanding
- to find out how others feel and think
- to clarify issues
- to identify and highlight significant areas of concern
- to check and confirm answers already given
- to enhance intimacy
- to start a conversation
- to put others at ease.

It is probably true to say that most people ask too many questions in their everyday interactions with others. We have already looked at the importance of listening and noted the fact that few people are adequately trained in listening and communication skills generally. Many of the questions which people ask in their daily exchanges are irrelevant or even sometimes unanswerable. This doesn't usually constitute a major problem when, for example, two friends are having an exchange of pleasantries, but when people are upset, unhappy or distressed, then irrelevant or unanswerable questions are not only useless but often harmful as well. The following is an example of the use of this kind of unhelpful question:

Sue: I have been feeling so depressed since yesterday. I simply can't seem to shake it off.

Garry: Why are you depressed?

In this instance the question asked is unhelpful because it is quite likely that Sue doesn't know why she feels that way; even if she is fully aware of the cause, the question is too stark and blunt in the way it is expressed. In addition to this, Garry is probably asking the question in order to gain information for himself and to satisfy personal curiosity. Ideally, he should be helping Sue to look more closely at her problem. Later in this chapter we will focus on more empathic forms of questioning and provide examples of how and when these might be used. In the example first given, it is quite possible that Sue will feel interrogated by the manner in which the question is asked, although this depends to some extent on the tone of voice and general demeanour of Garry when he asked it. In other words, the way people respond to questions depends on a variety of factors (see Fig. 4.1). The following are some of these factors.

- The person who is asking the question.

- The person's tone of voice, body language and general demeanour.

- When the question is asked.

- The type of question being asked.

- The context in which the question is asked.

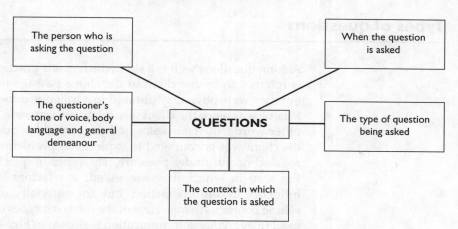

Fig. 4.1 *The way people respond to questions depends on a variety of factors.*

In the counselling situation, the person who is asking the question is, generally speaking, the counsellor, although clients frequently ask questions too, when they are seeking clarification of their problems. However, clients often come to counselling expecting to be asked questions by the counsellor, and because of this are sometimes reluctant to continue without some prompting in this way. It is important to remember that many people are unable to volunteer information without some help through questioning. This is partly related to early childhood and school experience, when children were expected to speak only when the teacher required or asked them to do so. The child's contribution then was directly elicited by the teacher, and the child's pattern of responding in this way is often carried forward into adult life. Another reason for this initial passivity in clients who come for counselling, in particular those who have had no prior experience of it, is that they expect counselling to take the form of an interview. Consequently, they react to it as such until they realize that the counsellor is there to listen to them, and to help them explore their problems. The following is an account of one such client's first experience of counselling:

'I had no idea what to expect when I went for counselling. As a matter of fact, I felt that there was a certain stigma attached to it and I didn't tell anyone I had made an appointment. The first time I met Paul [the counsellor] I couldn't understand why he didn't ask me more questions. He was friendly and very relaxed, but I got the impression at first that he couldn't really be interested since he didn't ask questions! After a while though, I found myself really opening up and talking to him, and I got the feeling that he was listening to me, and that he was genuinely interested in what I was saying. I couldn't really tell you how I got started, but I certainly knew that he was listening and interested.'

(Pam, 1995)

Types of questions

Asking questions well is a skill which needs practice. The counsellor who is referred to by the client in the above passage must have asked some, but they were obviously phrased in a friendly, non-threatening and unobtrusive way since the client was relatively unaware they had been used. In other words, the counsellor had developed his questioning skills so that the client was encouraged to explore her problems without feeling interrogated or put under pressure. The types of questions asked, as well as the way in which they are asked, are factors which have enormous influence in any interaction, but are especially important in the counselling context. An overview of the different types of questions commonly used in everyday communication is shown in Fig. 4.2.

CLOSED QUESTIONS

This type of question usually requires a simple 'yes' or 'no' answer, or a very specific reply. Closed questions give little scope or freedom in choosing responses. They are used when specific information is sought or needed, and they have the disadvantage that they do not elicit or require reflective or elaborative communication. Closed questions, therefore, should be avoided in counselling, since a fundamental purpose in

TYPES OF QUESTIONS

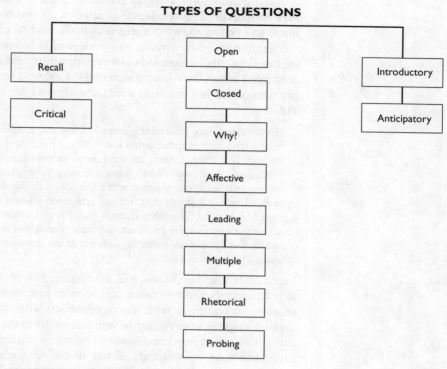

Fig. 4.2 *Types of questions.*

counselling is to enable clients to explore areas of concern reflectively, thoughtfully and in depth.

EXAMPLES OF
CLOSED QUESTIONS

- Do you like that colour?
- How long did you live there?
- Do you want to go?
- Did you understand what I said?
- Are you happy?
- Will you take the job?
- Do you want to make an appointment?
- Did you ask to speak to me?
- What's your husband's name?
- Can you swim?

The response to any of the above questions is likely to be monosyllabic in character, and whoever is being questioned will not feel that they have been invited to expand or discuss.

Asking questions is one of the most difficult skills for student counsellors to master. The tendency is always, at the beginning of training at least, to ask too many questions overall, and to phrase them in a closed rather than an open way. In any review of video practice work by student counsellors this weakness is always apparent, and students are frequently surprised when they hear themselves. Lesley, a student, gave the following account of her reaction when she viewed her first practice session on video.

'In the first place I hated the sound of my voice, and I had never realized how many irritating mannerisms I have. When I got over the initial shock of seeing myself like that, I then noticed how many questions I was asking. Poor Vivienne [the client] didn't have a chance to think or pause. We discussed it afterwards with our trainer, and I think one of the things I had been afraid of was silence. I just felt that if there had been silence between us then it meant that I had failed. The other thing which I kept thinking about was that I needed to help Viv solve the problem she had, therefore I must keep moving her forward. But I could see from the video that the questioning technique I was using didn't help in the least.'

From watching her video and discussing it with her trainer, Lesley was able to identify the two main problems in her approach to the counselling session. In common with many other students she was afraid of *silence* and was doing everything in her power to make sure it didn't happen. But clients often need and want to be silent during counselling because it gives them an opportunity either to collect their thoughts, to examine issues more carefully, or simply to experience a strong emotion in the presence of someone who is empathic and understanding. The second problem which Lesley identified was that of wanting to *solve* the client's problems for her; in other words, she was asking questions to allay her own anxieties about the pace of the counselling session, and not to facilitate the client. These are two pitfalls in counselling, but through practice they can be overcome. Practice in the use of **open questions** is helpful in this respect.

OPEN QUESTIONS

The following are examples of open questions.

- So how does that compare with the old routine?
- Could you say something more about that?
- What does that situation mean for you?
- Perhaps you could look at the things which trigger that feeling?
- How do you feel about it?
- What other areas could you look at?
- Is that something you could look at more closely?
- How does it feel now that you are away from home?

- In what way has the situation changed since then?

- How did you feel when you saw her again?

Open questions, like the examples just given, can afford clients the opportunity to answer at their own pace and to expand on and clarify significant areas of concern which perhaps need to be looked at in greater depth. When this happens the counsellor needs to listen attentively and to stay within the client's frame of reference. In other words, good listening and good questioning skills are inseparable in counselling. When the counsellor truly listens to the client, the temptation to question frequently or badly is diminished.

'WHY?' QUESTIONS

Questions which begin with 'why' are problematic in the counselling context because they are often difficult or impossible to answer. As well as this, they sometimes sound accusing and this has the effect of putting clients on the defensive. An example of a 'why' question was given at the beginning of this chapter when the client was asked by the counsellor why she was depressed. In addition to putting the client on the defensive, the question might also have the effect of making her feel inadequate because she is unable to answer. This, in turn, could lead to a situation in which she (the client) turns to the counsellor for 'expert' knowledge on the subject. This is one way in which clients can be robbed of their own innate ability to clarify, discuss and make sense of their own problems. 'Why' questions can be useful in some situations – for example, as part of an interview – but even then they are limiting as they tend to inhibit real communication instead of opening it up.

If we look again at the question and answer given at the beginning of this chapter, it is clear that a number of possible, more appropriate open responses to what the client has said could be formulated.

Sue: I have been feeling so depressed since yesterday. I simply can't seem to shake it off.

Garry: You say that you have felt like that since yesterday; could you say more about how it started?

This response invites Sue to look more closely at the origin of her depression. In this way, she can begin to make more sense of her feelings and what may have caused them.

QUESTIONS WHICH HELP CLIENTS TO LOOK MORE CLOSELY AT THEIR FEELINGS

Questions which invite clients to discuss feelings are also sometimes referred to as **affective** questions. They are especially useful in counselling because they facilitate the identification and expression of feelings and they stimulate reflection and thought. Clients who come for counselling often find it difficult to identify and acknowledge strong feelings in particular. This is sometimes linked to the fact that they have become out of touch with their own feelings, or because they believe that to acknowledge strong feelings is a sign of weakness. Some clients, especially those whose work or role involves caring for others on a day-to-day basis, seldom recognize or address their own affective needs. Marian, a client, describes her experience of counselling, and the way it helped her to identify some of her own needs:

MARIAN: Everything came to a head when Ian, my youngest, was taken into hospital. It came out of the blue because he had never been ill before, but suddenly it looked like he might need major surgery and my whole world fell apart. Then there was Laura at home and I was desperately trying to figure out how she could be looked after while I stayed at the hospital with Ian. She was so upset and didn't really want to stay with anyone else. My husband is away from home, so I had to do everything on my own. I don't have any family here, you see. We just moved here two months ago and I hardly even know my neighbours.

COUNSELLOR: So that must have been a very anxious, even frightening time for you?

MARIAN: Yes, it was. At the time I just kept going, but yes... (pause) it was terrible.

COUNSELLOR: With no one there who could support or help you?

MARIAN: That's right. Before, I didn't even think I could ask Helen [a neighbour] for help. I felt that it would be an admission that I couldn't cope, and I hardly knew her anyway.

COUNSELLOR: But now you have found that it's alright to ask for help when you need it, especially when things are fraught.

MARIAN: Yes. I wouldn't hesitate again.

It is not always all that easy for clients to cope with and identify feelings of distress, inadequacy, fear or anger. This is why it is essential for counsellors to formulate questions carefully and sensitively, and in this respect, timing is also important. To ask someone to look at strong, perhaps overwhelming, emotions when they are not ready to do so could cause even further distress or anxiety.

LEADING QUESTIONS

There are questions which are asked in a way that is designed to elicit a particular reply. Some simple examples of leading questions:

- Isn't it a good idea?
- Is your wife upset by your behaviour?
- That's a good plan of action, don't you think?
- Surely you feel happier about it now?
- The teacher knows best – doesn't she?

The person answering these questions might feel compelled to agree with what is being said, but often leading questions are more subtle than this and the answer is only vaguely implied. Occasionally an emotive word is used to indicate the response required, in which case the question is not only leading but loaded as well. Leading questions put the respondent under some pressure to agree, and if this happens in the counselling context then the counsellor is imposing his or her opinions, values and beliefs on the client. This goes against the whole ethos of the counselling relationship, and effectively sets the counsellor up as an authority or expert who tells the clients what to feel and think. For this reason, leading questions should be avoided in counselling. The only sure way for students to overcome any tendency they might have to use them is to practise frequently and on a regular basis with members of their peer group and with a trainer.

MULTIPLE QUESTIONS

Sometimes people ask several questions in the same breath. These multiple questions are awkward and inept, and very often serve to confuse clients especially those whose thinking processes have been disturbed through emotional upheaval and distress. Elderly people, in particular, might find it difficult to follow the thread of a multiple question. Very often only one part – usually the last – of the questions is answered. Multiple questions also sound interrogatory, and tend to put clients on the defensive. Occasionally clients ask to have the question repeated, but more often than not they simply give a non-committal reply. The following is an example of a multiple question which is unhelpful to the client:

Counsellor: When did you decide to leave? Where did you go? Was it far?
Client: Well no, not very.

It is not difficult to see that real communication will break down when this type of questioning is used. In fact, confusion is the usual response, and often it takes a great deal of laborious work in order to get communication re-established.

Nick, a counselling student, described a practice session with a fellow student, which they both reviewed afterwards on video.

'We just couldn't believe how bad it was at first. I was firing questions at David so fast that he was unable to answer them. We discussed it afterwards and he said that he felt under pressure and quite threatened by the sheer speed and number of questions I was asking. I know it was our first session on video, but still, I wouldn't have believed I could ask so many questions!'

Nick: When your boss became ill you were asked to take over. For how long was that? When did he come back?
David: I think it was about a month, no maybe six weeks.
Nick: You say you weren't sure about your ability to cope. Did you? How do you feel now when it's over and you've done it?
David: I don't know.
Nick: You seem to have done it well though.
David: Yes.

It can be seen from the above exchange that David has not been given any real opportunity to explore issues relating to his feelings about the work situation and his ability to cope in his boss's absence. Instead, he has confined himself to giving factual answers to the last question in each series. When asked directly about his feelings, he replies that he doesn't know, and this is understandable in view of the fact that he has not been given a chance to consider them. Often it is only the last part of a multiple question which is answered, and the answer given is usually non-committal and designed to deflect further interrogation.

RHETORICAL QUESTIONS

Questions which do not require an answer are referred to as rhetorical. The following are examples:

- Who wouldn't want to have a happy home life?
- What's the point of working if you can't have a good time spending the money?
- What's life worth if you don't have some fun?

It is seldom useful for counsellors to use rhetorical questions in the counselling situation; this is because such questions are usually an expression of the counsellor's own opinions, and if these are given too freely they can place pressure on the client to accept the views contained in them. Clients themselves frequently ask rhetorical questions, sometimes as an indirect way of soliciting advice or opinion. When rhetorical questions are asked in this way, a useful response from the counsellor is to invite the client to look more closely at the significance of what they are actually saying. For example:

Client: What's the point of working if you can't have a good time spending the money?
Counsellor: So perhaps you feel that you need to reward yourself for the fact that you work and run the home as well.
Client: Yes, because nobody else thanks me really. I do give myself rewards and I know I sometimes overdo it and get into debt.
Counsellor: And that produces more problems for you . . . ?

When the rhetorical question is approached in this way, the client is given the opportunity to look at areas which are causing anxiety or concern, but which are difficult to express directly. Bitterness, sarcasm or anger can also underlie the client's use of a rhetorical question; again, the counsellor can respond by inviting a closer examination of the real, but indirectly expressed, feeling. Certainly rhetorical questions asked by clients should never be ignored, because they are almost invariably prompted by a need for further discussion or consideration.

PROBING QUESTIONS WHICH ENCOURAGE ELABORATION

Often clients describe their problem situations in ways which – if they are to gain real insight – need further elaboration. The use of probing or prompting questions also enables clients to look beyond the obvious which they have stated, and to consider the various dimensions and implications involved. In *The Skilled Helper*, Gerard Egan makes the point that these prompting or probing questions can take the form of verbal or non-verbal communication; that even a nod of the counsellor's head or an expression of interest can give the client sufficient encouragement to carry on (Egan, 1990). Too much prompting, however, either verbal or non-verbal, can exert undue pressure on clients. It is important to remember also that clients need time for reflection before they move on to a further stage. When the atmosphere seems to be rushed, clients can easily lose their train of thought, and the value of the work accomplished earlier on can be sabotaged as well. The following client found it difficult to clarify his problems because of the emotional distress and confusion he had experienced as a result of them.

> **Client:** It wasn't the job really – I quite liked it. It's just that the pressure of it ... (*long pause*)
>
> **Counsellor:** (*nods encouragingly*) The pressures?
>
> **Client:** It was a combination of the pressures at work and the driving accident – the two things together were just too much. And yet ...
>
> **Counsellor:** And yet?
>
> **Client:** I've had pressures almost as bad and survived them. This time was different and I'm trying to figure out why that should be.

In this exchange the counsellor has confined himself to prompts, both verbal and non-verbal, as a way of giving affirmation to the client and encouragement to explore the issues further. As well as giving encouragement, however, the counsellor's use of prompts has the added effect of helping the client to focus attention on the real reasons behind his depression; thus giving him a deeper understanding of himself, and the way he reacted when under stress.

Asking questions too soon

The emphasis in this chapter has been on the use of questioning skills which are helpful to the client and sensitive to individual needs. At the beginning of the chapter we looked at the factors which influence the way people respond to questions, and noted that timing was an important element in this. Although some clients come to counselling expecting to be asked questions, there are others who need and want to talk straight away about the issues and problems which concern them. Often much of what clients say at first may seem inconsequential, and full of unnecessary circumstantial detail. From the client's point of view, however, this makes perfect sense because the counsellor is, after all, a stranger whose reliability, trustworthiness and respect have not been established or confirmed. One way of testing these important areas is to disclose very little at first, and then to gradually reveal more, as confidence and trust increase. When clients need to talk at length like this, it would be wrong and inept to interrupt them with questions; if such interruptions are made, the client is likely to feel irritated by them and to lose the thread of what they are saying. The counsellor needs to concentrate on the skill of listening in the initial phase; although sometimes clients themselves – especially those who are anxious and do not know what to expect – will want to ask questions at this stage. These questions often relate to factual details which need to be understood: for example, how long sessions will last, how often and so on. Even when these details have been established in advance – as they should be – clients may need to hear them again. Clients may come to the first sessions with a list of questions already prepared; if this is the case, then the counsellor should spend some time on these with the client, in order to facilitate understanding and establish a rapport. The most important point to remember about the initial stage of counselling is that clients should be allowed to proceed at their own pace, and disclose information by degrees if they wish. In addition, questions from the counsellor should be avoided as these tend to encourage dependence, and may even lead the session in a direction which is of more interest to the counsellor than the client.

OPENING QUESTIONS

Student counsellors are often concerned about the correct way to greet clients, especially during the first attendance at a counselling session. In this context, a brief question is usually appropriate, as a way of acknowledging the client's presence and establishing contact. The following are possible opening questions/statements which would serve this purpose.

- Would you like to start by telling me what's on your mind at the moment?

- We have fifty minutes together today. How would you like to use the time?

- Please tell me how I can help you.

- Would you like to tell me about the problem you mentioned when you made the appointment?

- How would you like to begin?

- Is there anything specific you would like to look at first?

- Perhaps we could look at the issues which concern you most right now?

The initial statement or question should be sufficiently 'open' to encourage the client to talk freely. In this respect it is like permission to talk, and signals to the client that the counsellor is there to listen and to help.

Other forms of questioning

QUESTIONS WHICH ENCOURAGE CRITICAL THINKING

In counselling, clients can be encouraged to become their own questioners with a view to enhancing their innate abilities to discriminate between various possibilities or courses of action. Some theoretical models of counselling place more emphasis than others on client self-questioning, and Albert Ellis's Rational Emotive Counselling is an example of a model which values this skill. In particular, Ellis refers to the irrational beliefs which people hold and which cause emotional problems. According to Ellis, these beliefs need to be identified and challenged (Ellis, 1990). Habits of critical thinking and questioning enable clients to gain confidence and independence – two of the most important goals of counselling. Clients can be encouraged to look more closely at some of the assumptions which they hold, and to establish whether these are really true. The belief that people should always be perfect and never make mistakes, for example, is one which clients sometimes hold, and one which they can be taught to challenge for themselves. In order to assist clients in developing the skill of critical thinking, however, it is essential that counsellors themselves develop some expertise in this area during their training. This field of questioning necessitates a great deal of sensitivity and insight, as well as the appropriate use of *challenging skills* which will be discussed more fully in the next chapter.

QUESTIONS RELATING TO THE PAST AND TO THE FUTURE

There are some models of counselling which emphasize the importance of reviewing the client's past experience, in order to highlight the origins of current problems and difficulties. In the Psychodynamic model of counselling, attention is focused on childhood experience and clients may be encouraged, through questioning, to examine early aspects of their lives, including their relationship with parents and siblings. However, the Psychodynamic model – in common with other models – stresses the importance of respect for clients, and this includes ensuring that they do not feel interrogated or placed under pressure through the counsellor's use of questions. For this reason, questions are asked only when they are relevant and will help the client gain insight. The principle of asking open-ended questions also applies, and empathy is considered to be an essential component of every stage of the counselling process.

Occasionally, clients need to look at the consequences of any changes which they are planning to make. This kind of questioning usually takes place in the later stages of counselling, when clients are establishing or setting goals for the future, and it will be dealt with more comprehensively in Chapter 6. A client could, for example, be asked to look at what might happen if certain plans were set in motion. If the various possibilities are examined in this way, clients will be helped to make better, more informed choices.

CREATING THE RIGHT EMOTIONAL ATMOSPHERE

In Chapter 3 we looked at the meaning of counsellor *warmth* and *empathy*, two characteristics which Rogers believed to be important if clients are to make progress in counselling (Rogers, 1991). It is difficult to say exactly how these attributes can be acquired, but most people have absolutely no doubt about their presence when they perceive them in another person. From the student counsellor's point of view, the most important prerequisite for the development of empathy in particular is personal self-development and self-awareness – processes which need to be addressed within counsellor training. Through these often painful processes, students can develop a deeper understanding of clients and their problems, and thereby cultivate their own innate reserves of empathy. Further development can be achieved through ongoing training and supervision, as well as through contact with clients in professional practice.

The emotional atmosphere which clients perceive when they first come for counselling is one of the factors which will determine their future commitment to the process of self-exploration. It goes without saying that clients will not be encouraged to continue in counselling if they feel that the counsellor does not understand them or their problems. Real understanding is obviously something which develops over a period of time. But during the initial phase of counselling, the counsellor needs to demonstrate a willingness to give the client individual attention so that this deeper understanding is fostered. Asking the client questions is one way of helping this process along, but as we have seen consideration needs to be given to the timing of questions as well as to their structure and formulation. Another important consideration is the reason for asking questions. In this respect the following checklist is a useful guide for student counsellors who experience difficulty in establishing when and how often to ask questions.

- Is it too soon to ask this question?

- Why do I want an answer to the question I am asking the client?

- Will the question help the client?

- Will the question satisfy some curiosity in me?

- Will the question help the client to become more open?

- Will the question help the client to explore the situation further?

- How many questions have I asked in this session?

- Have I given the client sufficient time to consider the previous question and to respond?

- What has the client *not* said in answer to a specific question?

In addition it is a good idea for students to become aware of their own body language, voice tone and general demeanour when asking questions. If these areas are observed and monitored, there is less likelihood that sessions will become interrogatory or superficial. When too many questions are asked, there is real danger that sessions will become superficial, since the client is given no real opportunity or time to explore problems in depth. One way of monitoring non-verbal communication and voice tone is through the use of video feedback and this has already been discussed in Chapter 2. Peer group appraisal is also useful in assessing the use of questioning skills. This assessment should also include the client's reactions and if students are encouraged in co-counselling – that is, with one student acting as the client – as part of their training, then these reactions should be discussed freely and openly. At the start of training, students are often reluctant to criticize their colleagues within the group, but this is an attitude which needs to be overcome if the real training needs of individual members are to be met.

CASE STUDY: GILLIAN

Gillian was sixteen years of age and lived at home with her grandparents and an older bother. She sought counselling initially because her brother was bullying and verbally aggressive in his attitude towards her. Her grandparents were unable or unwilling to help her deal with the situation. As a consequence of the depression which she felt, Gillian's school work suffered and she found it increasingly difficult to concentrate on her work, or to socialize with her friends. Her relationship with her brother was Gillian's major preoccupation or concern, but she also worried about her deteriorating social life and the many minor arguments or disputes which she had recently had with friends. During her first counselling session, Gillian described her problems in the following way:

'Everybody picks on me, not just my brother, but everybody. Vanessa, who used to be my friend, has started to go around with a really bad crowd. At least, I think they are a bad crowd, and yesterday when I got on the bus to go home I know they were laughing at me. I was really embarrassed and cheesed off with them, especially Vanessa. I can't believe she would act like that. She was my best friend right through school. And that's not all. I've got these funny pains in my legs and arms. Did I tell you about them? (*Doesn't wait for a response*) They are worse at night and all Gran can say is that I should go back to the doctor, which I did. He just kind of dismissed them and said that I had been through a lot recently and would have to give myself time.' (*pause*)

COUNSELLOR: You have had a lot of things to deal with recently, your brother, Vanessa and feeling unwell. Things have been very stressful for you.

GILLIAN: Yes, stressful is right. I can't believe that all these things have gone wrong on top of everything else.

COUNSELLOR: Everything else?

GILLIAN: Yes, my Mum died dix months ago (*lapses into silence*) . . . she had cancer.

COUNSELLOR: So you have had all this sadness to bear, and everything else becomes a burden as well.

GILLIAN: Yes, that's right. Everything else seems to get right out of proportion. I find it hard to cope, especially when Vanessa doesn't seem to care. She used to be my best friend.

COUNSELLOR: Someone you thought you could talk to?

GILLIAN: Yes.

COUNSELLOR: Maybe we could talk now about some of the things you would like to have talked about with Vanessa. About your Mum?

GILLIAN: Yes, I would like that.

It can be seen from the above exchange that the counsellor asked Gillian several questions during the first part of the session. This might seem a lot to start with, but the questions were asked tentatively and with great sensitivity. In common with many clients who come for counselling, Gillian was preoccupied with several problems, but the central problem was not mentioned until she had talked in some detail about the other events which were troubling her. These included her relationship with her brother, his bullying behaviour, her belief that she was being picked on by former friends, Vanessa's seemingly callous behaviour, her physical pains and her inability to secure her grandparents' support or help. Underlying all this, was the fundamental issue of bereavement and loss. Her mother had died six months previously, and Gillian had not been given an opportunity to talk about this with anyone. As so often happens, her grandparents tended to avoid the subject, so that Gillian felt increasingly isolated and lonely.

At first, Gillian was reluctant to mention her mother's death in case the counsellor would withdraw (as others had done) or fail to understand its significance or the depth of Gillian's feeling. The counsellor was able to empathize with Gillian, and she showed this is in the first instance by summing up the issues which Gillian had outlined, and by referring to the stress which must have accompanied these events. Gillian, in turn, responded to this and gradually started to approach the subject of her mother's death. Afterwards, the counsellor asked questions which had the effect of showing that she was indeed interested, and would listen attentively. This encouraged Gillian to open up further, and to talk at length about her mother.

With regard to Vanessa's reaction to her loss, Gillian was particularly upset. When she had discussed this with the counsellor during subsequent sessions, however, she came to understand that Vanessa lacked the experience and confidence to help her. Vanessa, too, had been overwhelmed and frightened by what had happened, and when Gillian realized this her relationship with her friend improved a great deal.

KEY WORDS AND PHRASES

FACILITATIVE QUESTIONS

The word facilitative is sometimes used in relation to the kind of questions which should be used in counselling. This means asking questions which encourage clients to speak freely, for example open-ended questions. It is also sometimes used in relation to challenging and confrontation, and these will be discussed in the next chapter. Facilitative question always aim to stay within the client's frame of reference, and are meant to help them clarify and make sense of the issues which are problematic for them.

HYPOTHETICAL QUESTIONS

Hypothetical questions are those which ask clients to use imaginative skills in order to look at a problem or problems from various angles. Questions like these can be effective in helping clients to determine how they might respond, for example in a particular situation, or how they might cope with possible changes in their lifestyle.

Janine, a client, wanted to establish a better, more communicative relationship with her mother. She wanted to be able to talk to her mother, but found this very difficult to do. The following exchange took place between Janine and her counsellor.

JANINE: The trouble is she is so busy when she gets home from work. She doesn't have much time for long talks.

COUNSELLOR: So perhaps a short talk to begin with? How would it be if you asked her for, say, ten minutes to begin with?

JANINE: Yes, that might work. If I approached it casually.

COUNSELLOR: And maybe build on that first talk in a gradual way, so that future talks are possible.

JANINE: Yes, it would probably be better if I didn't go over the top at the beginning.

Through the construction of several hypothetical scenarios, Janine was helped to look at the problem in different ways and to abandon her original conviction that communication with her mother was virtually impossible.

DEFENCE MECHANISMS

The term defence mechanisms refers to the strategies which people use in order to protect themselves from too much anxiety; they will be discussed in greater detail in the next chapter. It is important for student counsellors to realize that clients often use defence mechanisms in counselling, especially when questions are being asked. Examples of defence mechanisms which clients use include the following:

- joking
- intellectualization
- changing the subject
- denial
- distortion
- silence
- lack of response
- arriving late or leaving early.

These are just some of the ways in which defence mechanisms are manifest in counselling. Counsellors need to understand that it is not just clients who use defences, however; we all use them to some extent. It is true that people who are emotionally upset or overwhelmed by problems, tend to resort to them more readily. This is why it is so important to treat clients with real respect and sensitivity, to ask questions only when necessary and to phrase them in a way which will not force vulnerable people into immediate retreat through the use of these mechanisms.

EXERCISES

EXERCISE 1   CLOSED AND OPEN QUESTIONS

Read the following list of *closed* questions and rewrite them so that they become *open* questions:

a) Were you upset?
b) Did you see your father?
c) Are you going to stay at home?
d) Do you spend too much money?
e) Is your home life satisfactory?
f) Have you been ill long?
g) Do you understand what I am saying?
h) Does that make you angry?
i) Do you love your husband?
j) Is there anything else you want to say?

EXERCISE 2   'WHY?' QUESTIONS; LEADING QUESTIONS

Work with a partner and take turns to ask each other questions. One person acts as client, the other as counsellor. The client describes the events of the previous day; these could be events which have taken place at home or in the work situation. The counsellor listens and then asks a series of '*Why*?' questions. Afterwards, discuss how this felt for both of you, paying particular attention to the way in which the questions either helped or impeded the client's progress.

Reverse roles, and this time the person acting as counsellor should concentrate on asking *leading questions*, for example: 'So that seems like a good idea, doesn't it?' Try to maintain this interaction for about five minutes. Afterwards, discuss the use of these questions and how they affected the session. In particular, how was the client affected by the counsellor's use of leading questions? Did the client, for example, feel under any pressure to agree with the counsellor? Were the questions asked from the client's or from the counsellor's frame of reference?

EXERCISE 3   QUESTIONS WHICH ENCOURAGE SELF-EXPLORATION

Work with a partner and role play the following situation. One person acts as counsellor and the other person acts as client. The client has come to counselling and describes the problem outlined below:

'I don't want to go back to university next year. Last year was the worst time of my life. Everyone told me that university would be great, but it was a big disappointment as far as I am concerned. Failing my exams didn't help either, although things were bad before that. The problem is knowing what to do now. People keep telling me what I should do, but I don't know what I want myself. The only thing I do know is that I don't want to go back to university.'

Spend some time reading this passage. Afterwards, the person acting as counsellor asks the client questions in order to clarify the problem situation. Try to phrase the questions in a way which will encourage elaboration and reflective thinking. What are the kind of questions which would facilitate this process? Discuss.

(NB: although this is a role-play situation, it should give you some idea of the kinds of questions which would help a client in the difficult course of self-exploration.)

EXERCISE 4   CHANGING MULTIPLE QUESTIONS

Look at the following list of multiple questions. Say how you think they could be rearranged to form single open-ended questions. Write down your answers, or discuss them with a partner.

a) You did go to the party? What was it like? Who did you meet?
b) So was it a mistake? Did you regret it? Do you worry about it now?
c) How much did you pay? Did it cost a lot? How much have you left?
d) Do you love him? Do you miss him? Will you go back?
e) What are your prospects? Will you get promotion? Do you get on with the manager?
f) What was the final decision? Were you happy with it? Would you do it again?
g) Does your brother bully you? How long has he done this? Have you told your parents?
h) Will you leave home? Where will you go? Are you serious about it?
i) You can't sleep? How long have you been like that? When did it start?
j) Have you thought of another plan? What would you do if this one failed? Will you try again?

EXERCISE 5   WORDS AND PHRASES WHICH DESCRIBE FEELINGS

We have already seen that affective questions are useful in counselling because they help clients to identify and express feelings which they may not have been able to identify, acknowledge or express in the past. Counsellors need to use affective questions with sensitivity and good timing. As well as this, they need to be aware of their own range of feelings and to be familiar with the words which describe these feelings. Work on your own and write out a list of words, phrases or expressions which could describe the following states:

- happiness
- sadness
- excitement
- disappointment
- betrayal
- regret

- surprise
- anticipation
- anxiety
- fear

When you have completed the written exercise, discuss it with the other students in the group. Compare the different words or expressions which the members of the group have described.

EXERCISE 6   IDENTIFYING AND FOCUSING ON FEELINGS

Work with a partner. Each person should write three examples of questions which might help clients to identify and focus on their feelings; for example, *So how did you feel at the time it was happening?*

Discuss what you have written with each other. Are there any particular problems in formulating questions in this way?

EXERCISE 7   BECOMING MORE SPECIFIC

Using a video to record your session, work with a partner: one person acting as counsellor, the other as client. The client describes his/her personal views about a particular subject or topic. The following is a sample list of topics which could be used:

- ambition
- responsibility
- courage
- dedication
- endeavour
- achievement

The counsellor should listen attentively and then ask questions which will encourage the client to become more specific and focused about the views they express. For example:

> **Counsellor:** You say you dislike ruthless ambition. Could you say more about that word 'ruthless'?

Afterwards, review the video session together and note the timing of questions asked, the number and type of questions used, the counsellor's body language and tone of voice. Were the questions asked in a non-judgemental way, and was the client given sufficient time to consider them before replying? Note also the client's responses, their body language when responding, as well as their tone of voice and general reactions to questions. Discuss your individual reactions and how you felt during the session.

EXERCISE 8   HOMEWORK EXERCISE

This is an exercise which trainers can use to encourage students to become more aware of questioning skills and techniques in general. Students should be asked to watch an interview on television; this could be an interview with a politician, an interview with a member of the public as part of a news item, or an interview with a celebrity on a chat show.

Having watched the programme, students should then jot down their observations with particular reference to the following areas:

a) the type of questions asked
b) the number of questions asked
c) the timing of questions
d) the attitude of the interviewer, e.g. friendly, hostile, patronizing, bossy, deferential etc.
e) the response of the interviewer, e.g. defensive, expansive, aggressive, patronizing, explanatory.

Afterwards, students can discuss their observations with the rest of the group. If individual students have watched different programmes, this should generate even more discussion about questioning skills and techniques.

FURTHER READING

1 Dillon, J T, *The Practice of Questioning,* Routledge, London, 1990.
2 Brookfield, Stephen, *Developing Critical Thinkers,* Open University Press, Milton Keynes, 1987.
3 Long, Paradise and Long, *Questioning Skills for the Helping Process,* Brookes/Cole, Monterey CA, 1981.
4 Egan, Gerard, *The Skilled Helper,* Brookes/Cole, Monterey CA, 1986.
5 Rogers, Carl, *Client-Centred Therapy,* Constable, London, 1991.

REFERENCE LIST

1 *The Skilled Helper* by Gerard Egan (3rd edition), Brookes/Cole, Monterey CA, 1986.
2 *Reason and Emotion in Psychotherapy* by Dr Albert Ellis, Carol Publishing Group, NY, 1990.
3 *Client-Centred Therapy* by Carl Rogers, Constable, London, 1991.
4 *The Practice of Questioning* by J T Dillon, Routledge, London, 1990.
5 *Questioning Skills for the Helping Process* by Long, Paradise and Long, Brookes/Cole Monterey CA, 1981.

CHAPTER 5

Challenge and change

The need for change and readjustment arises at various stages throughout each person's life. This need may be linked to age-related stages of development, or it may be associated with new opportunities which require some measure of personal reorganization if they are to be successfully taken. On the other hand, people are often challenged to change when traumatic or stressful events have occurred in their lives. These events may include bereavement and loss, or they may be concerned with the erosion or ending of significant emotional and relational bonds. Sometimes people are prompted to change when outmoded or dysfunctional patterns of behaviour no longer seem tenable or justified. An unhealthy lifestyle may also act as a catalyst for change, and individuals often reappraise their lives when they realize that addiction has become a problem for them.

Clients bring a variety of problems to counselling, and their difficulties include at least some of the elements just mentioned. We have seen that in the initial phase of counselling, clients are concerned to talk about their problems in the presence of someone – in this case, the counsellor – who is willing to give them individual attention, respect, understanding and genuine support. It is at this stage that the basic skills of listening, paraphrasing, summarizing, reflecting clients' feelings and asking open-ended questions are used. These skills are also employed throughout the whole counselling process but when clients are given sufficient time to explore and make sense of their difficulties, a new phase of counselling begins. In this new phase, they are encouraged to look again at problems and to identify different ways of dealing with them. This is the second stage of counselling referred to in Chapter 1, under the heading of 'Development of new understanding – looking at goals and objectives' (Egan, 1990).

This reappraisal of problems and the subsequent development of some incentive to address them, presents a challenge to clients; very often this is the most difficult part of the counselling process for them. The reasons for this are numerous and diverse, but it is probably true to say that any change is daunting for most people, since it involves some element of risk-taking which always presents a threat. People often stay in situations which are clearly unsatisfactory or even shocking; for example, because change is seen by them as too unpredictable and frightening to contemplate. The following case study illustrates this last point.

Amanda's husband had physically abused her for many years of their married life. On several occasions she had tried to leave him for good, but she always returned after a short absence when he begged her to do so. This pattern continued for almost twelve years, and was disrupted only when Amanda's children began to develop behaviour problems and severe symptoms of stress. At this point, Amanda decided to leave home with her children. She sought refuge in a Women's Aid Centre, where she stayed for almost three months. During that time she received support and counselling, as well as legal advice, help with accommodation and educational guidance. Amanda was an intelligent thirty six year old woman, with many natural talents and abilities. She was good at art and had always wanted to study this at a higher level. With the support she received at the centre, she was able to secure a place on an art course which was run at the local college. One week before the course was due to start, she left the house she had just moved into and, taking her children with her, she went back to her husband. Some time later, she contacted the counsellor who had worked with her originally, in order to explain this sudden and quite unexpected decision. When Amanda met her counsellor to talk, she said that she had been so scared by all the major changes she had undertaken, and by the prospect of even greater ones, that she had opted to stay as she was rather than take any further risks.

There are complex reasons for women staying in the kind of abusive relationship just described, many of which are concerned with feelings of inadequacy and lack of self-esteem. However, the prospect of change is a major concern here too. In Amanda's case, several important changes had happened to her within a very short space of time; she left her family home and moved into cramped accommodation which, although hospitable, was unfamiliar to her and to her children. In addition to this, she lived in dread that her husband would find her and create a scene. The children missed their friends, and they often asked about home and their pets. The art course which Amanda was due to start at college, created a major challenge for her since she had not been in full-time education for twenty years.

This example is given in order to highlight the point that change can be especially difficult for some people. Not all client's situations are as problematic as this, however. But even those which on the surface appear relatively easy to deal with, can prove obdurate and difficult when change is needed to ameliorate them. In other words, clients may hesitate about change, even when it is the obvious and only way forward for them.

Challenge and confrontation

Egan lists a number of skills which can be used with clients in order to help them make progress in those areas of their lives which have been problematic for them. Before listing and describing the skills, however, he

is careful to point out that challenge can only be used effectively by counsellors who are honest and open with themselves both within their own
lives and in relation to their clients (Egan, 1990). Sensitivity, tact and good
timing are also essential for effective challenge in counselling, and the
relationship between client and counsellor needs to be firmly established
before challenging skills are used. An important point to make about
challenge is that it should evolve from the client's own insights gained
throughout the counselling process. It is most useful when it follows from
the client's own perception or awareness of what needs to be done.

The words *confrontation* and *challenge* are sometimes used interchangeably in counselling literature, but strictly speaking they are not the same.
The word confrontation has some unfortunate connotations since it tends
to imply a head-on collision between the two people involved, in this case
counsellor and client. However, confrontation in the counselling context
has nothing to do with aggression, blame or censure, but is used to help
clients identify areas of their lives where discrepancies or inconsistencies
exist. These may be related to the client's own behaviour, or to his behaviour in relation to others. In many instances, confrontation is used in
order to acquaint clients with positive aspects of themselves which they
may have missed or underplayed in the past. The following case study
illustrates this point.

Andrew joined a motor mechanics class at his local college. Shortly after joining,
he ran into trouble with the other students in the group who constantly teased
him and made frequent references to the fact that he was the oldest in the class.
Andrew was, in fact, at least five years older than the other – mainly sixteen year
old – students and he felt slightly awkward and embarrassed about this difference in age. He was also more experienced than the others, and had worked
with cars as long as he could remember. He was certainly capable of achieving
top grades in all the assessment procedures he was required to undertake, but
because of the difficulties he experienced with other students his work fell
behind and his overall mark for the course suffered. At the end of his first term,
he began to experience stress and anxiety and visited the college counsellor in
order to talk about his problems.

ANDREW: I have a quick temper naturally, but I've managed to restrain myself
with that lot. God knows how.
COUNSELLOR: You've bottled it all up inside you, and now you're beginning to
feel the effects . . .
ANDREW: I just wish I knew what's behind it all. I mean, why me? Is it just
because I'm older than the rest?
COUNSELLOR: You think there may be other things about you that are different . . .
ANDREW: Well, I have worked with cars for as long as I can remember. So I
have far more experience than any of the rest of them. Maybe that's why
they slag me off.
COUNSELLOR: So there may be an element of jealousy behind all the aggrava-
tion they are causing you . . .

ANDREW: I suppose so.

COUNSELLOR: And if that really is the case... that they envy your ability, perhaps you need to look at it in a different way, now that you understand the cause.

ANDREW: Yes, I can see what you mean. It's not my fault... it's more that they feel insecure?

COUNSELLOR: Perhaps that's it. Is there any way you could change the way you respond to them now, since you know what's behind it?

ANDREW: (thoughtfully) Yes, I think I could. I could probably help them more, instead of sticking to myself all the time. I do have a lot of experience they don't have...

Throughout this exchange with the counsellor, Andrew was encouraged to challenge himself and the way that he responded to the other students in the class. He was further encouraged to challenge his own strengths, and to recognise the extent to which his ability – which he kept to himself and felt apologetic about – had become a liability for him instead of the asset which it clearly should be. When he looked at himself and his own experience in a more positive, less blinkered way, it became clear to him that he was capable of dealing with the problem; subsequently he did deal with it quite effectively.

Challenge, therefore, works best when it stems from the client's own awareness and insight. Counsellors, however, need to encourage clients to look more critically at their problem situations, but this can only be achieved within a supportive and empathic relationship. One of the difficulties which can arise for student counsellors, in particular, is that they may be tempted to challenge clients when they themselves feel frustrated, confused or even impatient. Such a response to clients is clearly wrong, since it originates from the counsellor's own feelings of frustration or inadequacy. Effective and skilful challenge should always address the client's needs, and not the counsellor's. This is a maxim which student counsellors need to keep firmly in their minds when practising challenging skills in the training group. Once again, this involves discipline, self-awareness and the capacity to identify and separate one's own feelings from those of the client.

The most important aspect of effective challenge is that it enables clients to look at themselves and their problems in fresh and different ways. When new perspectives are gained through challenge, the client is in a much stronger position to tackle problems effectively, and with renewed creativity. It is important to wait for the client to initiate challenge himself; sometimes clients do this quite quickly, especially in the presence of a counsellor who listens well and clearly understands what they are trying to convey. The following client, named Rosemary, spoke to a counsellor about the difficulty she was having in communicating effectively with her sixteen year old daughter. She was able to challenge herself quite early on in the first session, once she had talked through her problems with the counsellor.

ROSEMARY: I suppose I could try setting some time aside to talk to her...

COUNSELLOR: You feel you could set a time when you are both free and fairly relaxed . . .

ROSEMARY: Yes, I should do that. Perhaps if I did do it, we could talk to each other more rationally.

Rosemary identified this need to set time aside for her daughter, and through this identification she challenged herself to approach their communications problem in a more creative way. Later on in counselling she challenged herself again, this time in relation to her need for 'control' within the home.

COUNSELLOR: So you feel that you need to keep the house a certain way . . . it needs to look right.

ROSEMARY: I can't bear to get behind with housework . . . it gets me into a panic when I feel I'm behind.

COUNSELLOR: It's very very important to you . . .

ROSEMARY: Yes, I suppose you might say it's over the top. (*laughs*) Perhaps I make it too important. I know that Abbie [her daughter] thinks I fuss too much.

COUNSELLOR: So that's something you might need to look at again . . .

ROSEMARY: I should try to put it in perspective. It's just a house after all. Over the years I've got into the habit of it [housework and cleaning] but I could afford to ease off a bit . . . everyone would be happier.

It may be the case that some clients (like Rosemary) are better at self-challenge than others, and it is certainly true to say that a capacity for reflection and self-criticism is helpful in challenging. However, many of the people who come for counselling have lost touch with these attributes – temporarily at least – because of the emotional turmoil they may be experiencing at the time. When that is the case, counsellors need to help clients in a way which does not undermine their *innate* ability to challenge themselves – an ability which may, in fact, be reactivated when support and empathy are demonstrated for them.

It goes without saying that clients should never be challenged in order to accelerate the counselling process. Earlier in this chapter we referred to the fact that timing is an important factor in the use of challenging skills. If clients are challenged too soon the effect will be to breach the defences which they, and all of us, use – at various times in our lives – to protect against painful or disturbing aspects of reality. There are various defences which clients may use in this way (see Fig. 5.1), but some of the most common include:

- humour
- denial
- intellectualization
- rationalization
- introjection
- projection.

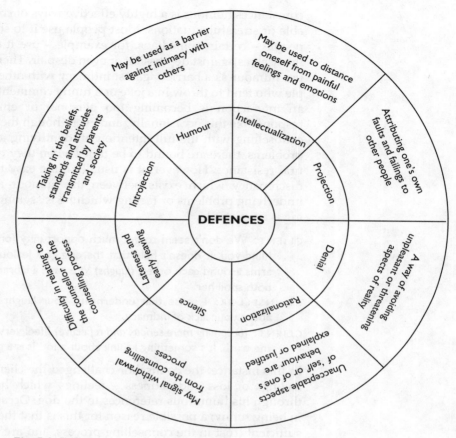

Fig. 5.1 *Defences.*

A number of other defences have been identified by Sigmund Freud (1922) and by his daughter Anna Freud (1937). It is worth looking in more detail at the above-mentioned defences, since they are fairly easy to identify – both within ourselves and in clients – and they help to explain a great deal about the anxieties and fears which they are designed to mask. Defence mechanisms – often referred to as *ego defence mechanisms* – are unconscious psychological and behavioural methods which people use to protect themselves against unpleasant emotions. We all use these mechanisms occasionally, but if we come to depend or rely on them over a long period of time problems can arise because overdependence will prevent us from seeing things clearly. The following is a brief description of several commonly used defences.

HUMOUR

Clients sometimes use humour to deflect attention from painful emotions or problematic issues which they are afraid to confront. In ordinary circumstances humour is a highly effective ways of coping with uncomfortable or stressful situations. Most people use it to some extent, and a few people – certain comedians, for example – use it extensively to defend themselves against depression or even despair. There are also people who use humour as a barrier against intimacy with others. These are the people who tend to throw in a joke or a funny comment when they sense that an interaction is becoming too personal or emotional. Clients, too, respond like this occasionally, and even though they may have come into counselling with the full intention of identifying and dealing with their problems, there are bound to be times when they come up against a natural resistance. However, it is usually quite easy to identify the kind of discrepancy which exists between the humour a client uses and the underlying problems or feeling which he is seeking to mask. The following is an example.

CLIENT: We don't seem to get much opportunity for intimate contact lately. Mind you, it doesn't help that the dog gets jealous each time we put our arms around each other. (*laughs*) We have a labrador . . . she's lovely . . . we both spoil her.

COUNSELLOR: I sense that underneath your laughter there is real sadness about your lack of intimacy.

CLIENT: (*becoming more serious and reflective*) I feel very sad about it, to tell you the truth. It's something I think about a lot. It is a great loss.

In this instance, the counsellor challenged the client to confront his own feelings of loss and sadness – feelings which he had tried to evade through his humorous references to the dog. Occasionally clients persist in being funny; a possible reason for this is that they have not developed sufficient trust in the counselling process, and are therefore unwilling to make themselves vulnerable and genuine to the counsellor.

INTELLECTUALIZATION

An effective way of distancing oneself from painful feelings and emotions is to talk about issues in coldly abstract terms. People who use intellectualization as a defence against strong feeling often subscribe to the belief that emotional issues are embarrassing and should therefore be kept under wraps. These people tend to engage in long discussions about conflict-related topics in terms which strip these topics of any real feeling. Abstract generalizations are frequently made, and there is a prevailing sense of diminished emotional experience and contact.

Why do people with this kind of intellectualizing tendency set out to explore emotional issues in the first place? It is possible that for some people the academic or cerebral approach is the only one which does not pose a threat to their affective equilibrium. Thus a client may embark on counselling or therapy with the express intention of exploring some of the theories which he has carefully studied through reading and research. A client with this kind of approach is certainly not doomed to failure in counselling, since an understanding, skilful and considerate counsellor should be able to guide him towards some awareness of his feelings, while carefully acknowledging the validity of his intellectual interest. In other words, respect for the client is paramount in counselling regardless of the initial approach which he chooses to make to his problems. The following is an example of one client's intellectual approach to his problems.

CLIENT: I suppose I've always considered myself to be a loyal person. Certainly I believe in the concept of loyalty to family and friends.

COUNSELLOR: Loyalty is very important to you...

CLIENT: Yes, I can't stand disloyalty of any kind. It's anathema to me.

COUNSELLOR: It's something you simply couldn't bear...something which would make you feel betrayed?

CLIENT: It would...it has made me feel totally betrayed when...when my wife left...I felt...

COUNSELLOR: You felt betrayed and...

CLIENT: Well devastated really.

The counsellor who worked with this client helped him move from his initial, fairly distanced reflections about the nature of loyalty, to a point where he was able to express his deepest feelings of loneliness and loss. Acknowledgement of feelings is important for clients, so too is understanding and the ability to integrate all aspects of personal experience. If this integration is achieved, clients are less likely to rely exclusively on intellectualization as a way of dealing – often ineffectively – with their problems.

INTROJECTION

The word introjection describes the process of 'taking in' the views, beliefs, standards, attitudes and behaviours transmitted by other people. This internalization of mainly parental and societal values is part of the socialization process which we all experience. Introjection is, therefore, a normal developmental process, although it can become a defence mechanism, especially when it is used as a way of avoiding responsibility for self. People who introject the views and values of other people, without ever seeking to questions these beliefs, are likely to have difficulty in achieving total independence. This can lead to numerous problems, especially in adult life. Clients who come into counselling often experience difficulty in identifying their own beliefs and values, and this is sometimes because they have not had sufficient opportunity to develop these in the past. Occasionally clients suffer for years from parental messages which were, for example, negative or even abusive. This can lead to depression, lack of confidence and an inability to make decisions without the approval of others. A client who was constantly told in childhood that he was 'stupid' or 'no good' will certainly experience some difficulty in believing that he is, in fact, ultimately capable of dealing with his own problems. A central belief of all the main approaches to counselling is that clients do have the inner resources necessary to deal with their own problems. This belief has been highlighted especially in the Person-Centred model described by Carl Rogers (1991).

The following short case study illustrates the point that some clients have more difficulty than others in locating their inner resources, although they can make progress in this respect through counselling.

Claire, who was twenty six years of age, wanted to rent a flat in the city where she worked. Her parents were adamant that she should stay at home and travel to work each day. Claire had a boyfriend, Clive, who also wanted her to stay at home, and both he and her parents frequently told Claire that she would never manage to cope alone in the city. Having argued unsuccessfully with them on numerous occasions, Claire gave up and began to suffer from depression. She found it increasingly difficult to make decisions of any kind, and eventually she came into counselling 'as a last resort'.

CLAIRE: Clive always says that I need a minder. He says I'm the most indecisive person he has ever met.

COUNSELLOR: Clive thinks you need to be looked after because you can't make decisions...

CLAIRE: He is a really bright person and I do respect his views about things...

COUNSELLOR: So you would accept his views about you...that you can't make decisions.

CLAIRE: Well no...that's his view, but I don't share it. It's just that I sometimes don't know what to think.

COUNSELLOR: So you need to identify what it is that *you* believe...rather than just accepting the views of others?

CLAIRE: Yes...I suppose so...it's just difficult to do.

COUNSELLOR: Difficult to identify your own views...especially since you are hearing so many views expressed by others...

CLAIRE: Yes.

COUNSELLOR: But you know you don't share these views, especially those of your boyfriend...you say you don't agree with him. Could we look a little more closely at how you do feel and think?

Throughout this exchange with Claire, the counsellor was concerned to help her identify her own thoughts and feelings. It is not always easy for clients to do this, and for some clients it often takes a while before they are willing to trust their own judgement.

PROJECTION

The word projection describes the practice of attributing one's own faults and failings to other people. A man who is angry with his wife might, for example, accuse her of bad temper instead of acknowledging the feeling in himself. This lack of acknowledgement has the effect of distancing people from themselves and their own feelings. When this happens, personal problems tend to go unresolved. People can continue to project their feelings over quite long periods of time; this is sometimes seen in counselling with clients who are unable to see that they themselves are responsible for some of the feelings or character traits which they ascribe to others. The following is an example.

CLIENT: My line manager is a difficult woman. She is manipulative, although she can be charming too. I always try to be one step ahead of her though ...

COUNSELLOR: You try to out-manoeuvre her?

CLIENT: I can't stand it when people are not upfront and honest ... I really can't. But with this woman it pays to box clever.

COUNSELLOR: It pays to be manipulative ...

This last response from the counsellor could certainly be described as confrontational, since it forces the clients to look critically at her own behaviour in relation to the line manager. It needs to be emphasized that this kind of response can only be made when a relationship of trust has been established between client and counsellor. One consequence, however, of not challenging the client who is clearly projecting character traits, is that the behaviour and the client's problems will simply continue and cause further communication problems for them. When this happens, counselling sessions are a waste of time and the client achieves no benefit from them. Challenge does work best when it stems from the client's own insight; in the example just given, the client was aware, to some extent – although she had not stated it explicitly – that she too was involved in a manipulative game with her boss.

DENIAL

One way of avoiding unpleasant or threatening aspects of reality is to simply deny that they actually exist. Denial is perhaps one of the most primitive of all defences, and most people use it at least occasionally. However, habitual use of denial leads to avoidance of whole areas of personal experience. Numbness and denial often accompany the grieving process, although it is generally agreed that long-term denial is problematic since it inhibits the healing which should take place after a bereavement (O'Flaherty, 1995). Loss and bereavement are not the only catalysts for denial though; aspects of the self are also sometimes denied, and it is often the case that clients reject their own feelings, especially when these feelings are intense or threaten to overwhelm them. One client who denied his own feelings, and subsequently came to terms with them, described his experience in the following way:

'When we were growing up, my brother, who is two years older, was always successful in everything he did. He was good looking, clever, with loads of personality, and compared to him, I always looked backward and clumsy, even though I managed to get reasonable grades in all the exams I sat. When I found out I was adopted things got worse between us, because by this stage. I felt that he had everything I didn't have – including our parents. As we got older, I became more and more envious of him, and this destroyed any chance of friendship between us. Looking back now, I know how bitter I felt, although I would. never have acknowledged it then. It was only years later, when my brother's first child died, that I began to see him in a more realistic and rational light, and to realize that he is – and always was – a likeable and decent person who always wanted to be closer to me as a brother. Once I was able to acknowledge my feelings of bitterness and envy, things became better between us straight away. What I regret now is the lost years between us, and the fact that I denied my own negative feelings for so long.'

RATIONALIZATION

Rationalization is a process whereby unacceptable or disturbing aspects of the self, or of behaviour, are 'explained away' or justified. The reasons which are given in these instances are not, of course, the real reasons, but are designed to protect the individual from painful reality. A person who is unsuccessful in a job application might, for example, rationalize his failure on the grounds that the job was 'fixed', or he might say that he had never really wanted it in the first place. These justifications serve to protect the applicant against anxiety or feelings of failure, and there are certain situation in every person's life when rationalization is used in this way. Clients often use rationalization as a means of justifying unacceptable behaviour either in themselves, or in others. In common with other defence mechanisms, however, prolonged use of rationalization can lead to chronic self-deception. When this happens, clients need to be challenged to look at issues in more realistic terms. The following client had been abusing alcohol and prescribed drugs for many years. She had come into counselling in order to talk about 'other' problems which she believed to be unconnected with her addiction.

CLIENT: Everybody knows I'm a bit mad at times. That's how I am. If I go overboard and say outrageous things at parties, people just think . . . here we go again. Everyone has a laugh. I provide the light relief really . . .

COUNSELLOR: Everyone expects you to act in a certain way, and this provides some entertainment for them.

CLIENT: Not for everyone of course. There is always the stuffed shirt who wants to object. That's what happened on Saturday night.

COUNSELLOR: Someone objected to your behaviour?

CLIENT: The person I went to the party with, as a matter of fact. She really upset me afterwards when she accused me of being drunk.

COUNSELLOR: She didn't find your remarks and behaviour funny . . . She thought it was the effects of the alcohol . . .

CLIENT: Look, I know that people expect me to provide the light relief. It's just the way I am. All those serious faces . . . everyone needs to let their hair down occasionally.

COUNSELLOR: So you drink at parties to help you cope with the serious faces . . .

CLIENT: (slowly) I suppose you could put it that way.

COUNSELLOR: And at home?

CLIENT: You mean the problems with the family? Well, yes, I do drink to help me cope with that too, at times.

COUNSELLOR: So the drinking, and the tablets which you take ... they become a habit to help you cope with all these other demands and people?

CLIENT: Yes.

The client in this example had been concerned about her communications difficulties within the family, and with friends. Over a period of time, she had rationalized her alcohol and drug abuse on the grounds that people 'expected' her to behave in a certain way. If she stopped behaving in that way, people might express disappointment in her, and this would in turn disturb the fun-loving image she liked to portray. There are elements of *denial* in this case study too. The client denied her addiction until challenged by the counsellor to look more realistically at her habits and general behaviour.

OTHER ASPECTS OF DEFENSIVE BEHAVIOUR

There are other ways in which clients exhibit defensive behaviour in counselling; some of these were mentioned briefly at the end of the last chapter. It is worth looking more closely at some of those aspects of client behaviour which may seem puzzling or incomprehensible, especially to student counsellors. Clients who *arrive late for appointments*, for example, or those who wish to *leave early*, may be particularly difficult to understand. On the other hand, there may be perfectly valid reasons for lateness and early leaving, and these include transport problems, or work and family difficulties. However, when certain patterns of behaviour become habitual, then the onus is on the counsellor to seek understanding of what might lie behind this particular response from the client.

Perhaps the most important thing which counsellors can do when they encounter the kind of client responses already described is to look more closely at their own attitudes to the client, and to consider what expectations – if any – they may be silently transmitting to him. Counsellors and clients do pick up unspoken messages from each other in this way, and clients frequently feel under pressure, especially when they sense that the counsellor is experiencing some difficulty in accepting or understanding the problems they describe. The following is an account given by a client who experienced this kind of silent message from his counsellor.

'After a while I couldn't bring myself to get there on time. I just kept arriving late, and making excuses to leave early, because I really didn't want to be there. It was fine in the beginning and we really got on well together, and he helped me a lot. When I told him about my gay lifestyle though, a mental block went up between us. I just know, he didn't – or couldn't – really accept it. Then finally we discussed things openly. He asked me why I always came late or left early, and that's when we really started to talk. It was a relief at the time, and now I'm with a female counsellor with whom I feel much more open and communicative ...'

Clients generally come into counselling because they want to make progress, but even when this is the initial ambition, subsequent self-exploration may prove so taxing that the desire to retreat is very compelling. Retreat may also take the form of *silence*, a subject which was considered from a different viewpoint in Chapter 2. Although *silence* is often used by clients as an aid to reflection and thought, it is also sometimes used to signal withdrawal from the counselling process. Clients may do this when they feel that they are under pressure in counselling, and this pressure may take the form of inept or intrusive questioning by the counsellor. It is sometimes the case that clients are 'advised' to have counselling, either by doctors or other professional people; when this happens, clients may be uncommitted to the counselling process from the outset. When lack of commitment is the case, other forms of retreat may also be evident, including *lack of response* in counselling, *changing the subject*, or *switching attention* to the counsellor and away from self. Occasionally a client may reject outright anything the counsellor says. When any of these forms of behaviour is evident, the counsellor should address the issue, by bringing it into the open in order to explore the underlying cause. The principle of active listening to all aspects of the client's communication is important here; so too are the core concepts of empathy and respect. Counsellors need to show clients that they understand the problems they experience in relation to counselling. When clients miss sessions or cancel appointments, these issues need to be discussed as well. The consequence of not addressing these issues is confusion, misunderstanding and wasted time for both counsellor and client.

Skills

IMMEDIACY

In this section, we shall look at some of the challenging skills described by Egan (1990), and consider the ways in which these can be used by counsellors to facilitate client progress in counselling. The word *immediacy* is used by Egan to refer to the process of discussing issues which are taking place in the 'here and now' between counsellor and client. An example of how this might work is contained in the following dialogue between counsellor and client.

Client: Things are not as bad as they sound though. There are some good things happening to me at the moment.

Counsellor: Could we just look again at some of the things we discussed... especially at what you have just said?

Client: What I have just said?

Counsellor: Yes, I get the feeling you might have said it to reassure me... could I be right about that?

Client: I don't want you to think I'm a hopeless case...

Counsellor:	I don't think that you are. You have gone through a particularly tough time...But you don't need to take care of me. I'm here to listen to you.
Client:	It's just that I'm conscious of not wanting to over-burden people...People can only take so much.
Counsellor:	I will listen to and try to understand all that you have to say. It is not a burden to me to hear these things. But perhaps other people have seemed unable to listen...?
Client:	That's part of the problem really. After Joe's [her husband] death people didn't seem to want to listen after a while. They would cross the street when they saw me coming. There was no one to talk to.

In the example just given, *immediacy* was used by the counsellor in order to engage the client in direct communication about the apprehension she was experiencing. She was apprehensive about the counsellor and his ability to 'stay with' her while she talked in detail about her husband's death. If the counsellor had chosen not to challenge these fears, the client would have continued to experience them, and might eventually have abandoned counselling because the issue had never been resolved. Immediacy may also be used to focus in a more direct way on the relationship between client and counsellor. In the first example given, immediacy was used to highlight a communication issue which existed at a particular time in a particular interaction. In the second use of immediacy, attention is directed towards the nature of the relationship between client and counsellor. The following is an example of immediacy used in this way.

Counsellor:	We have talked quite a bit about your illness and about your difficulty in talking to hospital staff...
Client:	It is difficult because they seem so far above me...
Counsellor:	That thought makes you inhibited...makes you hold back?
Client:	Yes, it does.
Counsellor:	Because the thought occurred to me that over these three sessions that we have talked together, you sometimes hold back in this way too...
Client:	Well, I suppose, yes...you're a professional too, like the others.
Counsellor:	With a difference though... I feel that we need to look more closely at that...

In this second example, the counsellor used immediacy in order to focus on the progress which had been made over a period of time between herself and the client. She highlighted the relationship itself, and in doing so encouraged the client to be more aware of the inhibitions she clearly expressed in relation to the counsellor – and to others.

COUNSELLOR SELF-DISCLOSURE

To disclose or not to disclose information about oneself is a central issue for student counsellors, and one which is discussed frequently at length within training groups. There are several important considerations in relation to self-disclosure, and these concern the nature of the counselling relationship, as well as the amount of information which is disclosed at any given time (see Fig. 5.2).

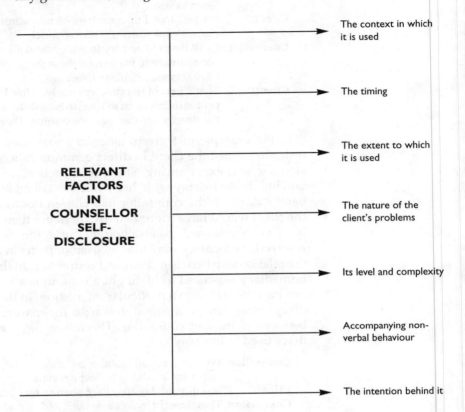

RELEVANT FACTORS IN COUNSELLOR SELF-DISCLOSURE

- The context in which it is used
- The timing
- The extent to which it is used
- The nature of the client's problems
- Its level and complexity
- Accompanying non-verbal behaviour
- The intention behind it

Fig. 5.2 *Counsellor self-disclosure.*

In certain specialized areas of counselling – for example, alcohol and drug abuse – self-disclosure may be used quite extensively by counsellors (Egan, 1990). Members of an Alcoholics Anonymous (AA) group will disclose a great deal of information about themselves, and even though this is a model of helping for which no formal training is usually undertaken or required, an enormous amount of therapeutic benefit is derived from it by participants. The success and staying power of AA as a support group is sufficient evidence of this last fact. When drug or alcohol abuse has been a problem for clients, they are often encouraged by some indication from former sufferers that the problems they experience are not insurmountable or hopeless. Other areas of addiction are also relevant in this respect, including smoking, gambling, sexual promiscuity, shopping, excessive exercise and comfort eating – to name just a few. Self-help groups also operate successfully for participants whose experiences have been similar in other ways; these include support groups for victims of trauma, sex abuse or rape, as well as groups which operate to support people who have been made redundant or those who experience high levels of stress or anxiety in everyday living. A more comprehensive overview of the way groups work will be given in Chapter 8, but it is important to indicate at this stage that self-disclosure and mutual support are integral aspects of group activity.

The nature of the counselling relationship is significant, therefore, in relation to self-disclosure. When a client experiences problems which are similar to those once experienced by the counsellor, self-disclosure by the counsellor may be appropriate and very helpful. Even here, however, certain problems can arise when the amount of personal information given to the client is either too great or too little to meet their individual needs. If small amounts of unconnected information are given in a random way, clients may be left confused and bewildered about their overall purpose and meaning. Enigmatic statements from the counsellor – such as 'Yes I know, I had that' – will serve only to switch attention from the client to the counsellor, without giving any concrete or helpful information to the client in the process. On the other hand, too much self-disclosure by the counsellor will certainly take the focus away from the client, and may even have the added disadvantage of making the client feel responsible for the counsellor. When such a reversal takes place, the client is placed in a truly intolerable position since the problems which he brought into counselling are now perceived – by him at least – as insignificant compared to those recounted by the helper.

When self-disclosure by the counsellor is measured, skilful and geared towards client needs, its effects are likely to be beneficial and therapeutic. In addition to this, self-disclosure may have a 'bonding' effect in the sense that client and counsellor may establish a deeper, more human relationship as a result of it. This deeper relationship may encourage greater self-disclosure on the client's part, and the example set by the counsellor may prove useful in helping clients to confront – in more resolute and constructive ways – the difficult and problematic aspects of their behaviour and living. When this happens, self-disclosure does fulfil its purpose as a challenging skill, but it needs to be used with the client's, and not the counsellor's, welfare in mind.

We have already indicated in Chapter 1 that the relationship between counsellor and client is very different in kind from that which exists between family, relatives or friends. Mutual self-disclosure occurs frequently between family members, or between friends, but in counselling the client is – or should be – the primary focus of attention. This means that the counsellor's level of self-disclosure should be accurately judged and well timed, and should be such that it does not serve to elicit diversionary curiosity on the client's part. Once such curiosity is aroused, questions may follow, and in this situation confusion about roles and responsibilities is often the result. The needs of the counsellor may come to dominate sessions, and the painful self-exploration which belongs to the client is neglected or even lost.

When considering the subject of self-disclosure, it is worth remembering also that even when it does seem appropriate and geared to client needs, it may not be as useful as the counsellor intended it to be. People's experiences are vastly different, even when they look the same on the surface, and the way that one person copes with a problem, may not be helpful to another, whose perception and circumstances are unique and personal. A summary of the benefits of self-disclosure includes the following.

- Through self-disclosure the counsellor shows herself to be human, experienced and understanding.

- Counsellor self-disclosure may encourage the client to be more courageous in confronting painful or difficult issues.

- Counsellor self-disclosure can bring client and counsellor closer together and this may result in deeper empathy on the counsellor's part.

- Counsellors working in specialized areas, for example addiction, can give useful personal information to clients which is based on experience.

A summary of the potential dangers of self-disclosure includes the following.

- Counsellor self-disclosure takes attention away from the client.

- No two people have exactly the same experience.

- Counsellor self-disclosure may worry the client.

- The client may start to feel responsible for the counsellor.

- Counsellor self-disclosure may confuse the client who may not understand why personal details are being given.

- Counselling is not a form of social exchange. It is a special therapeutic relationship in which the client's needs come first. Self-disclosure can upset the balance of the relationship.

- Clients may become envious if they feel that counsellors are boasting of personal achievements or success.

- Counsellors whose own problems are unresolved, may escape into self-disclosure to avoid listening to the client.

Student counsellors need to be aware that any self-disclosure will have some effect on clients; this can either be positive or negative, depending on a variety of factors. These are:

- The nature of the client's problem/problems.

- The timing of self-disclosure by the counsellor.

- The extent to which self-disclosure is used.

- The level and complexity of self-disclosure.

- The intention behind the self-disclosure.

- The non-verbal behaviour which accompanies the self-disclosure. This needs to be congruent and to match the words spoken.

Finally, it is worth remembering that even though clients are guaranteed confidentiality in counselling, there is no such reciprocal agreement in relation to any information which the counsellor may give to clients during sessions.

LOOKING BELOW THE SURFACE OF THINGS

In Chapter 3 we looked at the concept of empathy, and considered its importance in the counselling relationship. Empathy is essential if real understanding is to take place between counsellor and client; when it is absent, understanding is absent too.

Egan refers to 'advanced empathy' and details its use as a challenging skill which can be effective in helping clients identify aspects of themselves, their behaviour and their problems which they may not have been fully aware of before (Egan, 1990). Advanced empathy can be defined as a deeper, more intuitive awareness of another person's experience, and it is something which occurs between people in various situations in everyday life, especially when emotional bonds have been established. There are numerous examples of advanced empathy at work all around us. One has only to think of the nurse who clearly identifies the needs of her patient, even when those needs are not explicitly stated by him. This level of empathy is not just a result of knowledge which the nurse has acquired during her training; it is also related to her ability to identify, on a human level, with the patient's discomfort, distress or pain. Another way of stating this is to say that we often pick up signals from other people, especially when our mental antenna is deliberately tuned into their needs. Within the therapeutic relationship, the client's expressed, or unexpressed, difficulties need to be understood and appreciated by the counsellor, and development and use of advanced empathy is effective in achieving those aims.

The needs of the client, therefore, are paramount in counselling. The counsellor's task is to listen to what the client is saying, and to understand not only his words but also his unspoken concerns, especially when these are outside his immediate awareness. An underlying assumption in all this is that most people – including clients – have a strong desire and impulse to get at the truth, even when personal defences make such an undertaking difficult. Counsellors have a duty to help clients get at this truth, which is often elusive and frequently masked by numerous layers of self-deception or confusion. The following example should illustrate the use of advanced empathy as a challenging skill in counselling.

Client: It was lovely at first and very exciting. He seemed so interested in me, and the sexual side was great. It's only recently that he expressed these doubts. Anyway, I think we can get it back on course again, we have so much in common...

Counsellor: I can sense the excitement and happiness which you obviously feel about him. But I also get the feeling that deep down you are not so sure about it all – that you are hurt by the doubts he expressed.

Client: Well I suppose I don't want to admit it to myself...but at one level I'm terrified that he might have cooled off.

Counsellor: So you know that the possibility exists that he is not as interested as you would like him to be.

Client: Yes.

Throughout this exchange, the counsellor was tuned into the nuances and subtle shades of meaning which were expressed both verbally and non-verbally by the client.

At first the client sounded optimistic in her assertion that she and her boyfriend could get their relationship back on course. To some extent, she engaged in a form of wishful thinking, but the counsellor could identify the concern in her face and the hesitation in her voice when she spoke. If the counsellor had failed to challenge the client in this instance, then some degree of collusion and complicity would have taken place between them. In other words, the client would have gained no insight and the counsellor would have tacitly supported this self-deception and lack of courage.

GIVING INFORMATION TO CLIENTS

Occasionally clients ask for information in order to help them deal more effectively with the problems which they have. Giving information to clients is not the same thing as giving advice, although clients sometimes ask for advice when they feel that their own coping resources have been seriously depleted. The drawbacks of giving advice to clients was dealt with in Chapter 1, but it is important to emphasize here that there is often a slim dividing line between the practice of giving information and the temptation to offer advice or to recommend certain courses of action to clients. There are many examples of counselling situations in which it is entirely appropriate to give information about resources which are available to help them cope more effectively with specific problems. A client with a drug or alcohol problem might benefit from information about support groups within his area. Clients who suffer from severe depression are often reassured when they learn that medical treatment for the condition is effective and available. Information is also sometimes given in counselling about the specific and identifiable features of certain traumas, like bereavement and loss, for example. Clients frequently ask just how long it will take to get over the acute phase of bereavement, and counsellors can usefully discuss this with them, and give appropriate information to help them cope with their grief.

In addition to the examples given, clients often need further information as a form of challenge in counselling. It may be that they lack certain knowledge which, if it were provided, would substantially alter their perceptions of how things are, or should be. The following is an example of this last point.

Elaine, who was eighteen, wanted to become a social worker. She was frustrated in her attempts to gain a place at university, and she became angry and upset about the constant rejections she felt she was getting. Although her academic record was good, Elaine had no practical experience of working with people. When the counsellor discussed this with her, Elaine agreed that she had neglected the issue of work experience. She decided to apply to a voluntary agency for work during the summer, and resolved to try once again for a place at university when she had gained some confidence in working with people.

At one level, Elaine had been aware of the university entrance requirements, but she needed further information from the counsellor in order to challenge her view that social work places were being allocated unfairly.

CASE STUDY: MARTIN	Martin was a thirty five year old man, who was referred by his doctor to the practice counsellor at the surgery he attended. Martin suffered from psoriasis which had developed over a period of many years, and which caused him a great deal of anxiety and stress. Besides the itchy and irritating discomfort of the skin condition itself, psoriasis had also induced in him a deep feeling of self-disgust, and a belief that everyone else regarded him as unclean and unlovable. The quality of Martin's life had undoubtedly suffered as a result of the disfiguring skin condition he had; one of his main problems concerned the reactions of other people, especially when he participated in activities like swimming, which necessitated exposure of large areas of his body. He was also reluctant to sunbathe, or to take part in sports, even though he had a particular interest in sporting activities generally. On one occasion when he went swimming at the local pool, several teenagers had stared at him, and had made some comments about his appearance. After this incident, Martin's anxiety and depression grew more acute and he became increasingly reclusive in his lifestyle.

Over the years, Martin received various forms of treatment for his psoriasis including acupuncture, homeopathic remedies and eventually steroid ointment prescribed by his own doctor. None of these treatments was particularly effective, and he was referred to a skin specialist who recommended further drug treatment, which Martin refused. When asked by his General Practitioner if he would like to speak to the practice counsellor, Martin agreed at once. An appointment was made for him to meet her the following week.

During the first counselling session, Martin spent some time describing his disappointment about the failure of the treatments he had received to date. He then talked about his anxiety, and his inability to establish intimate relationships.

MARTIN: You can't imagine how it feels...how it is to feel ugly as I do. It's not exactly a turn-on for women...

COUNSELLOR: It is something which makes you lose confidence in yourself... especially in relationships.

MARTIN: It's not just relationships...it's so obvious, a skin condition...it's visible to everyone. The worst thing is that people don't understand it...most people think it's infectious.

COUNSELLOR: People are ignorant about it, and think they can catch it from you.

MARTIN: Nobody is going to get too close when that's on their minds...the more I worry the worse it becomes.

COUNSELLOR: I sense that underneath all the worry the saddest thing for you is the lack of a relationship, of real intimacy.

MARTIN: (*slowly*) It makes me despair at times. The whole world seems full of couples. I seem to be the only person on my own.

Throughout this exchange with Martin, the counsellor (Helen) was very aware of his loneliness and his regret about the lack of an intimate relationship. At one stage, Martin seemed keen to distance himself from this issue ('It's not just relationships...') but Helen brought him back to this using an empathic and challenging response. This had the effect of encouraging Martin to be more reflective, and to pay attention to his own feelings on the matter. Afterwards they discussed his reclusive lifestyle, and again the counsellor used challenging skills to encourage him to look at his behaviour more realistically.

MARTIN: I haven't been at a social function for God knows how long. I've lost the habit.

COUNSELLOR: So staying in has become a pattern for you...quite apart from the condition of your skin.

MARTIN: I suppose I just lost heart.

COUNSELLOR: So how to regain heart?

MARTIN: By trying again...it's very difficult...once you get out of the habit.

COUNSELLOR: Once you get out of the habit of going out?

MARTIN: That's right. I suppose I could always go somewhere I don't have to take any clothes off. (*laughs*)

COUNSELLOR: And perhaps gradually go to places where you do have to take them off...swimming, sunbathing?

MARTIN: I don't know about sunbathing...

COUNSELLOR: Yet Doctor Millar told you that certain kinds of sun exposure would be helpful.

MARTIN: He did say that...but I wouldn't go to see the specialist about it.

Helen re-enforced the information that Martin's doctor had given to him. This concerned the possibility of receiving treatments of Ultraviolet A light through consultation with the specialist. Martin decided to discuss this with his GP again, and eventually he agreed to see a specialist who told him about other available drug treatments. He learned that exposure of psoriasis to the sun can help to reduce the severity of the condition. As a result of this information, he booked a holiday abroad for two weeks. When he returned, he booked another counselling session with Helen. Although he realized that his condition was liable to return periodically, Martin was happy with the progress he had made and felt more confident about his general appearance. Through her use of challenging skills – including information giving – Helen had succeeded in helping him challenge his own assumptions about the limited help available for his condition.

KEY WORD   **CHANGE**

The word change has been used frequently throughout this chapter, with special reference to the challenging nature of change and to the difficulties which people often experience in coping with it. The problems which clients bring to counselling often involve some element of change which requires a certain level of adaptation if it is to be dealt with effectively. Even desirable changes in life can cause deep stress and anxiety. One example of this is the person who is promoted at work and who becomes, as a result of it, anxious and insomniac. The increased salary and status associated with promotion may be attractive, but the workload and associated pressure need physical and psychological adjustments to be made. Celebratory events like marriages, births and Christmas can also be deeply stressful, mainly because they require changes to be made to the normal routine of everyday life.

Unemployment, divorce, illness or death in the family cause major upheaval and change. Traumatic events and unemployment are also catalysts for change.

An important aspect of change, which is seldom appreciated at the time it is happening, is that positive as well as negative possibilities are integral to it. Another way of stating this is to say that change may present an individual with opportunities which were never experienced before. Clients often learn this as they struggle to deal with the more difficult elements of change, and it is often only when the acute phase of it has been mastered that the favourable dimension becomes apparent.

EXERCISES

EXERCISE 1   BENEFITS OF CHALLENGE

Working in groups of three, discuss the situations in which you think clients would benefit from challenge. Write down the suggestions made by each person, and discuss these within the larger training group.

EXERCISE 2   DANGERS OF CHALLENGE

Working in pairs, consider the potential dangers of challenge in counselling. What are the possible outcomes if challenge is used ineptly by counsellors?

EXERCISE 3   SELF-CHALLENGE

Spend about ten minutes working individually on a list of personal areas which you think might benefit from self-challenge. You might, for example, consider yourself to be a tolerant and accepting person. Try challenging this with a statement beginning with 'I', for example:

'I am not so tolerant when I'm tired, or when I'm in a bad mood.'

Discuss your chosen areas with other members of the group.

EXERCISE 4   POSITIVE CHALLENGE

This exercise is suitable for use with a group of students who know each other well. The idea is for students to challenge one another in a positive way. Students should take turns to address the person on their right with a positive challenge statement beginning with 'I', for example:

'I appreciate the way you express your views so clearly in the group.'

Students will probably find this form of challenge difficult to do at first, so it is useful to follow it up with some discussion about the problems clients experience in coping with challenge.

EXERCISE 5   EXPERIENCE OF CHALLENGE

Work with a partner: one person acting as client, the other as counsellor. The student in the client role should describe a personal experience of receiving challenge, while the student who is counsellor listens and gives the appropriate responses. Afterwards, discuss the situations in which challenge was given and received.

- What were the circumstances of the challenge?

- Who gave the challenge?

- Was the challenge effective?

- How did it feel to be challenged by someone else?

EXERCISE 6   DEEPER EMPATHY

One of the most important aspects of empathy is that, when it is present, it enables us to see beneath the surface of things and to appreciate the complexity of another person's character. This exercise is intended to give students some practice in looking at individuals in new and imaginative ways. Working individually, students should write out short descriptions of each of the following:

a) Jane, aged twenty five
b) An elderly woman
c) A ten year old boy
d) A middle aged couple
e) A man in prison.

EXERCISE 7   FURTHER EMPATHY

Working in groups of three or four, students should look at the following scenarios and brainstorm a list of the feelings and emotions which each of these people might experience.

- A teenage girl who has a date with the best-looking boy in her class.

- A woman who crashes her car while she is on her way to collect her child from school.

- A pregnant woman who has waited two hours in the outpatients' department of the hospital.

- A man who has just discovered his wife has been having an affair.

- An elderly man who lives alone and who has just been told that he needs hospital treatment.

EXERCISE 8   GIVING INFORMATION
Working in groups of two or three, brainstorm a list of situations in which it might be appropriate to give information to clients. Afterwards, discuss any situations in which you think information giving might also prove challenging for clients.

FURTHER READING

1 Dryden, Windy, *Questions and Answers on Counselling in Action,* Sage, London, 1993.
2 Hargie, O, Saunders, C and Dickson, D, *Social Skills in Interpersonal Communication,* Routledge, London, 1990.
3 Dryden, Windy, *Key Issues for Counselling in Action,* Sage, London, 1993.
4 Murphy, P M and Kupshik, G A, *Loneliness, Stress and Well-Being,* Routledge, London, 1992.
5 Culley, Sue, *Integrative Counselling Skills in Action,* Sage, London, 1991.
6 Egan, Gerard, *The Skilled Helper,* Brookes/Cole, Monterey CA, 1990.

REFERENCE LIST

1 *The Skilled Helper* by Gerard Egan (3rd edition), Brookes/Cole, Monterey CA, 1986.
2 *The Ego and the Mechanisms of Defence* by Anna Freud, Hogarth Press, London, 1937.
3 *The Discovery of the Unconscious* by Henri F Ellenberger, Fontana, London, 1994.
4 *A Critical Dictionary of Psychoanalysis* by Charles Rycroft, Penguin, London, 1972.
5 *On Becoming a Person* by Carl Rogers, Constable, London, 1991.
6 *Client-Centred Therapy* by Carl Rogers, Constable, London, 1991.
7 'Abnormal Grief' by A O'Flaherty in *Death and Dying,* edited by C Kean, Mercier, Dublin, 1995.
8 *Insight and Experience* by Michael Jacobs, Open University Press, Milton Keynes, 1991.
9 'Against Self-Disclosure' by J Segal in *Questions and Answers on Counselling in Action,* edited by Dryden, Sage, London, 1993.
10 *Social Skills in Interpersonal Communications* by Owen Hargie, Christine Saunders and David Dickson, Routledge, London, 1995.

CHAPTER 6

Action and management

A concern which is often expressed by members of the public in relation to counselling and therapy is that these activities can be used by people who wish to retreat from the harsh realities of living. Implicit in this concern is the idea that asking for help is a sign of weakness or ineptitude, and that only those individuals who are unable to act for themselves would ever resort to therapeutic assistance. What tends to be ignored in this argument is that asking for help is, in itself, a daunting prospect for many people, and one which requires a great deal of courage as well as a willingness to become proactive in addressing personal difficulties.

There can be no doubt that situations do sometimes arise in which clients in counselling are not actively encouraged to develop initiative in coping with problems. These situations usually occur when helpers themselves are inept, poorly trained, unsupervised, or quite simply lacking in personal awareness. However, one of the central aims of counselling is the development of client independence and autonomy, and it is to this end that all endeavours in therapy should be directed. The aims of counselling were identified in Chapter 1, but it is worth reiterating the point that clients in counselling need help in devising strategies for coping, and encouragement in planning programmes which will enable them to achieve the goals they wish to meet.

Although clients do not always progress through counselling in a series of neat and orderly stages, it is, nevertheless, useful to think of the counselling process in a fairly structured way. The advantage of this approach is that it gives counsellors – especially student counsellors – a frame of reference or schema which can provide some guidance for working in an organized way with clients. It is useful, therefore, to think in terms of a beginning, a middle and an end in counselling. The stages which were outlined in Chapter 1, derived from Egan's problem-solving approach, are particularly helpful in this respect. The third stage which Egan describes is concerned with action and the management of problems (Egan, 1990). This is the stage of counselling which we shall consider here, paying special attention to the ways in which clients can deal with their problems, through use of strategies like action planning, creative thinking, brainstorming, and the development of social and assertiveness skills. Attention will be focused on the importance of helping clients to become more confident in their own abilities to choose and to deal effectively with problems. The factors which impede goal setting or achievement will also be discussed.

Self-esteem

The term self-esteem has become almost a cliché in current phraseology, and is often used without understanding of its essential or true meaning. It is especially ubiquitous in books which deal with self-help or self-psychology, and in these contexts it is frequently promoted as an attitude of mind which is relatively easy to attain. Anyone who has worked closely with clients in counselling, however, will realize that this is a simplistic approach. Basic self-esteem can be greatly diminished or even absent when trauma or emotional damage has occurred early or frequently in people's lives.

A definition of the term is important at this stage because it is impossible to over-estimate the significance of self-esteem as a facilitating factor in the management of personal problems. One way in which people differ from other animals is in the human capacity to be aware of self.

This awareness of self begins to develop in infancy, and evolves as a result of the interactions which take place between a young child and the immediate environment. The most significant aspect of any child's environment is, of course, the parents, or primary caretakers. If the relationships which develop at this stage are positive, loving and supportive, the child is likely to internalize a good sense of self. Providing that the immediate environment continues to be supportive and nurturing, the individual growing up within it has a good chance of maintaining and enhancing this affirmative view of self. Adverse events will certainly occur at various stages throughout any individual's life, but if basic confidence is acquired early on, then appropriate coping strategies will also be present. When these coping strategies are effective and difficulties overcome, the sense of achievement which follows will further enhance a person's sense of worth or self-esteem.

Unfortunately, early relationships are not always loving and supportive, and children often grow up feeling lost and hopeless in a world which seems alien, uncaring and hostile to them. When the environment is negative in this way, it is almost impossible for a child to feel good about 'self' because the message which is habitually passed to her is that she has no value or worth. Obviously, any setbacks which occur later on in life will serve to accentuate the negative personal image already in place. This is a no-win situation which is familiar to many of the clients who seek counselling, although it would be wrong to imply that all clients have had negative early experiences. Events like bereavement, loss and trauma do happen in adult life, and many people need help and support when these experiences touch them personally. Even people who are confident and secure may temporarily lose self-assurance when traumatic events occur in their lives.

However, it is clearly the case that many people do seek help when their self-esteem is at a very low ebb. Counselling is one form of help which – to some extent at least – should assist in redressing a balance which has been upset through negative early experience. In *Self-Esteem*

Awareness of self develops in infancy and evolves as a result of the interaction between the young child and the environment.

(1988), McKay and Fanning refer to research carried out in America by Zilbergeld (1983) which clearly indicates that therapy does have a positive and beneficial effect in helping to raise self-esteem. In Zilbergeld's view, this raising of clients' self-esteem may be the most important function of counselling, for regardless of the problems which clients bring to counselling it is the development of personal worth, and the increase in confidence, which actually motivates people to change.

It goes without saying that action, problem management and the achievement of goals would be difficult – if not impossible – for clients, unless they arrive at a stage where they experience some measure of self-esteem and confidence. Counsellors need to provide the right condition for such changes to take place, and these conditions can only be present when the skills which have been discussed in previous chapters are used to effect. In addition to those skills already described, clients need to be encouraged to formulate goals for the future, to take action when necessary, and to develop a range of new measures which will enable them to deal more effectively with problems. Once clients have been given an opportunity to discuss their problems, and to consider the ways in which these might be overcome, a stage is reached which calls for more direct action and initiative, as well as commitment to short- and long-term goals. The ways in which goals and objectives are pursued will, of course, depend to some extent on the nature of clients' problems, and the resources available to them. There are, however, a range of possible strategies which can be used by many people with a variety of problems. The following is an outline of some of the approaches which are often effective in helping clients to devise management and action programmes.

GOALS

It should be emphasized that any plans which are made in counselling and any action taken by clients should be a direct result of their own personal choice. The counsellor's skills at this stage should be directed towards encouraging clients to think carefully before any action is taken, to support clients when they have made their choices, and to monitor – and help clients evaluate – any progress or gain which is made.

Throughout the middle phase of counselling, clients will have considered all the options available to them, and should have reached some conclusions about the changes which they need or wish to make. Action planning and goal setting are the next links in the sequence, for although clients may have some view of *what* might be done, they need to go further than this in order to establish *how* things will be done. At this stage, therefore, the words *what* and *how* are especially significant. Clients can be encouraged to look clearly at these by writing them down and listing appropriate responses beside them. The following is an example of how this is done.

Catherine, who was nineteen and overweight, wanted to change her eating habits, to take more exercise, and to become fit. In counselling she listed the words *what* and *how*, and wrote her response to these.

What?
I want to be fit.
I want to eat sensibly.
I want to get out and about and make friends.

How?
By joining the local ramblers association.
By joining Weight Watchers.
By becoming more involved in social activities at work.

It is a good idea to encourage clients to express their goals in positive, rather than negative, terms. Instead of saying 'I want to lose weight', Catherine was encouraged by her counsellor to state her ambitions in terms of outcomes which would be agreeable and of benefit to her. Sometimes it is also a good idea to add another question to the two already mentioned. If Catherine had asked herself *Why?* her intentions and her reasons for following certain courses of action would have been clarified further. For example:

What do I want?
I want to be fit.
I want to eat sensibly.
I want to get out and about and make friends.

How?
By joining the local ramblers association.
By joining Weight Watchers.
By becoming more involved in social activities at work.

Why should I do these things?
Being in the Ramblers means walking and getting exercise.
Weight Watchers will teach me how to eat sensibly.
Involvement in social activities means meeting a variety of people.

On the face of it, this technique may seem simplistic and repetitive, but it does help clients to look clearly at the problems they have and the steps which they need to take in order to overcome them. It also raises the question of whether the goals which have been set are realistic and attainable (see Fig. 6.1). Clients need to consider the resources which they have, either personally or within their environment. If the resources are lacking or inadequate then the goals which have been set are doomed to failure from the outset. In Catherine's case, there were plenty of environmental resources available to her. As well as this, she was personally committed to the course of action she had chosen so her inner resources were adequate too. Things are not always as straightforward as this, however, and many of the problems which clients have are complex, multi-dimensional and less amenable to any formula approaches to solving them.

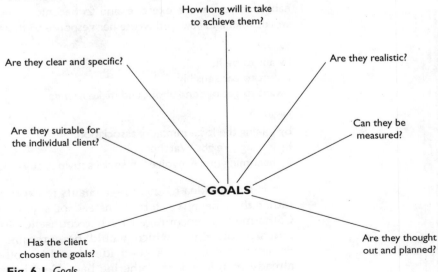

How long will it take
to achieve them?

Are they clear and specific?

Are they realistic?

Are they suitable for
the individual client?

Can they be
measured?

GOALS

Has the client
chosen the goals?

Are they thought
out and planned?

Fig. 6.1 *Goals.*

IMAGINATIVE AND CREATIVE THINKING

Anyone who has experienced severe emotional upset will be familiar with the diminished creativity which often accompanies it. It is difficult to be bright, imaginative and creative when all one's mental resources are preoccupied with feelings of distress, unhappiness or grief. Clients often experience a diminution in their imaginative or creative capacity, and this can seriously impede awareness of new and original ways of solving problems. Counselling is by no means the only way through which clients can recover some of their creative skills, but it is certainly helpful, especially since it offers the kind of individual support and attention which is important when people are involved in risk taking and change. New ways of tackling problems may seem very risky to clients, but if they are given the necessary encouragement and help, confidence and the courage to move forward will usually follow (see Fig. 6.2).

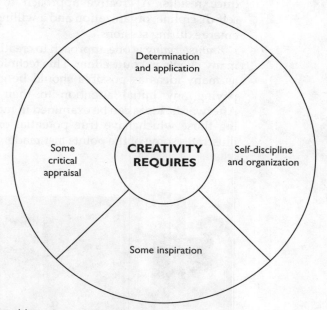

Fig. 6.2 *Creativity.*

The word 'creativity' used in the counselling context refers to the individual's ability to develop and realize full potential. Carl Rogers referred to this as the *actualizing tendency*. He described it as an innate urge to express oneself fully, and to utilize talents and abilities (Rogers, 1991). It also implies moving towards maturity, independence and autonomy, and although this impulse may be temporarily halted, it can be re-discovered and expressed again, once the right conditions are present. Abraham Maslow (1970) also referred to the process of self-actualization. He too described it in terms which emphasized its essentially creative and dynamic nature.

Imaginative thinking, originality and a willingness to venture into unknown territory are therefore closely linked with self-development and growth. When clients have been given the necessary conditions for exploring and defining their problems in counselling, some measure of personal growth and awareness should certainly develop. This enhanced self-awareness and confidence will then help them reclaim their innate abilities to judge, and make decisions. It should also enable them to become more innovative in the way they approach problem solving and goals.

SOME APPROACHES TO CREATIVE THINKING

An important point to remember in relation to creativity is that it requires determination and application in order to capture it and utilize its full potential. In other words, creative output does not evolve from inspiration alone, but requires effort and perseverance to make it work and produce results. A creative approach to problem solving also requires self-discipline, organization and a willingness to criticize any ideas which emerge during sessions.

Brainstorming is one approach to creative thinking which works well for many clients in counselling. This technique is based on the principle that as many ideas as possible should be generated fairly quickly, without paying any initial attention to their suitability or appropriateness. Afterwards, ideas can be examined in more detail, with a view to identifying those which have true potential or worth. The following example illustrates some of the points just made.

Creative output involves effort and perseverance to make it work.

Grace, a twenty year old university student, was addicted to shopping for clothes. She worked with her counsellor to identify the roots of her problem, and then moved on to looking at ways of dealing with it. Eventually, she set herself goals for the future, the most important of which – in her view – was to save enough money to buy a car. With the help of her counsellor, she brainstormed a list of ways she could control her spending on clothes. Her list included:

- Sort the clothes I already have and decide what I need or don't need.
- Open a savings account and put away some money each month.
- Go to town once a week instead of each day.
- Don't go into clothes shops.
- Meet a friend for coffee when I go into town. Tell her I want to avoid the shops.
- Take up a hobby which really interests me.
- Stop buying fashion magazines.
- Stop watching the Clothes Show.
- Put on weight.
- Give all my clothes away.
- Decide on the car I want and set a date for when I should have enough to buy it.
- Read more books.
- Cancel all catalogues.
- Mix with people who are not interested in fashion.
- Make a decision to buy a certain number of items per year, and stick to it.

While the counsellor was careful not to criticize any of the suggestions which Grace had made, she did encourage her to elaborate on these, and to identify the ideas which seemed most realistic and were likely to work for her. As a result of the work which they did together, Grace was able to select a number of real possibilities.

- Open a savings account and put away some money each month for a car.
- Decide on the car I want and set a date for buying it.
- Sort out my clothes. Wear the clothes I have not already worn. Give others to Oxfam.
- Enlist the help of a girlfriend. Tell her what I want to do.
- Read more.
- Make a decision to buy a certain number of clothes items per year, and stick to it.

Grace also decided to curtail her visits to town and to spend more time on her studies. Some of the ideas which she had come up with originally, now seemed unrealistic or even ridiculous. The idea that she should put on weight in order to inhibit her clothes shopping, for example, was clearly impracticable. However, the exercise did serve to open up more creative possibilities for her, and while she was engaged in it the counsellor offered support and encouraged her to focus on workable choices, or those with real potential.

VISUALIZATION

Visualization is another approach to creative thinking and can be used by clients to help them imagine what the achievement of specific goals would look like. Ian was a client whose ambition was to go to university to read for a degree. He was thirty years old and had been addicted to drugs, a habit which he managed to overcome with the help of a drugs counsellor. Ian's rehabilitation was difficult for him, but each time he felt in danger of relapse, he overcame the temptation with the help of visualization:

> 'I made myself think of what it would feel like to have the degree. That kept me going, the picture which I kept in the front of my mind. The picture was one of success and achievement. It was attractive and strong enough to help me overcome the temptation to go back to drugs. Without that picture of what I could do in the future, I would never have managed to stay clean.'

To enable him to sustain his resolve, Ian also visualized himself making small, positive steps towards his chosen goal. Besides thinking of the final degree, he thought of the interview which would secure him a place at university. The counsellor encouraged him to think of each step in confident, affirmative terms. This might seem like a technique for positive thinking, but there is nothing intrinsically wrong with that, especially if it works for certain clients. Egan uses the term *preferred scenarios* to describe the procedure for helping clients create mental pictures of a better future (Egan, 1990). The procedure is not just a facile one, but requires concentration, realism and a great deal of commitment to the achievement of goals.

PEOPLE WHO CAN HELP

Another method of helping clients to approach problem solving is to assist them in identifying the available resources which might be of use in the pursuit of their goals. These resources include people as well as things, for within any individual's social network there are usually others who are willing to help when help is needed. This is especially true when clients have specific problems like drug or alcohol addiction; in these instances, there are often whole groups of people who are available to help. The work carried out by support and self-help groups is described in some detail in Chapter 8, but it is important to emphasize at this stage that identifying others who can help is an essential skill in the goal-setting phase of counselling.

As well as people who can help, there are also unfortunately those who might hinder a client's progress. It is useful to identify any potential obstacles which exist, and to formulate ways of dealing with difficulties which may arise. One client who had been addicted to gambling joined a support group to help overcome his problem. He was still left, though, with the dilemma of dealing with the friendships he had established over a period of many years and which depended, to a large extent, on a common interest in gambling. He was able to resolve the problem with the help and encouragement of the support group, but it could have been a major stumbling block for him if he had not anticipated it beforehand. In the event, he explained his decision to quit gambling to his friends; one friend stayed, while the others gradually drifted away. Such obstacles to progress often inhibit a client's ability to sustain efforts for change.

OTHER ASPECTS OF THE ENVIRONMENT

Other aspects of the client's environment can also either inhibit or encourage progress. A client may, for example, be employed in a work situation which presents special problems in relation to change and improvement. Greg, a hotelier, found himself in a position which was especially difficult to resolve. Over a period of years he developed an alcohol dependency which was facilitated by his easy access to alcoholic drinks. As part of his decision to stop drinking, Greg tried for a different job and was successful in finding employment which presented less temptation to him. It was not easy for him to change so many aspects of his life at once, and in order to do so with any degree of success, he needed determination as well as the help and encouragement of a counsellor.

OTHER PEOPLE'S PROBLEMS

One important truth which clients often have to face when solving problems is that it is not always possible to exert control over *other* people or *their* problems. In fact, it is seldom possible to do so. Once clients have grasped this truth, it simplifies planning for the future because they realize then that they have to accept responsibility for themselves and for their behaviour. It is pointless for clients to spend time worrying about other people's problems if they do not address their own difficulties first. This is not to say that other people's problems are not important, or that clients should act in selfish or egotistical ways. What it does imply is that it is always useful to start from an individual viewpoint, and to consider what changes could be made to 'self' before seeking changes within the environment. Clients who have difficulties in personal relationships, for example, may be terrified to set goals which are unrealistic and involve some attempt to impose change on others. One client in group counselling expressed it this way:

'For years I thought my wife should change, that she should stop complaining so much and just get on with things. I was irritated with what I thought was her constant complaining. Then when I joined the group, I saw things from a different perspective. I began to understand what it was she was saying. Before that I wanted to change her. Now that I have changed my own behaviour, and help more with the children, things have become a lot better between us. Our relationship would have been happier if I had just looked carefully at myself. Now I can see how my lack of involvement in the family almost ruined things for us in the past.'

EFFECTS ON OTHER PEOPLE

Although it is important for clients to address their own problems and set their own goals, they also need to look closely at the cost to others if particular goals are accomplished. Since very few people live in total isolation from others, this is a significant point in relation to goals or objectives which are planned for the future. A client who decides to leave a marriage, for example, will need to consider the effects which such a decision will have on his family, including his children. Failure to address significant issues like this will tend to result in precipitate and disorganized action which is doomed to failure from the outset. The concept of self-actualization or self-fulfilment does not imply selfishness and a total disregard for the welfare of others. Although clients should be helped to identify their own individual needs first, they ought to consider how these will impinge on the lives of other people too. Counselling and therapy are sometimes criticized on the grounds that they encourage rampant individualism; while there is no doubt that such attitudes are occasionally fostered, therapeutic assistance should help clients to explore the issues of goals, not just in relation to self, but in relation to others as well.

It is also worth mentioning here that counsellors are sometimes surprised by the goals which clients wish to achieve. However, the goals which are set by clients are 'individual' in the sense that only they are aware of the circumstances surrounding the choices they have made, and their possible impact on others. Counsellors need to respect each client's unique view, while at the same time encouraging reflection and consideration of the consequences of any action taken.

Management skills

MAKING CONTRACTS

A more formal approach to goal setting with clients is one which includes making contracts, either at the beginning of counselling or later on when the client has a clearer picture of what he wants to achieve. The contract may be written or verbal, and should be subject to review sessions at different stages of the client's progress. These reviews serve to highlight any difficulties which have arisen since the original contract was made. When more than one goal is desired, the client should be encouraged to set these out in order of priority. Clients can also set out the advantages and disadvantages of various proposals for change.

Several theoretical approaches to counselling, including the *Cognitive* and Behavioural approaches, place a great deal of emphasis on contracts. These contracts are usually established early in counselling, and their working details are discussed in clear and specific terms.

There are several advantages to be gained from using formal contracts in counselling. In the first instance, they enable clients to focus attention explicitly on the goals they wish to achieve. As well as this, they help to establish order and mental preparation before any action is taken. When clients participate fully in setting out goals, they have a sense of ownership and commitment which are essential qualities for the attainment of goals. Clients are also less likely to under- or over-estimate their resources when they have been discussed beforehand. A formal contract relating to goals will address the issue of time as well. Clients need to have some idea about the length of time it will take to achieve certain goals. These ideas may need to be revised during a subsequent review session, but once they have been established through a contract clients should have some definite incentive for action.

LEARNING NEW SKILLS

Quite often clients need to learn new skills before they can take direct action to achieve their goals. In Ian's case (above), he needed to learn both interview and assertiveness skills before applying to the university for a place on a course. Some theoretical approaches to counselling are more geared than others to helping clients develop new skills in this way. *Cognitive behaviour* counselling, for example, employs a variety of methods including role play, reading, assignments and assertive techniques to help clients acquire skills. However, it is possible to provide clients with opportunities to develop aptitude and competence in different areas, regardless of the counselling orientation used.

Groupwork is an ideal form for encouraging the development or enhancement of social skills. This approach is described in some detail in Chapter 8 and is certainly effective in helping clients who lack confidence in communication, assertiveness or decision-making skills.

A person-centred or Rogerian approach to counselling – which is the approach we are mainly concerned with in this book – is also, by definition, geared to the needs of individual clients. It is therefore capable of offering a variety of helping activities to them, including encouragement to develop competence in whichever areas clients wish to improve.

GIVING ENCOURAGEMENT

Encouragement is an important aspect of the goal setting and action management stages of counselling. If clients are to sustain their effort to make progress and to reach their chosen goals, they need to be given the necessary support, encouragement and feedback to help them do so. Clients can also be helped to encourage and monitor themselves throughout this phase. Occasionally clients get stuck, or become too dependent on counsellors to help them achieve their goals. In instances like this, it can be useful to address the issue of dependence in an open and empathic way. This means encouraging clients to become more confident and trusting in their own abilities to cope. It also means helping them to identify supportive elements within their own environment. A client with a specific problem like panic attacks, for example, might derive a great deal of help from a support or self-help group. There is always a temptation to give advice to clients at this stage of counselling, especially when the counsellor is aware of the existence of various options which may not be known to the client. However, there is a difference between giving advice and supplying information to clients. Some of the disadvantages of giving advice to clients were dealt with in Chapter 1, but some of the benefits of supplying information when needed were highlighted in Chapter 5. It is important to reiterate that goals should always belong to the client. In order to ensure that this principle is respected, counsellors need to suppress any tendency to advice giving at this, and every other, stage of counselling.

Another important reason for giving encouragement to clients is that it often gives them the necessary impetus to continue when giving up looks like an attractive option to them. It sometimes happens that clients who are keen initially to set out and pursue their goals, lose enthusiasm and confidence when obstacles or impediments arise.

When situations like this arise, encouragement is vital if clients are to continue with the work they have started. To be truly effective, the encouragement given should highlight the client's personal resources and assets as well as the work which has already been achieved. Mistakes which have been made can be discussed in the light of experience. Some clients are particularly hard on themselves when it comes to making mistakes, but counsellors can help them to see that mistakes are not indicative of failure. On the contrary, it is difficult to see how any real learning could take place in the absence of at least some mistakes. This area of acceptance is important, especially for those clients who are self-punitive and perfectionist in regard to mistakes.

ENDINGS

When clients come to the end of counselling they are quite likely to experience a range of conflicting emotions. Some of these feelings may be negative, but others may be positive, optimistic and confident. To some extent the client's feelings at this stage will depend on the kind of problems which he brought to counselling in the first place. Those clients who have made real progress, even when their problems seemed intractable at the beginning, will obviously experience a sense of relief and achievement.

Even when success and achievement are dominant feelings, however, clients are also likely to feel some measure of apprehension, regret or loss because the relationship which helped them to get to this stage is now coming to an end. Clients who have become independent and quite confident about their ability to cope alone, may still need some time and assistance in order to help them accept the finality of this last phase of counselling.

The counselling relationship – unlike other relationships – is meant to end. One of the most important goals of counselling is that clients will – through the help they receive in the therapeutic relationship – develop confidence and autonomy, and the ability to cope effectively with their own problems. This makes counselling fundamentally different from friendships, for example. Friendships tend to develop over a period of time, and there is usually a great deal of mutual dependence as well as sharing. In the therapeutic relationship the counsellor does not expect or need to depend on the client, and the meetings which take place between counsellors and clients are for the client's benefit only. In addition to this, the work which is carried out between counsellor and client is designed to make the relationship unnecessary. Another way of putting this is to say that the *end* is the objective, right from the *beginning* of counselling. Clients need to be aware of finishing dates, if not at the outset, at least some time before the final sessions are due to take place.

Ideally, clients should be fully involved from the beginning in deciding the number of counselling sessions which they will need to help them deal effectively with their problems. Making a contract with clients is one way of involving them in decisions about the number of sessions they will attend. Contracts also help to focus attention on the limited amount of time available to clients, and in this respect they may also help to motivate action and change. It goes without saying that not all clients attend counselling for the same number of sessions; some clients may attend for three or four sessions depending on their problems, while others may need and request many more sessions than this, spread over a longer period of time.

When clients have explicit and achievable goals which are stated, clarified and addressed in counselling, then the ending phase should not seem traumatic, abrupt or disappointing for them. There is a possibility that clients may become dependent on counselling, but counselling can minimize this to some extent by consistently working to help them develop confidence and self-reliance, and some belief in their own abilities to cope. Issues relating to client dependence and transference will be discussed in more detail in Chapter 9, but it is important to emphasize that endings in counselling can be problematic when deep dependence is fostered or develops. When clients have developed some degree of dependency in counselling, they need time and preparation in order to adjust to the end of what has become for them a very important relationship. Clients also need to know that they have made real progress through their own efforts, before they can contemplate successful endings. Issues related to gains in counselling can be discussed with clients, as a necessary preparation to closure or termination.

Unless a clear contract has been established at the beginning, client and counsellor may not automatically agree about specific dates for ending counselling. From a counsellor's perspective, a client may appear to have made significant progress, while the client's opinion may be less optimistic or confident. The differing viewpoints need not present great problems, however, as long as they are acknowledged and openly discussed. Some agreement should then be reached concerning areas where discrepancies exist. Sensitivity, respect and empathy are as important in this last phase of counselling as they were in the beginning and middle stages. Indeed such qualities may be needed more at this time, especially for those clients who experience strong feelings about separation and leave taking. For some clients, endings are reminiscent of other losses or traumas which they have had to deal with in the past. In such instances, however, these particular vulnerabilities should have become evident in earlier sessions, long before the ending stage of counselling is reached. In other words, clients who are especially worried about ending relationships should have a chance to discuss their fears in some detail throughout counselling.

It is a good idea to spend some time with clients looking at the positive changes which have taken place for them, before the final stages of counselling are reached. In some instances, clients are given the opportunity to attend an additional session at some future date which is agreed upon by both counsellor and client. Even those clients who feel confident about their ability to cope alone, may welcome this possibility for future contact. On the other hand, counsellors should avoid giving clients the impression that therapy is a necessary part of one's lifestyle. Most people manage their lives effectively, and need help in specific circumstances only. Counselling is just one form of helping, and it has its limitations. As well as this, counselling has the potential to 'disempower' people, especially if it is viewed as an alternative to social involvement and the establishment of intimate and personal relationships. Student counsellors should also be aware that it is possible for therapists to become dependent on clients too. Such dependency, when it does arise, is usually linked to some area of deficit which exists in a counsellor's own life. This is just one issue which highlights the role and significance of supervision for counsellors. Other important aspects of supervision will be discussed at greater length in Chapter 9.

ENDING INDIVIDUAL SESSIONS

Counselling sessions usually last for fifty minutes to one hour, and may take place once a week, quite often on the same day each week. This is a routine which many counsellors try to establish although it is not always possible – or desirable – to stick rigidly to it. Some clients are reassured by the security which routine offers, while others may welcome a more flexible or varied approach. However, it is important that sessions should start and finish on time, regardless of how often or regularly meetings take place. This rule is especially important for counsellors who are meeting several clients one after the other, and there are obvious practical reasons for this. If sessions are allowed to run overtime, an atmosphere of stress and hurry is almost certain to result, with detrimental effects on both counsellor and clients. Most counsellors will allocate some free time for themselves between sessions in order to clarify their thoughts, re-arrange notes, go to the toilet or have some tea. These may seem like mundane tasks, but they do need attention. Counsellors have to take care of themselves if they are to be truly available and effective in helping clients.

REFERRAL

Sometimes clients are referred to counselling either by a general practitioner, psychiatrist, colleague or friend. When referral does take place, it is necessary to establish certain points of information relating to the client and the problem which he/she has. A referral may be made by word of mouth, telephone or letter. Regardless of the method of referral, however, the counsellor needs to know why therapy has been suggested, and how the client feels about the prospect of receiving it. Other important aspects of referral include the following:

- Has the client agreed to attend for counselling, or does he feel he has no choice?

- What does the client expect from counselling?

- What has the client been told to expect by the referring agent?

- Is the counselling approach which you offer the same as the one which has been recommended to the client?

- How does the referring agent view a counsellor's role? Is the counsellor seen as an adviser or expert?

- What are the problems which the client feels he needs to address?

- How much information are you expected to share with the referring agency? What are the rules regarding confidentiality? Is the client aware that information may be shared?

It is worth remembering that counsellors are not obliged to see every person who is referred to them. Sometimes counsellors do not have the time to see extra clients, in which case they should state this clearly to the referring agency, if possible before clients are sent to them. It is certainly best to avoid a situation in which clients are passed from one helper to another without proper consultation and liaison between agencies. Clients have a right to the best possible care, support and information, especially during referral procedures.

REFERRING CLIENTS ON

The fact that counselling has its limitations has already been highlighted within this chapter. Counsellors too have their limitations, and because of this they often have to refer clients to other helping agencies or personnel who have specific or specialized expertise which the client may need.

Ideally, referral should take place in the first stage of counselling, or just as soon as the client's individual needs become apparent. The process of referral requires tact and sensitivity on the counsellor's part since it can easily be interpreted as a rejection by the client. As soon as the need for referral becomes evident, the counsellor should discuss this with the client so that the decision becomes a joint one, rather than something which is imposed on the client. It may be that the client disagrees with the counsellor's suggestion of referral and such reluctance to meeting another helper or attending a different agency is understandable. It takes courage to disclose personal details about oneself, especially in the middle of emotional turmoil, and the prosect of repeating such disclosure may be daunting in the extreme. One reason it is important to refer early rather than later in counselling is that when left to a later stage the client may be unwilling to relinquish the relationship he has with a counsellor, in order to make another relationship with someone he has never met. However, it is essential to remember that clients should be given the most suitable help which is available for them, and counsellors have a duty to tell clients about any specialized support which might be of benefit to them. On the other hand, clients have the right to reject any offers of help which they do not regard as appropriate for them personally.

In order to refer successfully, counsellors need to be familiar with a wide range of counselling, helping and support services within their own areas. They also need to be aware of the agencies and specialized services operating at a national level, especially those in the areas of mental health, addiction, bereavement, sexual abuse, eating disorders and relationship problems. In-depth knowledge of all the helping agencies available can only be acquired over a period of time, but it does help to keep an up-to-date resources directory where important information, contacts and telephone numbers are clearly listed.

If referral is handled badly, there is a possibility that clients will come to believe their problems are too difficult for the original counsellor to deal with. It is important that clients should not label themselves in this way. In order to avoid such discouraging thinking, the reasons for referral need to be identified clearly by the counsellor. Counsellors should also be willing to acknowledge their own limitations to the client; in fact, this is probably an effective way of avoiding the kind of negative mental labelling already mentioned. Occasionally the problems which a client brings to counselling would be better dealt with by someone who works from a different theoretical perspective. Again, this needs to be explained to the client, along with some jargon-free details about the various approaches used. Sometimes clients specifically ask for referral because they feel that they could relate more easily to a counsellor of the same or opposite sex. There are various reasons for this kind of request, and counsellors should not interpret it as an indictment of their professional expertise. Clients with specific language difficulties may also benefit from referral, and the principle of consultation with the client beforehand applies here as it does in all other areas of referral.

Sometimes clients who are receiving individual counselling will be referred for groupwork too; and clients with specific health problems may benefit from medical treatment, in which case, referral to a doctor will be necessary. The two most important questions which counsellors should ask themselves in relation to referral are:

- What kind of help is best for this client?
- Where is this help available?

The client's financial situation is another consideration in referral. There is obviously no point in referring a client for specialist help, for example, when he cannot afford to pay for it. All the basic counselling skills which have been discussed in previous chapters should be used with clients when referral procedures are taking place.

CASE STUDY: LEN

Len was a fifty year old man who was referred by his General Practitioner for counselling because he had become increasingly depressed, and had developed obsessive behaviour which was directly related to his work. He was a builder who owned his own firm, and for many years he had worked successfully and established a good lifestyle with his wife, and his two teenage daughters who still lived at home. Len had been prescribed Prozac by his doctor, but found the drug unhelpful and asked if he could be allowed to see someone else who might be able to help him.

Len had consulted his doctor because he was worried about his preoccupation with checking the ceilings and walls of his home for any defects which might be apparent. His wife and family were continually harassed by his behaviour, and finally they convinced him that he needed to seek help from his doctor. When he arrived for his first appointment, Len was accompanied by his wife who was clearly very worried about his behaviour, and wanted to support and help him. Jim, who was the Practice Counsellor, asked if he could speak to Len on his own, and Len's wife readily agreed to this. Len talked at length about the origin of the obsession he had with checking for structural defects within his own home. He could trace his obsession to an incident which had occurred three years earlier, when he was involved in building a home for a friend. At that time, he had taken some short cuts in order to reduce costs. Later, certain defects appeared in the building and these cost his friend a great deal of time, effort and money to fix.

Len was extremely worried about these later developments, and he experienced enormous guilt about what he now regarded as the dishonest and 'shabby' treatment of his friend. After a while, he began to worry about his home and he started to check for defects and faults. Soon he was getting up in the middle of the night to check, until eventually his work started to suffer and his depression worsened.

Jim was concerned to gain as much information as possible about Len's problem, and the way it affected his home life, his work and his relationships with other people. In the first sessions, Jim also established a contract with Len to meet for a further six sessions. During that time he asked Len to keep a diary in which he would record his thinking and behaviour.

Jim wanted to gain an overall picture of Len's problems, so that he could formulate an individual action plan with him. The behaviours which Len found problematic had to be identified and related to the situations in which they occurred. It was also important to establish how often these problems occurred, and to identify some of the factors which affected them. Jim explained to Len that the diary recordings would help to highlight these factors.

Although Jim had trained as a person-centred counsellor, he was also a psychologist and in this instance used several techniques which are derived from a Behavioural approach to therapy. He also used the basic counselling skills of *active listening, paraphrasing, summarizing, asking open-ended question* and *reflecting feeling and content*, which are common to all theoretical approaches to counselling.

Once the initial assessment had been made, specific behavioural goals were considered by both Len and Jim, and strategies were developed to enable Len to deal more effectively with his problems. Issues of confidentiality were identified and Len stated that he had no objection to Jim discussing his progress with the GP. The role of counsellor supervision was also explained to Len, and he understood that some aspects of the work Jim was doing with him might be discussed with a supervisor.

Each counselling sessions entailed looking through the preceding week's diary and any areas of difficulty were discussed in detail. It soon became apparent that Len was anxious concerning several aspects of his domestic life, including his daughter's involvement with an 'unsuitable' boyfriend. Each time there was an argument at home about this issue, Len's depression became worse, and it seemed to act as a trigger for his obsessive behaviour. As the relationship between client and counsellor developed, Len also talked about other problems which he was having at work. Jim taught Len a simple relaxation technique which he could use when he felt most under stress, and this proved to be helpful in a variety of circumstances. Strategies for dealing with problems at work were discussed, using a problem-solving model (see Form A on page 131) and Len was also taught some assertiveness techniques to increase his effectiveness and confidence with colleagues.

After several counselling sessions, Len had gained some insight into the cause of his anxiety. He took a more relaxed view of his daughter's relationships, and some of his difficulties at work began to lessen. He was able to connect the short cuts he had taken when building his friend's house with his subsequent obsession for checking the structure of his own home. Once he identified the source of his guilt, and his fear of punishment, Len was able to become more rational in his thinking and more effective in dealing with potential difficulties.

Although in this instance Len was helped through counselling, there is no absolute guarantee that his problems would never surface again. On the contrary, it is quite possible that if circumstances became sufficiently stressful in the future, he might well develop obsessive behaviour again. However, the real benefit of his counselling is that it taught him some useful coping strategies which he could employ a second time round. In addition to this, he had the option of contacting the counsellor for further help if he needed it.

Form A

PROBLEM SOLVING

STEP 1   Write down exactly what the problem is.

STEP 2   List all possible solutions – write down **all** ideas, even bad ones.

1

2

3

4

5

STEP 3   Think about and discuss each possible solution, noting advantages and disadvantages of each.

STEP 4   Write down the best solution or **combination** of solutions.

1

2

3

STEP 5   Plan how to carry out the best solution.

1

2

3

4

5

Review how steps were implemented. Has this solved/dealt with your problem? If yes – **fine**. If no – **why? what's your next move?**

KEY WORD/ PHRASE

OBSESSIVE—COMPULSIVE DISORDER

The case study for this chapter described the problems of a client who was suffering from obsessive–compulsive disorder. This is a condition in which the individual has uncontrolled feelings and obsessive thoughts, along with a compulsion to carry out certain rituals or to do certain tasks. Anxiety is the basis of the condition, and obviously some people are more predisposed than others to become anxious in certain situations. The Behavioural approach to therapy would emphasize that obsessive–compulsive behaviours are learned habits which enable the person to avoid an anxiety-producing situation, including the anxiety which is caused by discussing personal feelings.

Compulsive behaviours may take many forms – perhaps the best known of all is compulsive handwashing. While in the grip of an obsession, the sufferer has no choice but to give in to it, since the anxiety which it is meant to control is relieved temporarily through the ritual. However, people with compulsions do know that their behaviour is excessive, tiresome and ultimately disruptive, since it interferes with various aspects of living and with personal relationships.

Treatment for obsessive–compulsive disorders is aimed at helping the sufferer to gain insight, and to understand the reason for the anxiety underlying the condition. *Cognitive Behavioural therapy* is often used successfully, along with social skills training, relaxation techniques and occasionally drug treatment.

EXERCISES

EXERCISE 1 GOALS

Working individually, think of a personal goal you would like to achieve. Consider the following points in relation to your goal:

- At what point in the future would you like to reach your goal? For example: how long will it take?

- How realistic is your goal? For example: is it within the bounds of possibility?

- How specific is your goal? For example: is it clear and unambiguous?

- In what way will the achievement of the goal change life for you? For example: what will you have gained from it?

- What are the factors which will hinder or help you in achieving your goal?

Discuss your conclusion with other members of the training group.

EXERCISE 2 GIVING ENCOURAGEMENT

Working in pairs, discuss the importance of encouragement in helping people to deal with their problems. Take turns to describe any memorable and encouraging experiences you have had. Consider the following points:

- Why did you need encouragement?
- What was it that encouraged you?
- Who encouraged you?
- How did the encouragement help you?

Discuss your experiences with each other, focusing on specific aspects of the encouragement you received.

EXERCISE 3   SELF-ESTEEM

Working in groups of three or four, list the characteristics of children with low self-esteem, and children with high self-esteem. For example:

Low self-esteem Poor performance at school	High self-esteem Resistance to peer group pressure

Discuss your findings, and consider the ways in which poor self-esteem in childhood can affect adult life.

EXERCISE 4   REFERRAL

Working in pairs, read the following descriptions of client problems, and discuss which clients you think might benefit from referral to another agency:

a) A seventy year old man whose wife died six months ago. He has started to drink heavily and says he is very lonely.

b) A thirty five year old single woman who has been suffering from depression and insomnia for the past two years.

c) A sixteen year old college student who is having problems with her parents and says she wants to leave home.

d) A twenty two year old man who is unemployed, and has become increasingly isolated from his friends and social network.

e) A thirty year old woman who has just had a miscarriage, and says that no one understands how she feels.

f) A middle-aged woman who has developed a phobia about leaving the house.

g) A young man who says he thinks he might be HIV positive, but he can't bring himself to have a test.

h) An eighteen year old college student who has expressed suicidal thoughts. Her mother died when she was fifteen, but she was told by her father that she must put the past behind her and get on with her education.

i) A twenty eight year old man who is having marital problems. He believes that his wife is mostly to blame.

j) A single mother with two young children who has a great difficulty living within a limited budget.

When discussing these case studies, consider the possible reactions of clients during referral. How might clients feel about being referred? What is the best way of making a referral without causing trauma or anxiety to clients?

EXERCISE 5   ENDINGS

Working in groups of two or three, discuss the issue of *endings* in counselling. What are the most important things to consider when ending a session with a client? Write out a list of boundaries or rules which might be useful in helping the counsellor to deal effectively with endings.

EXERCISE 6   PROBLEM SOLVING

Working individually, think about a minor problem which you currently have.

a) Write down exactly what the problem is.
b) List all possible solutions to the problem. Write down all ideas, even bad ones.
c) Consider the advantages and disadvantages of each of these solutions.
d) Write down the best solution, or combination of solutions.
e) Write a brief plan of how you will carry out the best solution.

EXERCISE 7   VISUALIZATION

Working individually, think of a personal goal which you have. Using the creative technique of visualization, imagine what scenarios would look like once you have achieved your goal. Write out a brief description of your scenario, and share this with the other members of your training group.

EXERCISE 8   CREATIVE THINKING

Work in pairs, and choose any object or item of furniture within the room. Observe your chosen object for three minutes, concentrating on colour, shape, proportion, texture, elements, lines, etc. Then, without looking at the object, or communicating with each other, write down as much detail as possible. Compare your description with that of your partner. Discuss the following points:

a) Which aspects did either or both of you omit?
b) Which aspects of the object or item did either or both of you highlight?
c) Was there anything which interfered with your observations, or with your recall of what you had observed?
d) Did either of you experience any difficulty in concentration?

e) Were there any aspects of the environment which inhibited concentration?

f) List any other methods which you think might help people to practise creative thinking.

g) Discuss the importance of creativity in problem solving. What are the factors which inhibit creativity?

FURTHER READING

1 Egan, Gerard, *The Skilled Helper,* Brookes/Code, Monterey CA, 1990.
2 Gray, Anne, *An Introduction to the Therapeutic Frame,* Routledge, London, 1994.
3 McKay, Matthew and Fanning, Patrick, *Self-Esteem,* New Harbinger Publications, Oakland CA, 1988.
4 Ellin, Jeanne, *Listening Helpfully,* Souvenir Press, London, 1994.
5 Dryden, Windy, *Key Issues for Counselling in Action,* Sage, London, 1993.
6 O'Farrell, Ursula, *First Steps in Counselling,* Veritas, Dublin, 1995.
7 Nelson-Jones, Richard, *The Theory and Practice of Counselling Psychology,* Cassell, London, 1990.
8 Culley, Sue, *Integrative Counselling Skills in Action,* Sage, London, 1991.

REFERENCE LIST

1 *The Skilled Helper* by Gerard Egan, Brookes/Cole, Monterey CA, 1990.
2 *Self-Esteem* by Matthew McKay and Patrick Fanning, New Harbinger Publications, Oakland CA, 1988.
3 *The Keys to Creativity* by Peter Evans and Geoff Deehan, Grafton Books, London, 1990.
4 *Developing Critical Thinkers* by Stephen D Brookfield, Open Univerisity Press, Milton Keynes, 1987.
5 *On Becoming a Person* by Carl Rogers, Constable, London, 1991.
6 *Motivation and Personality* by Abraham Maslow, Harper and Row, New York, 1970.

CHAPTER 7

Crisis situations

It would probably be impossible for any person to get through life without some involvement in at least one crisis situation. The word 'crisis' is generally used to describe a momentous event, a turning point, or a time of great danger and difficulty in an individual's life. Obviously, what constitutes a crisis for one person may not necessarily be viewed as such by another. How each person defines or interprets a crisis depends on a wide variety of factors. These factors include past experience, as well as the coping strategies and support systems, which people have at their disposal when significant events occur. Perhaps the most outstanding factor in defining crisis, however, is the individual's unique perception of events. In other words, it is how a person responds to circumstances, which is more important than anything else. An elderly woman who had lost all her material possessions in a flood described her reactions in the following way.

> 'The social workers and helpers were very concerned to make me comfortable. They took me to a temporary shelter, where I met many of the other people whose homes had been flooded. I knew all the furniture had been ruined in my house, as well as the carpets, the TV, all my clothes and everything else that I owned. It didn't really matter to me about those things. Even my family photographs had gone, and although I was sad about that, I accepted it. But I was devastated at losing Blackie [her cat]. Nobody seemed to listen to me when I asked about Blackie. They seemed to take the attitude that he was only a cat, although nobody actually said that. He was a great companion, and losing him was the worst thing that could have happened.'

This client's emotional trauma was compounded by the fact that the loss of her cat reminded her of a much earlier loss, which she had been unable to deal with at the time. Her daughter had died twenty years previously in a car accident, but she (Mrs Feldman) had been stoical and calm for the sake of her husband, who was devastated by his daughter's death. It is not unusual for one loss to trigger the memory of another in this way, and for some people this combination of losses – both present and remembered – will certainly constitute a major crisis.

Mrs Feldman received counselling shortly after the flood which destroyed her home and all her possessions in it. In common with many people who experience crisis in their lives, she wanted to talk about these events, over and over again. It was only when she made the connection between the death of her daughter and the trauma of losing her cat, that

Mrs Feldman was able to feel and express the deep sorrow which she had hidden for twenty years. If she had not been given the opportunity to make this important connection, she might well have continued to ruminate in a futile and distressing fashion, without any hope of ever resolving her grief.

Though a definition of crisis depends to a large extent on the individual's perception of events, there are nevertheless certain major experiences which seem to fit into the category, regardless of the person who is affected by them. Critical events like assault, burglary, rape, sudden bereavement and natural disasters, for example, would almost certainly affect the majority of people in adverse ways. However, a crucial factor in terms of response is the individual's attendant circumstances when a crisis situation occurs. Someone who receives immediate social support in the aftermath of a crisis will obviously fare better than someone else who is left to cope alone. A person who has experienced one car crash may take much longer to come to terms with another accident, especially if the second critical incident occurs close to the first. When several crisis events occur in close proximity, it is easy for people to get the impression that they are governed by forces outside their control. Such impressions can then give rise to feelings of hopelessness, futility and despair. If people are given the opportunity to express their feelings, they often say that their 'world has fallen apart' or they may remark that the 'ground opened up' beneath their feet.

The experience of crisis is also sometimes described as 'unbelievable' by the people who encounter or face it. Such reactions stem from the belief (common to all of us) that we are invincible, unassailable and special. This illusion of 'specialness' is shattered when critical and traumatic events happen in our lives, and shock and profound surprise are common reactions to them. The state of personal balance or equilibrium which most people sustain, without too much difficulty, is also impaired during crisis. It is this disequilibrium which causes the intense vulnerability which people in crisis feel. Caplan (1964) suggests that people are concerned to maintain stability in their lives: when this stability is threatened or disrupted through crisis, intense anxiety is the usual response.

Although the way in which people respond to crisis will obviously vary slightly, depending on the circumstances surrounding it, there are certain identifiable reactions which are common in most instances. People in crisis often feel totally overwhelmed and incapable of dealing with the situation they are in. The initial response is usually one of *shock*, followed by denial, alarm, depression, anger or disorientation, although not necessarily in that order. Thinking may also become muddled or impaired during periods of acute stress, and the person in crisis may engage in frantic activity in the hope of exerting some kind of control over the immediate environment. A woman whose sister and brother in-law were involved in a plane crash, described her immediate response to the news in the following way.

'We heard about the crash when my husband turned on the television news. At first, I would not believe that this was the plane my sister and her husband were on. I thought there must be some mistake, that they would have cancelled the trip beforehand, and therefore could not be on the plane. I was shocked and disbelieving, and physically very agitated. What made matters worse was the fact that we couldn't get any information about the crash, so we weren't even sure if my relatives were alive or dead. There was a very long period of waiting – about five or six hours – when we couldn't get any news at all. During that time I kept working at a frantic pace, washing and ironing clothes, hoovering the house and immersing myself in a multitude of physical tasks, as if everything depended on my keeping active. It was as if I wanted to impose some kind of order, at least on my immediate world. The events which had just taken place were so frightening to contemplate, and the possibilities so terrible, that I had to keep going in order to survive mentally. When I heard that they were alive, I was able to relax physically, although the mental stress was by no means over.'

Although the response described here is one of frantic activity, other reactions to intense stress include immobilization, resignation and despair. Some people simply give up when their ability to tolerate stress is severely challenged and when this happens, helping and support systems are vital. Most people do have the support they need within their family and friendship network. Others, however, may need the extra support and help which is available through counselling.

Developmental crisis

The word crisis is also sometimes used to describe the emotional upheaval which can accompany various developmental stages or turning points within a person's life. Perhaps the most common precipitating factors in terms of life crisis are the changes or adjustments which need to be made at these key stages.

ADOLESCENCE AND PUBERTY

Adolescence and puberty is usually regarded as an important period of transition and change. During this time, several choices have to be made, including choices of school subjects and career, choice of social activities, relationships and responsibilities. In addition, the physical changes taking place in adolescence and puberty often give the young person a feeling of being 'alien' within his or her own body. The development of sexual interest, along with psychological changes and mood swings, can also heighten feelings of disorientation, uncertainty and depression. There are many potential problems at this stage of development, including drug abuse, family conflict, eating disorders, unwanted pregnancy, running away, attempted suicide and violence. Most of these problems are routinely seen by counsellors who work in schools and colleges; whereas in the past young people were expected to muddle along as best they could, they are now receiving much more understanding and support.

ADULTHOOD

Specific problems arise in adulthood as well. Occupation, employment and choice of career are especially significant at this stage. They can prove problematic, particularly in view of today's economic climate. The other major aspect of life at this stage is commitment to an intimate and long-term relationship with another person. However, changes in the mores of contemporary Western Society have meant that relationships are now subjected to unprecedented stresses and strains. Separation and divorce are fairly commonplace; economic hardship, loneliness, insecurity and demands of childcare, all exert great pressures on young adults. The pressures may be felt more acutely by women, since there is often a conflict for them, which arises when the demands of childcare and work pull them in opposite directions. Guilt and anxiety are often felt by women in this dilemma, and unless support and help is available to them in the family or the community, the burden of coping alone can lead to intense frustration or even a crisis of confidence.

MIDLIFE

The term 'midlife crisis' is used so often and so casually that it is easy to forget that very real problems, connected with personal identity, work, family and health, do occur frequently and dramatically at this stage. Midlife is a transition during which people tend to re-appraise many aspects of their lives, and in doing so, frequently initiate radical changes in relationships, career and style of living. For women, the menopause marks both a beginning and an end; it signals the end of child-bearing years, and heralds the beginning of independence and freedom from child-bearing responsibilities. This freedom and responsibility is not always entirely welcome, however, and a midlife crisis may arise for the woman who feels that her primary function in life is now over. In addition to this, physical symptoms of the menopause may be debilitating and stressful, but the social and psychological problems of midlife are often more significant. This is true for men and women, since problems relating to adult children who are unable to find employment, or who need to be funded through college or university, affect both parents. At the other end of the generation spectrum, the deteriorating health of elderly parents may present extra difficulties and responsibilities. All these pressures are sufficient to precipitate midlife crisis, and it is very often at this stage that people seek help or counselling for the problems they encounter.

LATER LIFE

We are frequently told via the media that the elderly population in Great Britain is increasing. The usual implication is that increasing numbers and longevity are a problem for society as a whole, and to some extent this is true. Elderly people need younger people to care for them when they become incapacitated or ill, and the pensions which they have received need to be funded from some source. What tends to be neglected, however, are the personal problems which individual elderly people have, which are just as real and distressing as the problems encountered by people in the younger age bands. If we view elderly people solely in terms of 'a problem', then we strip them of human dignity and deny them the respect which everyone – young or old – deserves.

Elderly people do have many real problems, and counsellors who work in GP practices frequently meet older people whose lives are difficult, impoverished and often harsh. Many elderly people – who may not be physically well themselves – have to take care of a spouse who is ill. There are quite a few older people now who are having to cope with their grown-up and mentally ill children who have been discharged into the community. A psychological crisis is often precipitated in later life when acquaintances and friends of an elderly person die, thereby reminding them of their own mortality. Guilt, anxiety and despair are sometimes generated when older people review their own lives in an attempt to make sense of, or to integrate, all the experiences they have had. People who work with the elderly – whether in hospital, homes or day centres – are familiar with these patterns of reminiscence. Attention has not been focused sufficiently on the need to use good interpersonal and counselling skills to help older people make sense of these issues. However, there is a promising trend among nurses, occupational therapists, social workers and care assistants to undertake counsellor training.

Elderly people need younger people to care for them.

Erikson's Stages of Psychological Development

When considering the different crisis points occurring throughout the life cycle, it is useful to look at Erikson's model of psychological development which highlights the central issues arising from infancy onwards. Erikson (1963) believed that these are special challenges or crises which have to be confronted at all stages. If these challenges and crises – which are constringent upon relationships with other people, and the social environment – are not successfully negotiated, psychological development and progress will be impeded. The choices which we make at these stages are very important, and will determine the way we deal with – or fail to deal with – conflict.

The stages are as follows:

1 Trust versus Mistrust (infancy)

2 Autonomy versus Shame and doubt (1–3 years)

3 Initiative versus Guilt (3–6 years)

4 Industry versus Inferiority (6–12 years)

5 Identity versus Role confusion (12–18 years)

6 Intimacy versus Isolation (early adulthood)

7 Generativity versus Stagnation (middle age)

8 Integrity versus Despair (old age)

STAGE 1: TRUST VERSUS MISTRUST

At this early stage, the infant has a choice between trust and mistrust. If the mother, or primary caregiver, is able to satisfy the infant's emotional needs, feelings of trust will be fostered. On the other hand, if needs are not met, attitudes of mistrust especially towards other people will certainly develop.

STAGE 2: AUTONOMY VERSUS SHAME AND DOUBT

The development of autonomy and independence are central issues in the child's world at this stage (under 3). There is a need to build up confidence, to explore and to make mistakes, if necessary. Conflict arises when these needs are frustrated by parents who are unable or unwilling to provide the security and permission necessary for experimentation to take place. Lack of confidence in 'self' and inability to deal with the stresses of living will result if independence and freedom are inhibited at this stage.

STAGE 3: INITIATIVE VERSUS GUILT

Children need to learn and develop initiative at this stage. Curiosity and the desire to engage in satisfying activities are paramount. When these drives are denied through parental prohibition, a sense of guilt develops and initiative is deadened. The ability to make personal decisions and choices, which is essential for psychological health in adult life, is derived from the confidence which is gained at this stage. If opportunities for the development of confidence are not allowed, however, the ability to make personal choices will not develop.

The development of autonomy and independence are central issues in the child's world.

Children need to learn and develop initiative at stage 3. Curiosity and the desire to engage in satisfying activities are paramount.

STAGE 4: INDUSTRY VERSUS INFERIORITY

These are the school years for children, and a time during which curiosity and a willingness to learn are evident. When children are not given sufficient opportunities to develop basic skills, and to achieve some personal goals, they lose interest in tasks. This loss of interest will inhibit the child's sense of purpose and industry, and feelings of inferiority will inevitably result.

Curiosity and a willingness to learn are evident.

STAGE 5: IDENTITY VERSUS ROLE CONFUSION

Ages 12 to 18 is a time during which a clear sense of identity is striving to emerge. Conflict arises between the dependency of childhood which is being left behind, and the establishment of a new independent and adult persona. If adolescents are denied opportunities to achieve independence, to develop their own ideology and to ascribe some meaning to life, role confusion results.

STAGE 6: INTIMACY VERSUS ISOLATION

The establishment of intimate and satisfying relationships is a major preoccupation at this stage. When this goal is not achieved, there is a possibility that intense loneliness, isolation or even despair will follow.

STAGE 7: GENERATIVITY VERSUS STAGNATION

During the middle years, the adult is concerned to care for others, particularly for children and the next generation. There is also a need to achieve some sense of accomplishment in life, and there is often a renewed interest in work and activities outside 'self'. Without this sense of purpose and accomplishment, stagnation, self-absorption and a feeling of aimlessness will almost certainly be the outcome.

STAGE 8: INTEGRITY VERSUS DESPAIR

If a person is confident about having accomplished some chosen goals in life, then the later years will be a time of acceptance, equanimity and fulfilment. When realization of potential has been thwarted or frustrated, however, feelings of despair and failure will follow. Older people are

During the middle years, the adult is concerned to care for others, particularly for children and the next generation.

especially vulnerable at this stage, and need understanding, support and help in order to help them unravel these complex and often painful concerns.

The critical stages of development which Erikson describes are key points during which progress and integration are possible. Conflict is inevitable for the individual at these stages, but it is the way in which conflict or crisis is dealt with which is crucial. The solution which the individual chooses at each stage has far-reaching implications for the future. Personal integrity, happiness and a sense of achievement are all related to these choices and to the ways in which conflicts were resolved.

Bereavement

Some of the crisis situations which have been described in this chapter are often characterized by their sudden, unexpected and totally disruptive nature. Not all acutely stressful events are like this, however, and bereavement is one experience which may be sudden but is also often presumed or anticipated before it actually happens.

Responses to bereavement vary, just as they vary in an unexpected crisis situation. Some of the emotions which people experience as a result of bereavement may include shock, denial, self-blame, anger or even hatred (see Fig. 7.1). Most people feel numb following the death of a close relative or friend. This numbness often serves to protect against the harsh reality of what has happened. Numbness may then be replaced by intense sadness, yearning, loneliness and anger. Feelings of self-reproach and guilt are also quite common in bereavement; so too are the experiences of confusion, forgetfulness and preoccupation with thoughts of the deceased person. After a period of time, a process of renewal and reorganization should take place, when thoughts about the dead person become more realistic, and the intense sadness which was felt in the initial stage of bereavement is abated. It is worth remembering that the anger which bereaved people feel after a death is often directed against relatives, doctors and nurses, and anyone else who was involved in the care of the deceased. Alternatively, the bereaved person may direct anger against 'self' in the form of deep and prolonged depression. Counsellors working with people who have been bereaved need to understand these reactions which – on the surface – may seem very exaggerated, irrational or extreme.

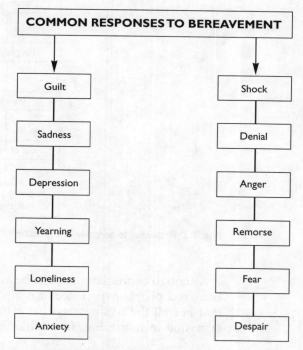

Fig. 7.1 *Responses to bereavement (common).*

The experience of grieving may also give rise to physical symptoms, insomnia, loss of appetite and a range of visual and auditory hallucinations (see Fig. 7.2). These may take the form of 'seeing' the deceased person in familiar places or hearing voices when there is no one else present. Fear is another common effect in bereavement, and this is often translated into panic, dread of being alone, fear of going out, and fear of madness.

The bereavement process is made more difficult by virtue of the fact that death is still a taboo subject in many cultures. It is a topic which is mainly avoided and when it is discussed, it is usually referred to in euphemistic terms which do nothing to help us accept or understand it. Thus it is common to speak of a deceased person having 'passed away', 'gone to sleep' or 'no longer with us'. These euphemisms certainly do not enable the bereaved person to cope in the long term, although they may very well aid the process of denial which tends to take place immediately following a death.

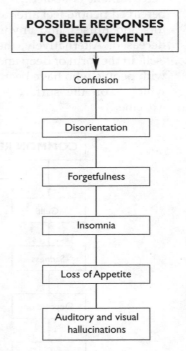

Fig. 7.2 *Responses to bereavement (possible).*

Although counsellors need to be aware of the range of reactions which bereaved people experience, it is also important for them to understand that not all the feelings and behaviours referred to will be common to everyone in mourning. In addition to this, not all the feelings will be expressed in the sequence outlined. Various writers, including Bowlby (1993), have described the bereavement process in terms of 'models' which can be useful in helping us to understand the different phases of grief. This understanding is essential if we are to be effective in helping bereaved people to accept and come to terms with their loss. Although Bowlby makes the point that the intensity and length of grief varies from one individual to another, he also adds that there is an overall discernible pattern which is familiar in most instances of bereavement. The following are the four stages described by Bowlby.

1 **Numbness:** this may be short or long term, and is sometimes interrupted by outbursts of distress and anger.

2 **Searching** and yearning for the person who is lost. This may last for months or years.

3 **Disorganization** and despair.

4 **Reorganization** and healing.

COMPLICATED GRIEF

Bereavement responses will also, of course, depend to some extent on the circumstances of the death, and the nature of the relationship between the bereaved person and the deceased. Sudden or premature death is obviously more shocking (initially at least) than a death which was expected. Chronic or abnormal grieving can occur when the relationship which existed between the bereaved person and the deceased was problematic or difficult in some way. Guilt, idealization, over-dependence and unresolved differences are all problems which can contribute to abnormal grieving. People who have experienced grief and loss during childhood, and those who have been separated from parents or family, may suffer special problems during subsequent bereavements. Accumulated losses in adult life also tend to complicate any further losses which occur later on.

DELAYED GRIEF

When other crisis events occur at the same time as a death, the process of grieving may be inhibited or delayed. It is difficult for people to cope effectively with several traumatic events occurring at once, and there is a tendency to suppress feelings of grief when other problems are pressing for attention. Some people are able to put their grieving 'on hold' in order to deal with immediate and compelling problems. This may work for a time, but later on the bereaved person may suffer a range of physical or psychological illnesses, including minor infections, depression and addiction.

ANNIVERSARY REACTIONS

These are common in the years following a death. They tend to be more pronounced when grieving has been inhibited or suppressed. Anniversaries and other significant dates can be times of great sadness for people who have been bereaved. Counsellors need to be aware of the importance of anniversaries, birthdays and other significant dates like Christmas and New Year, for those who have experienced the death of a relative or friend. Other life events, like births and marriages, may trigger excessive grief reactions; even minor losses may activate long forgotten memories of sadness and grief.

SUICIDE

When a relative or friend commits suicide, the bereaved person is confronted with special problems including profound shock, the possibility of media interest, speculation and gossip within the community, the harsh reality of police involvement, and, of course, an inquest. Anger against the deceased may be much more intense when suicide was the cause of death, and of course the greatest trauma is always suffered by the person who is first on the scene of a suicide (Kelleher, 1995).

Deep guilt is often experienced by relatives and friends following a suicide and, when the deceased was a young person, parents may blame themselves for not doing more to help and protect their child. People who have experienced the death of a relative through suicide may worry excessively that they might do the same. These fears and anxieties need to be expressed openly, and discussed in the presence of someone who will not become emotionally upset by them. This is why counselling is so important for those who have been bereaved in this way. Both Cruse and Compassionate Friends offer counselling services for bereavement, and they are trained to help clients deal with the intense and overwhelming feelings which relatives and friends usually experience when someone has committed suicide. The organization Compassionate Friends is more concerned to help parents whose children have died, while Cruse has a much wider brief and volunteers are willing to counsel anyone who seeks their help after a bereavement.

In addition to the factors mentioned above, relatives of suicide victims may also develop a deep distrust of other people and an inability to form close or lasting relationships. These responses are linked to the fact that a trust, which once existed, has been dramatically broken. The bereaved person may be scared to trust anyone again. There may also be a great deal of hidden resentment against the deceased. The presence of all these disturbing issues may give rise to chronic and distorted grief which can continue for many years, or indeed for the rest of a lifespan. Counselling can help clients who are in this position to unravel the complex and disturbing feelings which they have. It can also help clients to understand their feelings, and to forgive themselves and the person who has died for any breach of trust which they feel has taken place.

Crisis and bereavement: implications for counselling

Obviously, all the basic skills which have been described in previous chapters are used by counsellors when working with people in crisis, or with those who have been bereaved. In addition to these, other considerations need to be highlighted and these are especially relevant in acute crisis situations.

In the first instance, counsellors who are meeting clients in crisis need to be capable of dealing with the extreme anxiety and the urgency of the circumstances presented. At first glance, this might seem an unnecessary statement to make, since the role of the counsellor presupposes an ability to deal with people in distress. However, crisis intervention means dealing with distress on a grand scale, and to do this well counsellors need all the resources at their disposal, including the most important resources of all, which is regular supervision. A client in crisis can quite easily send a counsellor into crisis, unless adequate support is available. This does not imply that a counsellor who is helping a client in crisis should appeal at once for assistance or aid. What it does suggest is that the availability of support is, in itself, sufficient to give confidence to the counsellor who is working under this kind of stress. In other words, the counsellor knows that he/she does not need to carry an intolerable emotional burden alone. The knowledge that there is someone else there who is trained to give guidance and help will sustain the counsellor in dealing effectively and skilfully with crisis. This skill and effectiveness is, of course, dependent on the counsellor's own emotional equilibrium; a counsellor in distress will obviously be incapable of helping the client in crisis, and will certainly have a diminished capacity to help any client, whatever the circumstances. Attention to personal well-being is therefore important as well, and counsellors who are experiencing difficulties in their own lives need to seek help for themselves through counselling before they attempt to help clients in distress.

Aside from these important considerations of supervision and personal care, counsellors who are involved in crisis management need to be well informed about all the resources available within their own locality for helping with various aspects of crisis. People in crisis need practical help first; they also need information, and this means that counsellors should be reasonably knowledgeable about a range of problems as diverse as drug abuse, suicide attempt, violence in the home, problems with the law, and financial difficulties – to name just a few. However, this does not mean that an in-depth knowledge of all these areas is essential. What it does suggest is that counsellors should be in touch with other sources of information which can be used when the need arises. In addition to this, counsellors should know about the nature and range of work which is carried out by other professionals in the area, both voluntary and statutory. The client's own resources need to be identified as well, when a crisis situation arises. These may include family, friends and community, but the client's individual coping strategies are a point of focus too. In other words, the client can be helped to see that it is possible to gain management and control over the disturbing feelings which are evoked by the crisis. To help clients in this way, it is important that counsellors should be given the opportunity to express and accept their feelings in a supportive environment first. With help, acceptance and support, the client should become more confident in his own ability to cope, even though at the outset, the situation may have seemed extremely bleak. It is worth emphasizing the importance of helping clients to identify their own coping resources in a crisis, because once some confidence has returned the client is in the process of gaining some control over the situation.

It goes without saying that the counsellor who is helping a client in crisis needs to be calm throughout the process. Composure and dispassionate involvement may seem like a contradiction is terms, but these qualities are exactly what the distressed client needs to help him feel less agitated and disturbed himself. The client needs to know that the counsellor is not overwhelmed by the crisis, but is involved in helping.

In the immediate or initial stages of the crisis, the counsellor may have to adopt a more proactive approach to helping. This may prove difficult for some counsellors, especially those who believe that the client should always be encouraged to take personal control over all aspects of his life. However, in a crisis situation, the client may be unable temporarily to exercise control, and he may need some direction from the counsellor in order to regain his ability to do so. Active listening and empathy are especially important during crisis counselling, so too are the skills of reflecting back and responding to the very strong feelings which accompany distress. One of the things which makes a distressing situation more acute for most people is the inability to gain attention and understanding when they wish to express how they feel. Despair is a possible result of such neglect, and this is one of the reasons it is so crucial for counsellors to give the attention which clients in crisis need. People in crisis need a lifeline and instant help in order to help them make sense of the situation. Counsellors can also assist them in dealing with immediate problems first. This can be done by a process of separating out all the elements involved, into smaller more manageable units. Quite often the crisis situation has been precipitated by many factors, and may simply be the tip of the iceberg. A person who is suicidal, for example, will have reached that state of mind because of a variety of circumstances. These are factors which need to be taken into consideration, once the immediate crisis has been dealt with. This highlights another important point which is that the counsellor should clarify with clients just how much involvement they are willing/available to have with them in the future.

Threats of suicide and suicide attempts are obviously taxing for anyone involved with the person who is suffering. Unfortunately, families, friends and doctors have often been taxed to the limit by the time a client appeals to counselling for help. This places a heavy burden on the counsellor, since she is probably seen by the client as a last hope in a hopeless situation. Different schools of counselling have different approaches to helping clients who are suicidal, and in *Transactional Analysis*, for example, clients are asked to give an assurance that they will not harm themselves or others while they are in counselling. This forms part of the contract between counsellor and client, and seems to work effectively, since it lets the client know that someone cares enough to make such a request.

In the Person-centred approach to counselling, the helper is concerned to understand the client, and to convey this understanding to him. If this is done effectively, it should go a long way towards showing the client that he has value and worth in another person's eyes, and this knowledge alone may be sufficient to deter a suicide attempt. Most counsellors – whatever their approach – will probably experience some anxiety and guilt when faced with the possibility that someone will die in spite of their attempts to help. Even the knowledge that a suicidal client has the ultimate choice in this matter is not enough to assuage the tension and stress which counsellors feel when presented with the problem. One of the reasons for this is that suicide is an aggressive act; it is aggressive to the person who takes his own life, and it is aggressive towards the people who are left behind. The possibility that such aggression could have been avoided through human intervention, support and understanding means that people who work with suicidal clients feel a great deal of responsibility to avert the disaster if they possibly can.

Occasionally trainee counsellors express doubts about the wisdom of discussing suicide with vulnerable clients, in case such discussion will prompt them to do it. These doubts are misplaced, however, because people in despair are usually relieved to voice their worst fears to someone who is willing to listen, without showing alarm or dismay. The most important thing which the counsellor can offer a suicidal client is a safe and accepting environment in which to express his worst fears and concerns. Once these are out in the open, work can be done to enlist help for the depression which usually causes suicidal thoughts. (See Fig. 7.3 for various effects of depression.) It is important to remember also that clients who feel desperate sometimes talk about suicide in oblique terms, which may be difficult to decipher, unless direct questions are clearly asked.

Clients who are suicidal, or indeed clients in any other crisis, will not benefit from the kind of easy reassurance which is so often given when minor problems occur. In fact, reassurance may be quite out of place, since the message which it tends to transmit to people is that what they are suffering is not being taken seriously. However, there is a natural tendency after a crisis to operate in emotional, instead of rational terms, and the counsellor's task is to encourage a more objective viewpoint so that the client will begin to gain some mastery and control over the situation.

Reassurance, then, is inappropriate in crisis counselling since it tends to distort reality, and creates the impression that the client's distress is not taken seriously. However, this does not mean that the client in crisis should not feel some measure of reassurance as a result of his interaction with the counsellor. On the contrary, he should certainly experience restored confidence, and some encouragement that the situation can be dealt with. But this restoration of confidence can best be achieved through

EFFECTS OF DEPRESSION CAN BE:

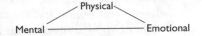

DEPRESSIVE SLEEP DISTURBANCE

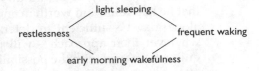

MENTAL EFFECTS OF DEPRESSION

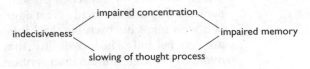

PHYSICAL EFFECTS OF DEPRESSION

headaches and muscle aches

extreme tiredness

overeating

loss of appetite

EMOTIONAL FEATURES OF DEPRESSION

feelings of guilt and failure

feelings of hopelessness

apathy or agitation

feelings of apprehension and fear

Fig. 7.3 *Depression.*

an objective, rational and realistic appraisal of events, and the counsellor can help the client to maintain this kind of focus.

We have already seen that short-term management is more important than long-term management in crisis situations. This means that people in crisis need immediate help to deal with immediate problems. People in crisis also frequently need to be told to take care of themselves, to rest more, to eat and to get enough sleep. Although these are basic points, they are significant because people who are deeply distressed often neglect their own welfare, and such neglect is almost sure to exacerbate the problem. When people are excessively tired, or emotionally drained, they are not in a position to manage their problems, or to gain control over the situation. Later on, when the immediate situation has been dealt with, and some measure of normality re-established, the client may wish to discuss the crisis in order to understand or make sense of it. This is the stage at which both counsellor and client need to discuss future contact, and the possibility of working together to look at these issues. It is important to emphasize here that clients need to come to this decision in their own time. There would be little point in trying to engage a client in philosophical discussion about a crisis, unless and before he is willing to do so. Immediate problems need to be addressed and managed before the theoretical implications and long-term outcomes are considered. The emotional shock, anger and grief which people experience in the immediate aftermath of a crisis would preclude this kind of theoretical discussion in any case.

A point which is often highlighted in the media when there is a major crisis like flooding or a plane crash is that groups of counsellors have made themselves available to help in the emergency. These counsellors are often criticized on the grounds that their presence constitutes interference and is ultimately intrusive. It is certainly true that a great deal of sensitivity and tact needs to be exercised by anyone who offers help in a crisis, but a fact which is often overlooked is that counselling personnel tend to make themselves 'available' only in these circumstances. In other words, counselling is available to anyone who needs it, and any suggestion that a service like this is superfluous is really missing the point. Some of the issues which were raised in Chapter 1 concerning the suitability of family and friends as counsellors is relevant in this context. Family and friends do help in a crisis, but the trauma is often so great for victims that they can only unburden themselves to people who are emotionally uninvolved, and trained to listen. If people are not given the opportunity to talk and to express strong feelings after a crisis, then they may find themselves unable to come to terms with it for a very long time.

CASE STUDY: EMMA

Emma, an eighteen year old student, was referred by one of her lecturers to the student counsellor at the university which she attended. The lecturer had noticed that Emma looked increasingly depressed during tutorials and seminars, and on one occasion had burst into tears towards the end of a lecture.

Emma's parents had divorced when she was fifteen, and her father re-married a short time later. Her mother had gone to live abroad with her boyfriend, and Emma felt that she had no real choice but to stay with her father. However, she did not get on well with her stepmother. There was constant tension, and sometimes bouts of outright hostility within the home. Emma was glad to come to university, but sometime after arrival she began to feel alienated from the other students, especially when they talked about parents, family life or relationships. These conversations made Emma feel isolated and occasionally she was overwhelmed with panic, and a sense of deep loneliness.

Since Emma had been referred by her lecturer because of feelings of despair and isolation, the counsellor's initial assessment was focused on these thoughts. Using the core conditions of the person-centred approach, she encouraged Emma to express her feelings of hopelessness and despair. She was concerned to establish just how severe Emma's depression might be, and to identify any suicidal thoughts she might be having. Emma explained that she had indeed thought of suicide, although she had not considered this in any detail. The counsellor approached the subject with her in the following way.

COUNSELLOR: The depression you describe...when you get really low...is it bad enough to make you feel you can't go on?

EMMA:...Sometimes it's like that. But I've not thought really seriously of killing myself...I mean, not in detail or anything.

COUNSELLOR:...But it's bad enough to make you consider it sometimes...

EMMA: Yes.

The counsellor (Theresa) made arrangements to see Emma weekly during term time. A contract was established in which Emma agreed to make an immediate appointment, either with Theresa or any other available counsellor, if she found herself experiencing suicidal thoughts. In addition to this, Emma agreed to visit her GP for an assessment of the severity of her depression. Once this was done, she felt greatly relieved, and she continued to attend her counselling sessions at the university.

The university counselling service operated a system whereby students who had attempted suicide in the past, or those who were experiencing suicidal thoughts, could be given an immediate appointment with any one of the counsellors. Emma agreed that her name could be entered in a diary which other members of staff could check if an emergency appointment needed to be made. This is a system which appeared to work well for students; it seemed to give vulnerable students a sense of security and acted as a safety net for them. The issue of confidentiality was discussed between client and counsellor, and it was agreed that if Theresa believed Emma's safety to be in danger she would speak to the GP about it. The subject of supervision was also discussed, and Emma understood that some aspects of the counselling sessions might be brought to supervision by Theresa.

The content of subsequent counselling sessions were taken up with issues relating to Emma's depression, her low self-esteem, and her feelings of alienation from her friends and family. The counsellor encouraged her to express the feelings of anger and grief which she had suppressed after her parents' divorce. Rapport and an empathic relationship developed between Emma and the counsellor. It became clear that there were many questions which Emma needed to ask, especially regarding the nature of her mother's departure. She had always viewed this as a form of 'desertion', and although she did keep in touch with her mother by letter, Emma had never really discussed the issue of her departure with her. A later counselling session was spent in exploration of ways whereby Emma could broach the subject with her mother. She resolved to visit her abroad and when she mentioned this in a letter to her mother, she received a warm and welcoming reply. Time was also spent in exploring ways in which Emma could establish better relations at home with her father and stepmother.

The counsellor (Theresa) saw Emma for twelve sessions in all. During that time, other important issues were discussed, especially those surrounding the transition from teenage years to adult life. Emma showed a marked improvement and her depression lessened. Her problems were by no means solved, but at least she had received the support and help which she needed at a very critical stage of her life.

KEY WORDS AND PHRASES	**DEPRESSION** Depression is a condition which affects most people – in varying degrees of severity – at different stages throughout life. It can be short term or long term, and is prompted by myriad causes, including loss, disappointment, life change and many others. It is also common after physical illness, and frequently accompanies loneliness, boredom, relationship difficulties and high levels of stress.

ENDOGENOUS DEPRESSION

There are some forms of depression which are more problematic that others. The clinical term *endogenous depression* describes a serious condition in which the sufferer may experience feelings of utter hopelessness, despair, self-blame, sleep and/or appetite disturbance, and sometimes suicidal thoughts. People who suffer from endogenous depression (depression from within) may also feel considerably worse in the morning. They also tend to wake up early in the morning, and find it impossible to get back to sleep again. The world seems utterly bleak for people in the grip of this kind of depression, but because of the feelings of guilt, self-blame and worthlessness which they often experience, they may find it quite difficult to ask for help. People who suffer from endogenous depression need medical help straightaway. Counsellors who meet clients with this condition should refer them to a General Practitioner as soon as possible. Obviously, this needs to be done in a sensitive and supportive way, and clients who receive medical treatment for the problem will usually benefit from counselling too. In fact, clients who are helped to locate the origins of their depression are probably in a much better position to overcome it in the long term.

REACTIVE DEPRESSION

The term 'reactive depression' is generally used to describe the individual's reaction to an external event. The external event may be a death, redundancy, job loss or any significant change in a person's lifestyle or circumstances. This form of depression was traditionally seen as less serious than the endogenous type, but there is a tendency now to regard some of these categories as misleading, and to view all forms of depression as potentially serious. This does not mean, however, that all forms of depression require medication, but it does mean that counsellors should be especially observant and attentive when helping clients who appear to be depressed. Clients who are deeply depressed may not necessarily experience the symptoms of endogenous depression, and it takes skills and fine judgment, on the counsellor's part, to assess the level of risk involved in such circumstances. The policy of open-ended discussion with the client is relevant here, so that suicidal or despairing thoughts are clearly identified.

EXERCISES

EXERCISE 1   ADOLESCENCE

Work in groups of three or four. Using a large sheet of paper, brainstorm a list of what you consider to be the central issues for adolescents of both sexes. For example:

> **Adolescent concerns**
> Relationships
> Looks etc.

Discuss the issues which concerned each of you individually, highlighting the people, events or circumstances which helped you to resolve any problems you had.

EXERCISE 2   ASPIRATIONS

Working in pairs, read the following list of objectives. Discuss the importance of each of these in childhood, adolescence, early adulthood, middle age and old age.

- To establish relationships
- To have emotional security
- To work hard
- To build a career
- To achieve status
- To acquire material goals
- To help others
- To stay healthy
- To understand life
- To help in the community
- To become more individual
- To compete with others
- To become more spiritual

- To develop independence

- To co-operate

- To achieve emotional stability

- To be more self-aware

- To have freedom

- To develop wider interests

- To have a sense of purpose

This is certainly not an exhaustive list. Discuss with your partner any other aspirations which you think might be characteristic of each developmental stage.

EXERCISE 3   EVERYDAY CRISES

Working in groups of two or three, look at the following list of everyday crisis situations. How many of these are familiar to members of your group? Discuss the feelings evoked by these crises and describe individual reactions to them.

- Loss of money and credit cards

- Car breakdown

- Being locked out of the house

- Dog goes missing

- Alarm clock fails to go off

- Car runs out of petrol

- Babysitter is ill

- Mortgage increases significantly

- Holiday sickness

- Loss of luggage

What were the factors which helped you deal with your crisis? What were the characteristics of people who helped you in a crisis?

EXERCISE 4   SHOWING EMOTION

People in crisis and people who have been bereaved are often afraid to show emotion in case this upsets the people around them. Working in pairs, discuss the reasons for this inhibition, and say in what ways counsellors can help clients to deal with strong emotions. The following are some examples of why people are often afraid to express their feelings:

- 'If I become upset, other people will become upset too.'

- 'If I become upset, people will be impatient with me.'

- 'If I cry or show strong feelings, people will avoid me.'

- 'If I cry, I might not be able to stop myself.'

Discuss any other reasons which you can think of for avoiding displays of emotion.

EXERCISE 5   LOSSES
Working in pairs, look at the following experiences and discuss the losses which each one of these entails.

- Redundancy

- Early retirement

- Moving house

- Changing schools

- Going through the menopause

- Exam failure

- Break up of a relationship

- Illness

- Moving to a home for the elderly

- Decrease in income

- Promotion

- Leaving home

EXERCISE 6   LONELINESS
Working in groups of three or four, take a large sheet of paper and make a list of the people who, in the opinion of group members, are most likely to suffer from loneliness. Then discuss the following points:

- Loneliness is a fundamental cause of many problems.

- It is possible to be lonely, even when surrounded by other people.

- Loneliness is most likely to be a problem at certain age-related stages of life.

- People who are lonely can benefit from counselling.

EXERCISE 7   RESPONSES TO LOSS

Working individually, look at the following comments and say which you think might be (a) helpful, (b) unhelpful.

1 I know how you feel.

2 This must be hard to accept.

3 Life must go on.

4 It's God's will.

5 He had a good life.

6 It's alright to cry.

7 Would you like to talk about it?

8 Tell me how I can help you.

9 Time will heal.

10 I think about you and pray for you.

11 You must have been devastated.

12 Come and talk to me any time.

13 You have to keep on going.

14 I'm very worried about you.

15 Are there any practical things I can do to help?

16 At least you have your friends.

17 There's no answer to these things.

18 You must have been very close.

19 I really liked him too.

20 Other people suffer terribly.

Afterwards, discuss your views with other members of the training group. Are there any common responses which people find helpful/unhelpful?

EXERCISE 8   ASPECTS OF HELPING

Working in groups of three or four, brainstorm a list of what you consider to be the most important aspects of help for the client in crisis. What are the most helpful responses from a counsellor, and what are the least helpful?

Discuss the ways in which counsellors can take care of their own needs while working with clients in crisis.

REFERENCE LIST

1 Caplan, G, *Principles of Preventive Psychiatry,* New York Basic Books, NY, 1964.
2 Bowlby, John, *Loss, Sadness and Depression,* Hogarth Press, London, 1980.
3 Kelleher, MJ, 'Death by Suicide' in Keane, Colin (ed), *Death and Dying,* Mercier Press in association with RTE, Dublin, 1995.
4 Bowlby, John, *The Making and Breaking of Affectionate Bonds,* Routledge, London, 1993.
5 Littlewood, Jane, *Aspects of Grief – Bereavement in Adult Life,* Routledge, London, 1993.
6 Erikson, Erik, *Childhood and Society* (2nd ed.), Norton, NY, 1963.
7 Tatelbaum, Judy, *The Courage to Grieve,* Cedar Press, London, 1988.
8 Murgatroyd, Stephen and Wolfe, Ray, *Coping With Crisis,* Open University Press, Milton Keynes, 1989.

FURTHER READING

1 *Coping With Crisis* by Stephen Murgatroyd and Ray Woolfe, Open University Press, Milton Keynes, 1989.
2 *Necessary Losses* by Judith Viorst, Simon and Schuster, London, 1989.
3 *The Making and Breaking of Affectional Bonds* by John Bowlby, Routledge, London, 1993.
4 *Good Grief – Experiencing Loss* by Carol Lee, Fourth Estate, London, 1994.
5 *Healing Pain – Attachment, Loss and Grief Therapy* by Nini Leick and Marianne Davidson-Nielsen, Routledge, London, 1991.
6 *Death and Dying* by Colin Keane, Mercier Press in association with RTE, Dublin, 1995.
7 *On the Death of a Parent* edited by Jane McLoughlin, Virago Press, London, 1994.
8 *Aspects of Grief* by Jane Littlewood, Routledge, London, 1993.

CHAPTER 8

Group communication

Throughout the preceding chapters, attention has been focused on inter-personal skills and the specific way that these are used in a one-to-one relationship between helper and client in the counselling context. However, the development and possession of good communication skills is a recognized necessity for increasing numbers of people, especially for those who work closely with others in a caring or helping capacity.

It goes without saying that a substantial part of the communication which takes place among people in a range of work situations is not exclusively conducted on a one-to-one basis, but may include groups of people. Sometimes these groups are small, sometimes large, depending on a variety of factors, including the function and purpose of the group, as well as its overall aims and objectives. In this chapter, we shall consider the composition and purpose of groups, the roles of individuals within them, the function and style of group leaders, the dynamics of communication, and the problems which can arise when several or more people are interacting in this way. Group counselling will also be discussed, along with its unique characteristics, and the factors which distinguish it from individual counselling. The advantages and disadvantages of both group and individual therapy will be highlighted in order to indicate the contexts in which each can be used most appropriately for the benefit of the clients.

Group membership

Perhaps the most significant aspect of group membership is that all of us have some experience of it. We grow up within the family group, and we mix with other people when we go to school. In addition to this, we usually belong to local communities, and we are involved – at least occasionally – in a range of social activities which take place in groups. Other activities, like going to work or to church, may also form an important part of the relational or friendship networks which are central to many people's lives, and through which they participate in group communication. It would be impossible to list all the groups to which people might belong at various stages throughout their lives. Obviously these are different for each individual, but the central point here is that none of us lives in isolation from other people. We all belong to groups and communicate in groups. The skills which we learn in early life, through membership of the family group, are transferred into adulthood and form essential building blocks for the evolution of later more refined interpersonal skills. This is not to say that the skills which we acquire in early childhood are always perfect. On the contrary, people often grow up within family environments which are not conducive to the development of skilful communication. In families like this, a high premium may not be placed on an ability to relate well and easily to others. Members of such families may be unaware of their skills deficit until later life, when they find themselves working with other people in any of the group situations already mentioned. The development and acquisition of interpersonal skills is, of course, a continuous process. So even when faulty or dysfunctional patterns of relating have been established early in life, there is always the possibility of reversing some of these effects through further training and self-awareness later on. Social behaviour, therefore, is amenable to change and modification in adult life, especially when amelioration of early problems is identified as a priority by the individual.

We all belong to groups and communicate in groups.

The socializing effects of school experience is also significant, in the way that it serves to modify some of the more problematic aspects of faulty communication. Through group interaction at school, children develop and refine their communication skills, and this process in turn helps to inculcate the fundamental rules of co-operation and support. From school to college, university, work or marriage, the task of learning to relate effectively to others continues, although not always in that sequence for many people. Numerous problems can arise when opportunities to participate in group interaction are decreased, and this is sometimes the case with people who are unable to secure employment, for example. The difficulties and problems which can result from social isolation of this kind are complex, and could not be adequately described within the scope of this chapter. However, some of the more specific emotional problems like agoraphobia, stress and depression, which are exacerbated by loneliness and isolation, have been referred to in previous chapters.

WHAT IS A GROUP?

When asked to suggest definitions of the word 'group', students invariably differ in the numbers of people which they believe would comprise one. Occasionally the numbers three to four are volunteered as minimum and necessary to make up a small group, and a maximum number of twenty to twenty five is often regarded as the upper limit. Anything over twenty five tends to resemble a crowd, although there is no rigid line of demarcation which separates a certain number of people and defines it as a group rather than a crowd. There are, however, certain characteristics which groups possess, and which set them apart from, say, a queue of people outside a cinema or a line of people waiting at a supermarket checkout. In the first place, people who make up group membership are aware of their existence as part of the group, and they also expect to interact with one another over a period of time in order to achieve certain goals. The goals are agreed upon within the group, and are shared among its members. Each person in the group has a role which helps to define individual behaviour. In some instances, more than one role is assigned to a particular person; when this is the case, role conflict can, and often does, occur. Affective relations exist within a group, which means that members experience a range of feelings for one another. These feelings are never static, but tend to change at various stages throughout group life. There is a clear expectation within groups that members will conform to certain norms, rules or standards which are often explicitly stated, and sometimes only implied.

A group, moreover, is more than just the sum of its parts, because its collective behaviour is quite different from that of any individual member working separately. Since groups often form for the specific purpose of achieving goals, an underlying assumption is that these goals are only attainable through common effort and endeavour.

Different groups

Within the health and caring services there is a wide spectrum of groups which operate for different purposes. There are, for example, groups which have been formed by people who suffer from the same illness, like diabetes, high blood pressure or eczema. In addition to these, groups have been formed by people with common disabilities, problems or addictions. Increasing numbers of people now join self-help groups whenever they feel that extra support is essential to help them deal with, or resolve, specific problems.

The evolution of group counselling and therapy is of particular interest in the context of groupwork generally. During and after the Second World War, extensive work was carried out by the German psychologist Kurt Lewin, who was instrumental in setting up the first *Training* or *T groups* in America in 1947. Much of the work carried out by Lewin, and by the National Training laboratories in Washington DC, was intended to facilitate the development of interpersonal skills which would then enhance relationships generally within organizations. Individuals in training were encouraged to become more sensitive to their own and other people's feelings and attitudes, and to develop spontaneity in the expression of these feelings. Issues of authority and leadership, and the dynamics of change within organizations were highlighted throughout training. Although the original focus of the work was on interpersonal communication, participants also experienced individual benefits from the training they had received.

ENCOUNTER GROUPS

Encounter groups also became popular in America before the idea was transferred to Britain. They were developed as a result of the work carried out by Carl Rogers and his person-centred philosophy which emphasizes personal growth and effective communication. These groups were meant to provide the right conditions for openness and honesty, and to facilitate the expression of authentic feelings in a supportive and non-authoritarian setting. This expression of feelings in a permissive and accepting environment was seen as an aid to self-discovery, and as an important step in overcoming isolation and alienation for the individual participants. Non-verbal expression of feelings was also encouraged and *catharsis*, which was regarded as beneficial, became a common feature of encounter group experience. Some discussion about the meaning of the word catharsis is included at the end of this chapter under the heading of 'Key words and phrases'.

An essential difference between the first Training groups pioneered by Lewin and the Encounter groups favoured by Rogers is that the former did not emphasize personal growth in the way that Rogers' model was intended to do. However, in both models of groupwork, stress is laid on the importance of improving individual communication skills used *outside* the groupwork setting. People who participate in training and encounter groups do so on a voluntary basis, and are not usually ill or emotionally incapacitated. Enhanced social and communication skills are the desired outcomes in both Training and Encounter group work, and the feedback which members receive from one another is usually effective in achieving these aims.

TASK GROUPS

Task groups, as the name implies, are usually formed in response to a particular need, and to address a specific task or problem. They might, for example, be set up in order to work on research or community projects, or to develop initiatives and to formulate plans. Members of the group are aware of the goals from the outset, and there is usually a high level of commitment to achieving these goals. No special significance is attached to the development of personal or communication skills, although task group experience often augments the skills which members already possess. In fact, it is probably true to say that membership of any group with clearly defined and legitimate goals is almost certain to enhance the individual's overall social skills. This last point will be discussed in greater detail later in the chapter.

SELF-HELP GROUPS

Self-help groups have been in existence for a long time, and certainly predate the emergence of counselling and psychotherapy groups as a way of offering support to people who need it. Perhaps the most famous self-help group of all is Alcoholics Anonymous, which was formed in 1935 in Ohio. It evolved as a highly successful organization to meet the needs of people with specific addictive problems. People who are in crisis, and who seek mutual support from fellow sufferers, often find that self-help groups are the most effective way of dealing with their difficulties. At present there are thousands of self-help groups throughout the world which have been set up to meet the needs of people with a wide variety of problems. It is possible for any person with a specific need to start a self-help group and thereby attract attention and support, not just from the members, but from the general public as well.

Self-help groups vary a great deal in terms of organization, size, structure, duration and mode of functioning, but their main attraction and strength lies in the fact that members understand one another in a way that no outsider could possibly do. When people share a common problem, a sense of support and community is fostered, and coping abilities are enhanced through group membership and communication. Personal growth and self-awareness are also facilitated as a result of participation in a self-help group. The idea that members can help and support one another without 'expert' intervention or help is also beneficial and serves to enhance self-confidence in participants generally. The fact that there are no 'experts' and very often no formal leadership either is significant for the successful functioning of self-help group. When people realize that they can deal with their own problems, through personal effort and through co-operation with others who share their concerns, individual empowerment and raised self-esteem are almost sure to follow.

Self-help groups place a high priority on the sharing of information among members. Advice giving, as well as discussion about practical issues and ways of achieving goals, are also emphasized. Emotional release is certainly facilitated, and members of self-help groups are likely to comfort one another when strong emotions are being expressed.

MULTIDISCIPLINARY GROUPS

Within both hospital and community contexts, there are now increased moves towards multidisciplinary care of patients. In addition to this, initiatives have evolved partly in response to guidelines laid down in the Patients' Charter, which stipulate that a named nurse should be assigned to each patient in hospital with the responsibility for assessing and managing that patient's care. This nurse is, therefore, the key person to liaise with doctors and other staff personnel who are part of the multidisciplinary team. Other team members may include the occupational therapist, physiotherapist and medical social worker, depending on the specific needs of individual patients. Multidisciplinary meetings take place at frequent intervals, and are especially important when rehabilitation of patients needs to be addressed. Nursing care in hospitals has now focused attention on the significance of good interpersonal skills. An interesting extension of this emphasis on improved communication is the move towards multidisciplinary recording and sharing of patient notes, a move which should enhance understanding and provide better patient care generally.

Counselling and psychotherapy groups

People who join counselling and psychotherapy groups do so for a wide variety of emotional or relational problems. A common experience among group member is that they have reached a stage when they feel the need for help and support in order to resolve these problems. This position is not any different from that experienced by the client who comes for individual counselling or therapy; indeed, some of the participants in a therapy group may also receive individual help as part of their programme. Some group members may be patients in hospital, or they might be outpatients who attend for treatment on a regular basis.

An important dimension of the groupwork experience is to help members cope with – and hopefully overcome – their emotional, psychological and relationship problems. Many of these problems have evolved as a direct result of faulty or dysfunctional relationships with other people, usually – though not always – within the immediate family. The group, therefore, becomes a positive and supportive medium in which to explore and resolve relationship difficulties. Since a group is made up of a number of people, all giving and receiving feedback, there is a good chance that individual members will achieve some measure of self-awareness and insight as a result of their participation in it. Although some group members may be reluctant to participate at first, this reluctance is usually overcome when the experience of openness, sharing and acceptance is communicated to, and accepted by, them.

A significant point of difference between encounter and therapy groups is that in the former the emphasis is on individual growth and development, while in the latter a more therapeutic and remedial approach – which is also developmental – is fostered throughout. Another way of stating this is to say that members of a counselling or psychotherapy group may feel the need to remedy some of the emotional or relationship traumas which exist in their lives. This requires a more sustained, concentrated and intense endeavour than is generally associated with either training or encounter groupwork experience.

Obviously individual members vary in their reactions to groupwork involvement. Personal perceptions of the benefits or otherwise of groupwork participation will depend, to a large extent, on individual problems, expectations and needs. In the first instance, membership of groups – like individual counselling – should be a voluntary commitment for each person attending. People who are reluctant to become involved should not be put under pressure to do so. As already indicated, individual counselling is often given in addition to groupwork therapy. For vulnerable clients who fear the social and perhaps threatening atmosphere of groups, individual counselling may provide a much needed preparation for groupwork exposure.

A practical aspect of groupwork, and one which is frequently mentioned by groupwork facilitators, is that therapeutic time is saved when a number of people meet together in this way (Ellis, 1991). As well as this, counselling and therapy are still expensive for the majority of people, but when a group of people receive therapy together it should be possible to reduce the cost considerably and thereby provide a service which is less élitist than it has tended to be. These considerations should not be taken lightly, since it is still the case that in many areas of the country it is difficult for people to find an affordable counselling service when they need it.

We have already seen that groupwork experience tends to encourage participants to widen and enhance their range of social and interpersonal skills. This phenomenon takes place as a result of direct interaction among members, but it also occurs as a response to modelling behaviour within the group. A shy or inhibited member of a group may learn to overcome this reticence once it has been shown that others are willing to take the risk of being friendly, responsive and open. This responsive and open behaviour helps to establish a sense of community among group members, and is perhaps one of the most therapeutic effects provided by groupwork experience. Members of the group effectively support and teach one another, and in doing so become additional therapists working alongside a skilful facilitator or leader. Indeed, it is probably true to say that in the context of the group setting, members may be more effective as helpers than any leader or facilitator could ever be. A principal reason for this is that members often share a common problem, and when this is the case a great deal of experiential understanding is bound to be present. When people encounter problems in their lives they sometimes assume that they, and only they, have ever experienced these particular problems. While it is true that no two people ever perceive things in quite the same way, it is nevertheless reassuring to know that others have endured difficulties similar to our own. It is even more encouraging and therapeutic to realize that there are different ways of tackling problems – ways which sometimes fail, but are worth trying anyway. The loss of courage and initiative which often accompanies emotional problems can be stultifying and obstructive; when examples of perseverence, creativity and resolution are shown within the group, all group members benefit as a result of it.

We have already seen that in some respects group members may be more effective therapists for one another than the counsellor who is actually leading the group. Even when members do not share a common problem, however, there are other benefits to be derived from group interaction and communication. Within the context of individual therapy, for example, clients may develop strong transference feelings for the counsellor. In the groupwork setting, transference feelings tend to be less tenacious and problematic, although they do exist and apply not just to feelings which members experience for the group leader, but also apply to relationships established among members themselves. However, there is less opportunity for the kind of intense and dependent transference which is easily developed when only one person exists to receive it. Groupwork, therefore, tends to be more democratic and egalitarian, and may foster a greater sense of autonomy and power among its individual members. Group members are given the opportunity to achieve independence, and mastery of their problems in a way that might be more difficult to accomplish in individual therapy. As well as this, there are people who find group interaction more satisfying and acceptable than individual work, and they may not be especially interested in establishing a close working relationship on a one-to-one basis with a counsellor.

Group membership may be drawn from a wide variety of occupations and backgrounds. When this is the case, there is much greater scope for acceptance, support and identification. This is very therapeutic for people who suffer from problems of loneliness and isolation in particular, but it is also beneficial for those group members who simply want to create new and more effective ways of relating to others. A person who experiences problems in communicating with others in positions of authority will probably develop greater confidence as a result of group participation, especially if other, more confident members of the group display positive attitudes of self-assurance and challenge towards the leader. In a similar way, individual members who need to feel in charge within relationships, and who seek to control and manipulate others, may learn to modify or even change these attitudes once they realize that acceptance within the group is likely to be enhanced by such change.

In Chapter 5, we considered some of the defences which clients may use in individual counselling. Such defences are used by participants in groupwork too, but in this context they are less likely to be sustained since group interaction works effectively to challenge them. A group member who uses humour, for example, in order to distance himself from emotional experience, is unlikely to continue with his defence once he observes the emotional vulnerability displayed by others in the groups. Intellectualization is less likely to continue either in such an environment, and defences like projection, introjection and denial are sure to be picked up and questioned by other group members. Clients who arrive late or leave early will only succeed in doing so on a few occasions at most. When such behaviour is observed by participants in groupwork they are certain to want some explanation for it. This accountability to the group exerts some pressure on individuals to observe group rules, whether stated or unstated. The following example illustrates this last point.

Stephanie, who suffered from anxiety and panic attacks, joined a therapy group which she attended regularly and punctually for the first three sessions. In the fourth session she arrived late, and sat down without offering an explanation for her absence. Another member of the group commented on this and said how disappointed she had been when she thought that Stephanie might not come. Several other members made similar comments, and encouraged Stephanie to talk about her feelings and her general reactions to the group. As a result of the dialogue which followed, Stephanie gained new confidence in herself, and her behaviour changed accordingly, especially when she realized the value and importance which others placed on her presence in the group.

Although the advantages of groupwork are certainly considerable, it is not always a suitable or appropriate mode of therapy for every client. There are quite a few people who tend to make more progress in a close and supportive relationship with just one other person. Extreme anxiety, sensitivity or deep depression may also militate against group participation, and clients who are totally withdrawn are unlikely to benefit from therapy in groups. In the same way, people who are oblivious to the needs of others, and those who claim a disproportionate amount of attention for themselves, may experience great difficulty in terms of integration and acceptance in the group. Intense or excessive hostility is hardly conducive to group therapy either, and certain acute forms of illness like paranoia or schizophrenia may mean that clients who suffer from them are so out of touch with reality that they are incapable – temporarily at least – of gaining any benefit from participation in groups.

The clients most likely to benefit from working in groups are those who have some enthusiasm and commitment to it, and those who have some awareness of their relational and social skills deficits. Although high intelligence is not a prerequisite for successful group participation, it is nevertheless important that members possess some aptitude for self-awareness, self-criticism, observation, reflection and thought. The ability to work through the often painful processes of self-development and personal growth is also important, and clients need to be able to tolerate quite high levels of anxiety at various stages throughout group therapy.

ADVANTAGES OF GROUPWORK

Groupwork has several advantages over individual counselling, and some of these have been highlighted in this chapter. A summary of the main advantages of groupwork includes the following:

- Counselling groups help clients to develop and extend their social skills.
- Groupwork tends to be less expensive for clients, and it may be more readily available for them on the NHS.
- Groupwork allows counsellors to help a number of clients together. This saves time, and makes counselling more accessible for clients.
- Clients who share the same problems in groups, provide emotional support for one another.
- Support groups can be set up by clients themselves. This is empowering for them and tends to enhance confidence and self-esteem.
- Insight may be gained more readily in groups. This is linked to the fact that a number of people are making contributions and offering help.
- When problems are shared within a group, it helps to dispel feelings of isolation, guilt and shame.
- Connections which are made within the group can be transferred and linked to relationships and problems which exist outside it.
- Clients can develop and use new ways of relating and communicating within the group.
- Clients' defences are less likely to be sustained within a groupwork setting.
- Transference reactions may be less intense and problematic in groupwork. Over-dependence on the counsellor is less likely to develop.
- Clients may develop assertiveness skills more easily in groupwork. The solidarity of a group enables even timid clients to question the leader and voice disagreements.
- A sense of belonging and community is fostered in groups.
- Clients experience themselves as helpers in groupwork. They not only receive help, but effectively extend it to others as well.
- Feedback can be shared among members of a group. In individual

counselling, feedback is given by only one person – the counsellor to the client.

- Clients learn to become more sensitive to the needs and feelings of others.

- In groupwork, traumatic and emotionally charged issues may be discussed. This may be a new and liberating experience for many clients.

- Clients in groupwork may come from a variety of backgrounds. This means that a diversity of opinion and cultural experience is shared and acknowledged.

- Clients in groups may differ in their sexual orientations. This is an educative and therapeutic experience for many people.

- Self-disclosure within groups can have lasting and beneficial effects, especially when it leads to support and acceptance from the whole group.

- A group leader with unresolved problems of her own is less likely to cause individual damage to clients in groupwork. On a one-to-one basis with a client, unresolved counsellor problems can pose a real threat to the client, and may inhibit his progress.

DISADVANTAGES OF GROUPWORK

Some of the disadvantages of groupwork have also been mentioned in this chapter. A more extensive list includes the following:

- Individual counselling is safer for those clients who are excessively withdrawn and who find it difficult to lower their defences. Group counselling may prove too threatening for them.

- Groupwork may be too confrontational for clients with very low self-esteem. People who are deeply depressed may be unable to contribute.

- Every person in a group may not, automatically, respect and value contributions made by others. This may lead to destructive hostility or scapegoating.

- Although confidentiality is discussed and agreed upon among group members, it may be more difficult to safeguard and guarantee than it would be in individual counselling.

- When a number of people in the group experience emotional catharsis, they may not receive adequate individual attention from the therapist.

- The group may become an end in itself for certain needy clients. It may be difficult for them to extricate themselves from the relative safety of the group to the real world outside.

- Vulnerable clients may feel under pressure to disclose personal problems before they are ready to do so.

- Vulnerable clients may be unable to bear the emotional discomfort and critical feedback which are integral to groupwork.

- Certain people may want to monopolize the group. This can be problematic for the group leader, and disconcerting for other members.

- Humour or intellectualization may be used persistently by some group members. This can impede the progress of the group.

- Some members may attempt to sabotage the work of the group. This can be especially difficult for group leaders to deal with.

- Clients who have special problems in relating to others may not do well in groupwork. Such clients may need a period of individual counselling before they are ready to join a group.

- Within the group setting, certain clients may not receive enough time to enable them to deal with their problems.

- Groupwork is unlikely to be suitable for acutely ill, schizophrenic, paranoid or deeply depressed clients.

GROUPWORK SKILLS

It should be emphasized that problems which arise in the groupwork context can usually be dealt with effectively by a skilful leader. However, facilitating groups is a specialized area of work – one which requires not just theoretical knowledge, but experiential and practical training as well. In other words, counsellors who hope to work with groups should endeavour to gain as much experience as possible of actually *being* in groups.

The skills which are necessary for working with groups include those which are used in individual counselling, but since a group leader is dealing with more than one person it is obviously much more difficult to monitor sessions and to give sufficient attention to each member participating.

In addition to the skills of listening, paraphrasing, asking appropriate and well-timed questions, summarizing, and reflecting back what individuals say, group leaders need to be adept at co-ordinating, linking and monitoring all contributions within the group. They need to show respect and empathy for individual members of the group, and they should be willing to be honest in relation to their own personal feelings and actions. Competence in making use of specific examples is also important, so too is the ability to use empathic challenge when it is needed. Clarifying comments made by group members is a significant aspect of the leader's role, and since group participants need to see some connection between the experiences which they have in the group and those which they have outside it, a skilful group leader will help to identify and highlight those links when they appear.

Group leaders need to be clear about the purpose of the group, and the tasks which have to be achieved within it. They need to be confident about the work which they are doing. The ability to impart this confidence and sense of purpose to the group is also important.

Contributions made by individual group members should be valued and accepted by the leader, and skill in both dealing with silent and dominant group members is essential in this respect. Non-verbal communication is an important dimension of groupwork – as it is in individual counselling – and a competent leader should be attuned to the non-verbal cues and nuances within the group.

PLANNING

In addition to the leadership skills which are necessary for successful groupwork functioning, several important issues relating to planning need to be addressed before the group starts. These include the following:

THE COMPOSITION OF THE GROUP
Who is it for?

THE PURPOSE OF THE GROUP
What is it for?

THE VENUE
Where will meetings take place?

THE SIZE OF THE GROUP
How many people?

GROUP LEADERS
One or two?

FREQUENCY, NUMBER AND DURATION OF MEETINGS
How often should meetings take place, how many, and how long should they last?

OPEN OR CLOSED
Will the group admit new members during the time that it functions, or will it be closed to new members once it has started?

PROGRAMME OF ACTIVITIES
How is the group to operate, and what is the leader's role? Is there a programme of activities?

MONITORING
How will group progress be monitored?

EVALUATION
What form of evaluation will be used for the group?

RESOURCES
What resources are needed and who will supply them?

SUPERVISION FOR LEADERS
Is adequate ongoing supervision available for leaders?

GROUP LEADERSHIP

In groupwork it is quite common to have two leaders working together. Co-leadership has its advantages over individual leadership, the most obvious of which is that in the former counsellors can share responsibility and give each other support. Occasionally one group leader is more experienced than the other, and in this situation, the less experienced counsellor is given the opportunity to work and learn in a relatively safe environment. The presence of the more experienced counsellor should also ensure that members of the group are not placed at a disadvantage because a trainee is acting as facilitator. Co-leaders are in a better position to give more time and individual attention to group members, and nervous or vulnerable clients may feel more secure when this is the case. Co-leaders can give valuable feedback to each other between sessions, and observation and monitoring of group processes is much easier when two people are involved.

It is not always the case, however, that two people will work in perfect harmony together. Some disagreement is inevitable in co-leadership, although this is not necessarily an insurmountable problem if leaders decide beforehand to communicate freely about all their difficulties. This is an important point to bear in mind because any unresolved problems and tensions between leaders will be picked up by group members, and will almost inevitably cast a negative and stultifying shadow over the whole group. Members can also exploit disagreements which exist between leaders. This is the case even when such disagreements are disguised or well masked. Free and honest discussion about all aspects of group life is essential at regular points between meetings. Co-leaders need to be well prepared for their work beforehand, and each person should be confident about roles and responsibilities during group sessions. When two people work together to facilitate a group, planning should be shared equally between them. All those fundamental issues relating to purpose, composition, programme, size and monitoring of the group should be discussed and agreed upon well before sessions begin.

STYLES OF GROUP LEADERSHIP

It goes without saying that individual leaders will vary a great deal in their general approach to groupwork, and to the way in which they personally propose to facilitate sessions. If one leader is male and the other female this can be a positive advantage for members of the group, since some people may relate more easily to one sex than the other. Quite apart from sexual identity, however, leaders will obviously differ from each other in terms of attitude, manner and style. Perhaps the best known and frequently quoted study of leadership styles is that which was carried out by Lewin, Lippitt and White (1939). As a result of their work, three leadership approaches were identified and these were seen to affect significantly the members of the group to which the leaders belonged. The leadership styles described were:

- Authoritarian
- Democratic
- Laissez-faire (see Fig. 8.1).

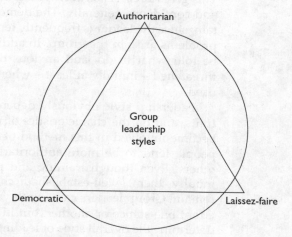

Fig. 8.1 *Group leadership styles.*

AUTHORITARIAN
LEADERSHIP

An authoritarian leader is one who tends to make most of the decisions for the group. This approach certainly provides structure and direction, but allows little opportunity for group members to develop independence or autonomy. This style of leadership does have some advantages, since participants know exactly where they stand and confusion is kept to a minimum.

LAISSEZ-FAIRE
LEADERSHIP

The laissez-faire style of leadership is in direct contrast to the authoritarian approach. It is concerned with encouraging members to express their views, opinions and suggestions at every stage throughout group life. No firm rules are imposed on the group. The advantage of this approach is that it can encourage a sense of freedom, and provide greater potential for creative thinking. On the other hand, group members can feel aimless and disconcerted with this style of leadership since little feedback is directly given, and no *obvious* attempt is made to co-ordinate the group. This last point is important because a laissez-faire style does not necessarily lack purpose. On the contrary, it may conceal a great deal of purpose and planning, but since these are not obvious to participants, considerable frustration is often the result.

DEMOCRATIC
LEADERSHIP

A democratic leader is concerned to include all group members in the decision-making process. Although such a leader will provide structure and planning – which is usually obvious to participants – consultation and participation are characteristic of the approach. Help is offered to group members if and when required, and feedback is freely given throughout sessions. A democratic leader is flexible and adaptable, and will usually take the view that members have innate potential to help themselves. The advantage of this approach is that participants are treated as equals, and given the opportunity to determine their own rules and behaviour. This gives a real sense of empowerment and tends to increase self-esteem and confidence generally. The democratic style is not a easy one to sustain, since the leader is frequently tempted to become authoritarian when problems arise in the group. In addition to this, members often want to be told what to do, and anxious or vulnerable clients may feel quite threatened – initially at least – when this kind of leadership approach is used.

Leadership style obviously depends, to a large extent, on personality traits, and on the characteristics of individual counsellors who chose to become involved in this method of helping. It is a fact of life that some people tend to be more authoritarian, democratic or laissez-faire than others. Even though training and personal development may serve to modify them, well-established characteristics are almost certain to remain. Group leaders can – with varying degrees of success – decide to adopt one stance or another, but in the end inherent personal traits will determine the overall style of leading the group.

Regardless of leadership style, however, planning and ongoing supervision are aspects of groupwork which leaders cannot afford to neglect. Group processes are difficult and complex, and without these essential elements of planning and supervision, members of the group will be adversely affected.

PROBLEMS IN LEADERSHIP

Some of the problems which can arise in groupwork have already been indicated within this chapter. Certain behaviours displayed by leaders can also be problematic or unhelpful. A summary of those aspects of behaviour which can be counterproductive includes the following:

- Poor or inadequate planning and failure to be explicit about the goals of the group. Talking too much and interrupting group members when they speak. Using specialist jargon which may confuse group members, or dominating the group and expecting members to accept only the leaders' views and perceptions.

- Asking too many questions, showing impatience, boredom or hostility, favouring certain members of the group and allowing them to dominate, are all counter-productive in groupwork. A leader who is judgemental, condescending or patronizing will also inhibit the work of the group. Showing discomfort with silence, drawing excessive attention to 'self', offering too many interpretations, or drawing premature conclusions are all aspects of poor leadership skills.

- Failure to deal with any evidence of scapegoating will undermine the possible benefits of groupwork; while placing too much emphasis on catharsis will also create an imbalance. Unspoken problems which exist in the group need to be identified by the leader, and failure to challenge constructively when such challenge is needed will result in frustration and neglect of important issues which arise in the group.

- Any failure to communicate adequately with a partner when two people are involved in leading the group would obviously create problems in groupwork. Any show of defensive or resentful behaviour towards one another – whether verbal or non-verbal – is also destructive.

It would be impossible to enumerate all the problems which can arise for group leaders. In the groupwork context most of the more obvious problems can be avoided when the leader is engaged in active and perceptive listening, not only to the words which are spoken by participants, but also to the feelings and ideas which are left unsaid. This is obviously the most significant skill in individual counselling too, but in groupwork it becomes much more difficult to sustain since it involves giving attention to a group of people, instead of just one. In addition to this, connections and links have to be made between individual contributions from group members, and all this requires the ability to balance each person's needs – whether expressed or unexpressed – within the group. The skills, and the avoidance of problems, can only be achieved through a programme of training which includes experiential participation in groups as well as a sound base of theoretical knowledge.

Stages of group development

Tuckman (1965) described the various stages or phases through which he believed groups develop over a period of time. He referred to these as *Forming*, *Storming*, *Norming* and *Performing*. In the first developmental stage members are coming together to form the group, and they are preoccupied with its purpose, and the need to establish relationships within it. During the second or storming stage, differences of opinion begin to emerge and members may compete with each other for roles and positions: sub-groups may form and the leader may be criticized and her authority challenged. Group cohesion is achieved at the norming stage, and a new closeness develops among group participants. Co-operation, bonding and sharing of experiences is usual at this stage, and a common perspective with regard to the group and how it will function is now in evidence. In the last or performing stage of group development, members concentrate on working together. Personal issues are explored and individual members now feel safe enough to express differences of opinion and a high degree of energy is generated within the group. It is at this stage that real work is accomplished; members begin to act as counsellors for one another and in doing so, become aware of the similarities in many of their experiences.

Tuckman's outline of the emotional and developmental stages of group life is just one of a number of models concerned with the subject. Individual writers have described the stages of development in various ways. Those students who are interested in group counselling will need to research the subject in a great deal more detail than is possible within this chapter. Figure 8.2 shows one model.

Finally, it should be emphasized that the ending or adjourning stage of any group is just as important as all the phases which have gone before. Group members often feel a sense of loss or bereavement when this stage is reached, and group leaders need to be sensitive and supportive in the way they deal with issues of separation and closure.

Fig. 8.2 *The developmental stages of group life.*

THE INDIVIDUAL AND THE GROUP

Since a group is composed of a number of people, all of whom are unique in terms of personality and characteristics, it is obvious that the individual contributions they make to the group will differ. We have already considered the group as a whole, along with the various stages through which it evolves. Some of the problems which can arise in groupwork have also been highlighted in this chapter. It is clear that certain aspects of individual behaviour can be unhelpful or problematic, but in fact most of the contributions made by group members are positive and productive. The majority of clients who participate in groupwork do so through a genuine desire to acquire self-knowledge, and some measure of control over the more problematic aspects of their lives.

Contributions made by group members often serve to facilitate the work of the whole group. Each member of the group has a role within it, and in some instances group members may have a number of flexible roles which are used at different stages throughout group life. The two most obvious examples of roles within groups are those of the leader and the scapegoat. While the role of the leader is usually high status, that of the scapegoat is, by definition, low status, since it tends to be assigned to someone who is disliked by the rest of the group (Benson, 1987).

It is important for counsellors – especially those who wish to participate in groupwork – to understand the significance of the roles which emerge when a number of people work together. Understanding leads to acceptance of the contributions made by the group members, and interventions which might otherwise seem negative or invaluable are given the recognition they deserve.

Bales (1950) identified several kinds of behaviour which were demonstrated by group members, and which can be observed in almost any groupwork situation. These aspects of behaviour include information giving, asking questions, providing summaries, giving support to others, sharing experiences, being humorous, clarifying contributions, making suggestions, giving opinions and showing acceptance. Other, less positive aspects of behaviour were also identified by Bales, including withdrawal and antagonism, excluding others and rejecting the group. There are various and complex reasons for these less positive aspects of behaviour, but it is important to remember that they do not occur without some underlying cause. The task for the group leader is to help individual clients to identify the problems which they have in relation to the group – and very often to others outside it – and to encourage these clients to develop more constructive ways of relating to others, both inside and outside the group.

| CASE STUDY: KEITH | Keith, who was thirty five years of age, joined a local support group for people suffering from stress, in the area where he lived. He heard about the group through a colleague at work who had already decided to join, and who was keen to have someone accompany him to the first meeting. Keith, who was sceptical at first, mentioned it to his GP who was treating him for slightly raised blood pressure and insomnia. His doctor was enthusiastic about the idea, and |

encouraged Keith to contact the counsellor who was running the group, in order to ensure membership of it.

The group which Keith joined was held at the local hospital on a Tuesday evening. Members were enrolled for it through a process of individual interviews with Mark, the group facilitator. This system of interviewing applicants for the group served a dual purpose, since it gave Mark the opportunity to assess an individual's suitability for groupwork, and allowed prospective members to ask questions about the purpose and function of this approach to therapy. In addition to this, the initial interview helped to establish a relationship between Keith and the group leader. By the end of the interview, Keith felt much happier about his decision to join. Issues relating to attendance at group meetings, confidentiality, objectives and general aspects of group behaviour were also discussed at the interview, and Mark explained in some detail what his role as facilitator would be. He also encouraged Keith to talk about his reasons for wanting to join the group, and asked him to identify any specific areas of his life that he felt he needed to work on.

A verbal contract was established between Keith and the group leader, and at the first meeting of the group, another collective contract was made which everyone agreed to uphold. The group was made up of twelve people, all of whom were suffering from the effects of stress in their lives, or from some form of stress-related illness which had not responded to medical treatment. Mark, the group leader, was a trained psychiatric nurse as well as a qualified counsellor and he had considerable experience of working with groups. He had spent some time in preparing for the first group session, and he was very aware that members would be shy, awkward and ill at ease with one another. He introduced himself to group members, and they in turn introduced themselves to one another. Participants then talked about their expectations and hopes for the sessions and Mark encouraged them to discuss any previous experiences they had of being in a new situation which made them nervous. The chairs in the room were arranged in a circle, and Keith was surprised at first that he found this quite comfortable. Everyone seemed to communicate on an equal basis, and even the group decision about tea time was reached quite quickly, with everyone opting for a halfway break in the two-hour session.

Over the next eight sessions the climate in the group was such that the members felt safe enough to disclose personal information about themselves and their problems. Many of the participants had experienced difficulties in their family relationships, and this became a subject for discussion at most sessions. Mark was concerned to co-ordinate the contributions made by the group members, and to make connections and links between the various issues raised. Disagreements also surfaced within the group, but these were usually discussed and resolved before the end of each session. Occasionally members of the group became emotional, especially when problems relating to childhood surfaced in discussions. Keith, who had grown up in a family which totally discouraged emotional expressions, found the atmosphere strange at first, but gradually became more aware of his own feelings and was able to share these with other participants. He realized how much more anxiety and stress he had endured in the previous six months, mostly as a result of promotion at work and the breakdown of a long-standing and important relationship.

Keith had been an only child. His early life, with older than average parents, was lonely and isolated. The experience of communicating in an intimate way with a group of trusted and supportive people was entirely new to him, and one which he grew to appreciate. He learned to be more responsive to the feelings of others in the group, and gradually he began to transfer this responsiveness to other significant relationships at home and at work. As a result of discussions with his fellow group members, Keith also learned about new ways of coping with stress. He took up swimming and cycling again – activities he once loved but had neglected recently.

Perhaps the most significant benefit which Keith derived from the groupwork experience was a heightened awareness of the similarities which exist in almost everyone's problems. The therapeutic effects of sharing experiences also became evident to him, and he found himself much more willing to talk to people about subjects which he would previously have considered taboo. He enjoyed the 'helping' aspect of groupwork, and on occasions when he gave support to another member of the group, he felt especially confident about his new-found ability and talent. As a result of all these changes, Keith developed a more accepting, less negative view of himself and his capabilities, and this awareness stayed with him even when the groupwork experience had ended. On a more prosaic level, he enjoyed the friendliness of the group which helped him to feel less lonely. He had not realized the extent of his loneliness in the past, and the group experience encouraged him to become more socially involved, at work and in the community.

The ending of the groupwork experience was difficult for Keith – and for the other participants – although they had all been aware from the outset that meetings would end on a certain date. Attention was focused on the achievements of the group, and Mark encouraged participants to discuss these openly. Some people expressed anger and sadness that the group was ending, and a great deal of reflection and reminiscing took place at this stage. It is important during this phase of group life to give members sufficient time to work through a broad spectrum of often quite powerful and negative feelings. Discussions relating to separation and loss frequently trigger memories of other losses which group members have experienced in the past. Adequate planning for the end of group life is therefore as important as planning for the start.

KEY WORD

CATHARSIS

The word catharsis – which literally means purging – is often used in relation to groupwork. It refers to the expression of strong feeling or emotion by participants. This expression of feeling is usually brought about when a group member relives traumatic or painful events from the past. Several group members may share the experience, since what is remembered and recounted by one member may well trigger similar memories from others. The feelings expressed may be various, but usually include those of extreme sadness, anger or regret.

Once strong feelings have been expressed within a safe and supportive environment, some degree of emotional insight is often achieved as a result. This insight may then lead to beneficial change for individuals, especially when they are given the opportunity to discuss the original event which caused their emotional trauma. Insight, as well as catharsis, is therefore important, and group leaders need to bear this in mind when working with members of a group who express strong feelings. On the other hand, it is also true that beneficial effects are unlikely to occur when group members recall past experiences *without* any expression of the painful feelings associated with these. This raises the question of how much emphasis group leaders should place on catharsis.

Perhaps the most important aspect of catharsis is that it should never be forced; certainly group members should never be put under pressure to express strong feelings when they have no wish to do so. It is sometimes the case that group leaders deliberately – though not always overtly – engineer displays of emotion, and the most likely reason for this is that they themselves have unresolved problems stemming from the past which need to be addressed.

EXERCISES

EXERCISE 1   JOINING A GROUP

Working in groups of three or four, identify the anxieties and expectations which people might experience when joining a group. Accept all the suggestions made by members of your own group, and list these under two separate headings: ANXIETIES and EXPECTATIONS. Discuss with other members of the training group.

EXERCISE 2   THE CONTRACT

Working in pairs, write out a contract or set of ground rules which could be used when group members meet for the first time. Some of the issues raised may include:

- confidentiality

- timekeeping

- responsibilities of the leader.

Discuss your contract with other members of the training group.

EXERCISE 3   PROBLEM BEHAVIOUR

Working in groups of five or six, discuss the following aspects of behaviour which might become apparent in groups.

- Hostility

- Withdrawal

- Persistent joking

- Poor timekeeping

- Scapegoating
- Breaking up into sub-groups or pairs
- Blaming the leader
- Defensiveness
- Talking too much
- Being critical of other group members.

Try to determine the causes of the behaviours mentioned and discuss the best and most effective ways of dealing with them.

EXERCISE 4 WORKING AS A GROUP

This exercise is best done with an observer taking notes. Working in groups of between six and eight, spend thirty minutes deciding how you would accomplish the following task.

You have been asked to raise money for an overseas charity, but you have only a week in which to do it.

You need to approach this as a group task, and any decisions you come to must be arrived at through group effort. The observer should note the behaviour of the individuals within it. Points of discussion might include the following:

a) Who emerged as group leader?
b) What roles did individuals take on in the group?
c) How was the final decision reached in the group?

EXERCISE 5 GROUPWORK SETTING

Working in pairs, draw a diagram showing seating arrangements for a support group which is meeting for the first time. Include the layout for the whole room, taking into consideration size and shape, lighting, decoration, furniture and privacy. Discuss your ideas with other members of the training group and say why you think these aspects of groupwork setting are important.

EXERCISE 6 SETTING UP A GROUP

Working in groups of three or four, discuss how you would set up and run a support group within your area. Individual trainees may have different ideas about what is needed in their own areas. For the purpose of this exercise, all that is needed is one idea on which everyone else in the group can work. For example, one person may make a suggestion that a support group for teenage mothers might be appropriate. Consider the following points:

- The purpose of the group.

- Who can join?

- Where will it be?

- When and how often will it meet? What time?

- What resources will be needed?

- What are the aims and objectives?

- Will the group be open or closed?

Discuss any other points which you think are relevant to the setting up of a group.

EXERCISE 7   PROBLEMS TO AVOID
Working in pairs, discuss the factors which you think might impede or inhibit interaction in groups. Some of the factors might include obvious distractions like extraneous noise or constant interruption, but other less obvious impediments also exist. Discuss your suggestions with other members of the training group.

EXERCISE 8   INDIVIDUAL CONTRIBUTIONS
Consider the contributions which you make as an individual to groups. Can you identify any particular role or roles which you tend to adopt. Work with a partner and discuss these roles. Can you identify any similarities between the roles which you adopt in groups, and those which you have within the family?

FURTHER READING

1   Conyne, Robert K, 'How Personal Growth and Task Groups Work', *Sage Human Services Guides* vol. 35, London, 1989.
2   Benson, Jarlath F, *Working More Creatively with Groups,* Tavistock, London, 1987.
3   Stock Whittaker, Dorothy, *Using Groups to Help People,* Routledge, London, 1995.
4   Aveline, Mark and Dryden, Windy (eds), *Group Therapy in Britain,* Open University Press, Milton Keynes, 1988.
5   Yalom, I D, *The Theory and Practice of Group Psychotherapy,* Basic Books, NY, 1970.
6   Peck, M S, *The Different Drum,* Rider Press, London, 1987.
7   Douglas, T, *Basic Groupwork,* Tavistock, London, 1978.
8   Rogers, Carl, *On Becoming a Person,* Constable, London, 1991.

REFERENCE LIST

1   *The Oxford Companion to the Mind* by Richard L Gregory, Oxford University Press, Oxford, 1987.
2   *Encounter Groups* by Carl Rogers, Penguin, Harmondsworth, 1971.
3   *Reason and Emotion in Psychotherapy* by Albert Ellis, Carol Group, NY, 1991.

4 'Patterns of Aggressive Behaviour in Experimentally Created Social Climates' by K Lewin, R Lippitt and RK White in *Journal of Social Psychology,* 10, pp 271–299, 1939.

5 'Developmental Sequence in Small Groups' by B W Tuckman in *Psychological Bulletin* vol. 63, pp 384–399, 1965.

6 *Working More Creatively with Groups* by Jarlath F Benson, Tavistock, London, 1987.

7 *Interactive Process Analysis: A Method for the Study of Small Groups* by R F Bales, Addison-Wesley, Cambridge, Massachusetts, 1950.

CHAPTER 9

Some ethical issues in counselling

This chapter will deal with some of the ethical issues relating to counselling and therapy. In philosophy, the word ethics refers to the study of moral conduct and the fundamental question – which has concerned philosophers for thousands of years – of what constitutes right and wrong behaviour. Most people are familiar with the term as it is used in reference to medicine and other branches of science. However, within recent years, it is increasingly used in relation to counselling and therapy. The British Association for Counselling has, for example, produced its own code of ethics and practice for counsellors, and although it is not my intention to describe this in detail here, I would certainly recommend that all student counsellors acquaint themselves with it.

Confidentiality

One of the subjects which should be addressed early on in counsellor training is that of confidentiality in relation to clients. Students are usually very concerned about this issue, and much animated discussion tends to be generated when it is the topic for group consideration. Most students are able to define the word *confidence* with a fair degree of certainty. It is often described as a 'firm trust' in another person, a trust which is freely given and freely accepted and one which should never be abused. There is an underlying assumption in almost all these discussions that the issue of confidentiality is so important that both client and counsellor will simply take it for granted. Such total and tacit acceptance of confidentiality is, of course, the ideal, but it is also an over-simplification of a complex and many-sided subject.

Nevertheless, it is probably true to say that the majority of people who seek counselling do so in the hope that what they have to say will be respected by the counsellor, and that nothing will be repeated outside the counselling interview. Occasionally, clients broach the subject of confidentiality themselves early on in counselling, and when this happens it is relatively easy to clarify its limitation for them. The following is an example of how one client introduced the topic of confidentiality, almost as soon as she sat down. The client, whose thirty year old daughter suffered from mental illness, was distraught by the pressures of caring for her unpredictable, grown-up child at home.

CLIENT: The worst part of it all is that I don't think people really believe me when I say how bad it is. It's hard to get anyone to take it seriously.

COUNSELLOR: The frustration of not having anyone believe you...all this makes it more difficult for you.

CLIENT: Yes. (pause) And I know I can trust you not to repeat what I tell you...it's so difficult for me to talk about it.

COUNSELLOR: I can see that it's difficult for you. But what you say to me is confidential. I wouldn't repeat what is said to me in counselling, except when someone is in danger of being harmed.

CLIENT: Well, Jackie hasn't harmed anyone thank goodness. It's my nerves that are getting punished...

There are two important issues which are highlighted in this exchange. The first concerns the limits of confidentiality itself, while the second concerns the client's worries about gossip and the possibility that things might be repeated outside the counselling situation. The counsellor in this instance addressed both issues with the client, but she did not give a lengthy explanation initially. Instead, she explained in brief what confidentiality in counselling meant and later – towards the end of the sessions – she spoke in more detail about it. She explained to the client that total confidentiality would not be possible if someone was threatening to harm either herself or another person. The client understood and accepted this. Concerns about gossip were also discussed, and it emerged that the client had encountered problems in the past when she had tried to enlist the help of people who had subsequently talked about her and her problems to others.

Issues of confidentiality should be clarified with clients before counselling begins. In crisis or emergency situations, however, this is not always possible or feasible. Clients can come to counselling in highly distraught or emotional states, and often they are not ready to absorb a great deal of factual information straightaway. Tact and sensitivity are needed, on the counsellor's part, in order to gauge the right moment for clarification of the subject. The important point to make is that issues relating to confidentiality should be discussed with the client, as soon as possible. Although many clients do not mention it themselves, they are, nevertheless, bound to have some feelings about it. Not all clients will be as explicit about their feelings as the client just mentioned. In fact, it is sometimes the case that clients are reluctant to introduce the subject of confidentiality for fear of seeming to question the counsellor's professionalism.

When absolute confidentiality cannot be guaranteed in counselling, clients should be aware of this fact. In other words, when there is a good reason to believe that a client will injure himself or someone else, the limits of confidentiality should be made clear to him. Different agencies have different rules relating to confidentiality, but most stipulate that absolute confidentiality will not be maintained when there is a real risk that someone will be injured. This raises another important point, however, and relates to the degree of risk which is actually present when clients impart information about their own or someone else's potential injury. Most people have experienced strong or even violent emotions at certain crisis points in life, but few ever really act out these fantasies in harmful or threatening ways. A mother who is harassed with the demands of a new baby, for example, might confide that she sometimes feels like shaking it even though she has no real compulsion to harm her baby. The very act of confiding this information to a counsellor may be sufficient to relieve the pressure which such a client may have experienced. On the other hand, there may be some danger that she will be driven to harm her baby. In either case, the counsellor has a clear duty to discuss the matter in detail with the client, and to refer her for further professional help if necessary.

Student counsellors should be aware that problems relating to confidentiality can be discussed during supervision. Once again, this highlights the importance of regular supervision for counsellors, especially for students who are likely to encounter difficulties not only in relation to confidentiality, but in other areas as well. Needless to say, clients should also be told about supervision arrangements. If information about a client is to be communicated to a supervisor then the client has a right to know beforehand. However, clients can be assured that discussions which take place between counsellor and supervisor will not reveal *individual* client identity. This assurance is generally sufficient to assuage any doubts which clients may have, although it still leaves the problem of how best to impart all this information to them without sounding officious or obtrusive. Tact, sensitivity and good timing are again needed in order to ensure that the client is given enough information, without switching attention away from him and his problems.

Counsellors who work in a multidisciplinary context – primary care or General Practice, for example – will usually arrive at an agreement with colleagues about the degree of client information to be shared. In real terms, this may mean sharing vital information with the client's doctor only. Again, clients should be told when this is liable to happen. Any rules relating to confidentiality and its limitations within a team need to be made clear to them. However, it is probably true to say that most of the problems which clients discuss, whether in General Practice or any other counselling context, can and should be regarded as absolutely confidential. Clients often need to summon up a great deal of courage in order to talk about their problems in the first place, and the onus is on the counsellor to provide a safe and trusting environment in which confidentiality is a basic and guiding principle.

Confidentiality is an essential part of the process of helping clients to engage in the often difficult and painful exploration of themselves and their problems. Anything which would limit, threaten or impede it must therefore be avoided, if at all possible. Occasionally the principle of confidentiality is breached by counsellors in ways which are not intended and certainly do not constitute infringements in the obvious or usual sense. Bernie, a university counsellor, described how she met one of her clients – a young man – at a social event on the campus. She said hello to him, addressing him by name, but he was obviously reluctant to acknowledge her and turned away. Since the young man was in the company of his friends, he was keen to distance himself from any acquaintance with the university counsellor. It is not difficult to understand how such a mistake could be made, but it does serve as a warning to student counsellors who may not realize just how many pitfalls there are in the area of confidentiality.

Issues of confidentiality are potentially so complex that it is important for counsellors to be aware of all the rules and expectations pertaining to it within their own agencies or specialisms of work.

Transference and countertransference

It is important for student counsellors to understand the twin concepts of *transference* and *countertransference* which are central to the counselling relationship. Although the terms are most often considered in a psychodynamic context, they are by no means exclusive to that particular theory. All theoretical approaches to counselling have their own views about transference and countertransference, but in the main they all agree that the relationship between counsellor and client is a crucial factor in the therapeutic process.

TRANSFERENCE

The word transference refers to a common human tendency to transfer ideas, beliefs and attitudes from the past to the present, and from the particular to the general. Everything we have learned in childhood stays with us throughout adult life, and is influential in determining the ways we respond to other people. Parents, who are usually the two most significant people in a child's life, are therefore the 'models' or blueprints for all subsequent relationships – whether casual or intimate. Transference occurs not just in counselling and therapy, but in other relationships too. However, it has special meaning in the therapeutic context, where its effect is heightened considerably. The images which clients transfer from the past are, by their nature, stereotyped which means that they are inappropriate when applied to the counselling relationship. A client may, for example, experience the counsellor as an all-knowing authority figure who will provide answers and take care of problems in the way that a mother or father might do. Doctors and nurses are also familiar with this kind of response from patients, and clergymen who work closely with members of their congregation also encounter it daily.

It is important to stress from the outset that transference reactions are unconsciously motivated, so clients and patients do not set out deliberately to form strong attachments to the people who help them. Moreover, the feelings which are projected by the client onto the therapist can also be hostile, anxious, idealizing, aggressive, intensely loving or dependent. They may be critical too or blaming, but regardless of the exact nature of the feelings, they are repetitions and stem from early interactions which the client experienced in childhood. Freud first observed the phenomenon of transference, and it was through his observance that he began to understand the importance which his patients attached to their relationship with him. Freud quickly came to realize that the transference reactions which he observed were not connected to any particular characteristics which he himself possessed. In this sense, they were unrealistic and out of date, but nevertheless very real to the people who experienced them.

At the beginning of this section, we observed that transference has special meaning in the therapeutic context. There are several reasons for this, but one of the most important concerns the heightened emotional and sometimes anxious state which clients are in when they first seek counselling. It is very easy for people to become dependent on others who help them when they are vulnerable, and it is especially easy for clients in counselling since they are often very grateful for even the slightest support which they are given. In addition to this, the counselling relationship – unlike friendship, for example – develops quickly, and clients often disclose their deepest thoughts, feelings and anxieties, some of which they may never have entrusted to anyone else before. The counsellor, on the other hand, does not disclose this kind of information about herself, so the client has to use his imagination to invest her with the qualities or attributes which he chooses. Without consciously thinking it over, he draws on his past experience of relationships in order to help him paint a fuller picture of the person who is helping him.

For the client, therefore, the counsellor is someone who has (on account of her training) knowledge and 'expertise' which he needs at this particular time. In view of his vulnerability and initial dependence on the counsellor, the client's responses will generally mirror the responses which he gave to the people on whom he depended in the past. In some instances, transference reactions by clients are mild; in other instances, they may be more pronounced, and sometimes even exaggerated. Obviously the degree of transference elicited in any particular client will depend on a variety of factors, including the level of apprehension or anxiety which he experiences before he actually meets the counsellor.

In the Psychodynamic approach to counselling, the concept of transference is central to the model. It is regarded as a valuable starting point in the counselling process since it clearly reveals the problems which clients have had in their relationships, especially in their relationships with significant adults in the past. In contrast to this, a fundamental aim of the Person-centred model of counselling is to help clients move quickly towards independence and autonomy. In effect this means that transference reactions, though tacitly acknowledged by the counsellor, are never deliberately fostered or encouraged. The Person-centred counsellor works towards understanding the client and providing the kind of acceptance and respect which should signal attitudes of equality and lessen the possibility of transference reactions being sustained. The client who is treated as an equal is much less likely to continue with inappropriate – and largely dependent – responses derived from childhood. Instead, such a client is encouraged to view the counsellor as a flesh-and-blood individual who is fallible, though certainly willing to help. In this way, the therapeutic relationship is placed in a more realistic light, and is no longer distorted by emotive images and feelings emanating from the past.

POTENTIAL ABUSE

Student counsellors need to understand the concept of transference if they are to avoid some of the pitfalls and areas of potential abuse which are directly contingent upon it. It would be quite easy, for example, to encourage unwittingly the kind of dependence which could certainly work against the client's best interests and progress. There are other more alarming possibilities which also have to be considered, and these include the possibility of sexual and emotional abuse of clients. The intense and intimate emotions which clients often experience and express in therapy can lead to a desire for greater closeness with the person who is helping. It is not difficult to see how this kind of situation could be exploited by unscrupulous – or even naive – counsellors. If a client's need for affection and love is not being met outside the counselling situation, it is likely and even probable that he will direct his attentions to the counsellor. The counsellor's task is, of course, to resist any unprofessional involvement with the client, while at the same time giving him the best possible assistance to help him deal with his problems. It goes without saying that the counsellor who becomes sexually involved with a client is taking advantage of his transference feelings, and is selfishly satisfying her own needs at his expense.

Unfortunately, clients can be hurt in other ways too. Even the most conscientious counsellors are sometimes capable of behaviour which can cause problems for the people they sincerely wish to help. Perhaps one of the most common mistakes made is premature termination of therapy by the counsellor, a situation which can cause untold distress and anxiety to the client. What tends to happen in these instances is that there is a lack of proper communication between client and counsellor. On the one hand, the counsellor believes that the client has made progress and is ready to finish therapy; while on the other hand, the client's perception is quite different for he may feel that he needs more time in order to deal with his problems.

It goes without saying, that a situation like the one described is unlikely to happen when counsellors receive adequate supervision for their work. The point needs to be emphasized, however, that the counselling relationship is built on trust. When clients put their faith in counsellors, clumsy termination of therapy is unforgivable. Of course, lack of respect for clients is possible in numerous other ways; counsellors who do not adhere to appointment times, for example, are certainly guilty of breach of trust. Lack of clarity about money is another area of central concern;

counsellors who charge for private work should ensure that clients are aware of their terms in advance of therapy. They should also know if terms are fixed or negotiable, and whether there is any provision for special concessions (for example, for people on low income, those who are unemployed, or those who are retired or likely to become redundant).

Clients should be given sufficient time to acquire information about all aspects of therapy. Although it is impossible to anticipate every question which clients might wish to ask, the following is an outline of some of the areas which should be of interest to them.

- Counsellor qualification, training and method of working; experience and supervision details.

- How long therapy is likely to last, and how often the client should attend for sessions.

- Whether notes and records will be kept and whether the client can see them.

- What happens in the event of a missed appointment by the client – can another appointment be made?

- Will it be possible for the client to contact the counsellor between sessions?

- Details of how payments should be made.

- Details about any research which is being carried out by the counsellor (if this affects the client; whose permissions is, of course, needed).

It is impossible to be specific about the best time for imparting this information to clients, but sooner, rather than later, is the general rule. Ideally, a clear contract should be made with the client before counselling begins. This may be updated or revised by mutual agreement, but it remains as an important reference point for the work to be carried out between counsellor and client in the course of therapy.

COUNTERTRANSFERENCE

Countertransference could be described as the opposite of transference in the sense that it belongs to, and affects the counsellor, rather than the client. Counsellors are also susceptible to feelings, beliefs and attitudes – and other unconscious material – which stem from their own past relationships and experiences.

It is possible for clients to elicit a wide spectrum of feelings from their counsellor; some of these may be pleasant, while others may be unpleasant. Like transference, this is something which occurs in all relationships, and is certainly not peculiar only to counselling or the counsellor. However, countertransference feelings may become problematic, especially when they interfere with the primary focus of therapy which is to help the client deal more effectively with his/her difficulties. A client who is very dependent, for example, may elicit from the counsellor warm feelings of being needed and loved. These emotions obviously originate in the counsellor's own need for affection and attachment, and unless they are identified (through discussion in supervision, for example) they are likely to sabotage the client's progress. They could be instrumental in keeping the client in a dependent and vulnerable role. It is worth remembering that counsellors are often drawn to their work because they themselves have suffered in the past. Although such experience can be an asset when it comes to helping others, it needs to be clearly identified first, understood and, if possible, resolved or ameliorated. In a study of counsellors' negative past experiences and their effects on present counselling practice, James Farrell (1995) discovered that almost half the group with whom he conducted the research felt that 'the stresses experienced in their counselling practice bore a relationship to negative past experience, and there was a tendency to work to over-identify with the client, or there were feelings of countertransference'. A high level of self-awareness is essential if past problems are to be dealt with successfully in this way. Unless steps are taken through self-development, supervision and personal counselling when necessary, there is a likelihood that therapy with the client will be contaminated by the counsellor's own unresolved and unmet needs.

The following account was given by a counsellor who realized that transference and countertransference feelings were in danger of blurring the boundaries of her work with one particular client:

'My client was an eighteen year old girl whose mother had died when she was fifteen. She was suffering from depression, and felt increasingly alienated from her friends who talked about their mothers and their relationships with them. I worked with this client on a weekly basis, helping her to deal with issues of grief and feelings of low self-esteem often associated with adolescence and young adulthood. We spent a good deal of time looking at concerns relating to the transition from childhood to adult life, and as the counselling sessions progressed, I became aware that the issue of transference and countertransference was emerging quite strongly. I felt that my client was beginning to see me as a replacement mother; she saved all her decisions and minor problems until her appointment with me, and I could see that I wanted to take care of her, protect her and make these decisions for her. My own mother died when I was fifteen years old, and I could see myself in my client. I identified with all her problems, and was in danger of over-stepping the mark and making her dependent on me. Fortunately, I became aware, throughout supervision, of what was happening, and was able to continue working successfully with this client, and to see her as a totally separate individual who needed to gain confidence, independence and a belief in her own ability to cope while she benefited from my help and encouragement. She would certainly not have made any progress if I had continued to treat her as a helpless and vulnerable child.'

A significant point which is highlighted in this account is that the counsellor concerned was unaware of her countertransference feelings until these were identified through supervision. She had, at one stage, received counselling for her own bereavement, but even this kind of help does not guarantee that important experiences from the past will not impinge on the counsellor's current work with clients. Once countertransference issues are identified, however, they become easier to deal with in ways which do not inhibit client progress.

Student counsellors – especially those who are just at the beginning of their studies – often ask what is wrong with the kind of identification which this counsellor described in her account. Surely, they argue, it is the basis of real empathy when a counsellor identifies so strongly with a client in this way? The answer is that true empathy does not cause a blurring of boundaries, nor does it focus attention on the counsellor at the expense of the client and his needs. Counsellors should have an appreciation of the way clients feel, but this appreciation must look outward towards the client, and not inwards towards the counsellor and the counsellor's requirements.

We have already seen that it is crucial for counsellors to understand their client's transferred responses to them. It is equally important that they understand the corollary to this, which is the nature of their own responses to clients. The emergence of feelings which are difficult or impossible to explain means that counsellors need the help of professional supervision on a regular basis, to ensure that their work is carried out safely and with maximum benefit to clients.

However, it should be emphasized that the responses experienced by counsellors are not *invariably* related to their own emotional difficulties, past experiences or unmet needs. On the contrary, it is often the case that a counsellor's reactions are indicative of the reactions which a client generally produces in other people. Sometimes a client will provoke a certain reaction in almost everyone he meets; if this pattern is identified in counselling, a lot can be done to help him change those aspects of his behaviour which are causing problems for him, especially in relation to other people. The counselling relationship can, therefore, act as a mirror in which the client sees a reflection of all his relationships outside the therapeutic setting. The following is an example of how one client was helped in this way.

'People often told me that I made them feel "unsettled". I thought they meant that I was too active for them and I tended to despise them for their own lack of initiative and drive. My wife also complained about my constant activity, and my colleagues at work sometimes commented too. After the accident, I went for counselling, and one of the things the counsellor helped me to look at was the need to be active all the time. She could see I had difficulty sitting still in the chair and when we discussed this she told me how "unsettling" my behaviour was for her. I then looked more closely at myself, at my posture, my nervousness and my inability to just do nothing for more that a few minutes at a time. I could quite easily connect all this to events in my childhood, but the important thing for me was that the counsellor highlighted aspects of my behaviour and my relationships with other people which, in fact, needed to be addressed and understood. Before that, I just took the view that other people didn't have the kind of drive and energy which I was privileged to possess.'

Supervision: what is it?

Numerous references have been made, in previous chapters, to the subject of professional supervision and its importance in relation to good counselling practice. However, since the concept of supervision may be new to students who are just starting out in training, it is worth looking more closely at what it entails.

The practice of supervision has been in existence for a long time, and probably had its origins in the work carried out by Freud and his followers in the early part of this century. It is a process whereby the therapist is given the opportunity to discuss her work with a trained and experienced colleague, so that areas of concern or indecision are identified and guidance given where necessary. Supervision forms an essential part of client care and is therefore not an option which counsellors can make use of, when and if they wish. It is important for trained counsellors, as well as for trainees. The BAC Code of Ethics and Practice for counsellors makes it quite clear that 'it is a breach of the ethical requirements for counsellors to practise without regular counselling supervision/consultative support' (B.3.1, 1993).

Although supervision is mandatory for all counsellors who are working with clients, it is especially relevant to the needs of trainees. They are the people who are most likely to experience fears, anxieties and doubts, especially when they are beginning to work with clients. This is not to say that trained counsellors do not have similar experiences, but students who are at the start of their career are certain to want a great deal of support, suggestion and guidance for the counselling which they do. In addition to the needs of students, however, attention should be focused on the interest and well-being of the clients with whom they work. Clients need to be protected from damaging ineptitude on the learner's part, and professional supervision is one way of ensuring that clients' interests are safeguarded.

IN WHAT WAYS DOES SUPERVISION HELP THE COUNSELLOR?

Professional supervision helps counsellors in a number of important ways. In the first place, most conscientious practitioners are concerned to help and protect their clients, and regular supervision enables them to look at their work in a more objective, dispassionate and judicial way. The factors which make such an approach possible are the support, guidance and differing perspective which is offered by the supervisor. Supervision provides an opportunity for the counsellor to reflect on the work which she is doing with clients. During reflection, the counsellor should try to identify those areas of concern which may be clarified through discussion with another person. The skills and approach which the counsellor is using can also be highlighted in supervision, actual or potential difficulties identified, and encouragement or challenge given as and when appropriate.

Although the supervisor's principal task is to work on the client's behalf, there is a corresponding commitment to help and support the counsellor in the work she is doing. Another way of stating this is to say that the supervisor helps the counsellor to deliver a quality service to the client. In this way, professional standards and integrity are also maintained and the counsellor is given the opportunity to grow and develop personally, academically and in the area of counselling skills.

In more specific terms, the tasks of supervision include teaching, giving support and feedback, exchanging information, focusing attention on the therapeutic relationship between counsellor and client, and discussing the feelings which are evoked in the counsellor by the client (the counter-transference). The relationship between supervisor and counsellor is another point of interest, and will often serve to mirror or reflect certain aspects of the relationship between counsellor and client.

Consideration of all these areas will underline any problems or difficulties which the counsellor experiences in her work with clients. However, counsellors – especially students – also need to receive other things from professional supervision. As well as understanding and support, counsellors should have the kind of experience which is rewarding for them, both intellectually and emotionally. Effective supervision should also help the counsellor to feel more confident about her ability to work competently with clients; any anxiety which she has experienced in her work, should be addressed and modified throughout contact with her supervisor.

HOW DOES SUPERVISION DIFFER FROM COUNSELLING?

Supervision differs from counselling in several important respects. Perhaps the most significant point of difference is that the supervisor's task is to help the counsellor understand and deal with issues relating to clients. The supervisor is not, therefore, *directly* involved in helping the counsellor deal with personal problems, although there are occasional overlaps when it is difficult to differentiate between problems which belong to the client and those which belong to the counsellor. A counsellor might, for example, experience some difficulty in working with a client whose problem or problems are similar to those which she herself has encountered. The task for the supervisor in a situation like this is to help the counsellor identify her own countertransference feelings in relation to the client and, when appropriate, suggest to her that she might benefit from personal therapy. When a counsellor's personal issues have been re-awakened through contact with a client, it is important that these are discussed in supervision, and any remedial action recommended and undertaken. However, it is not the supervisor's responsibility to give counselling in these instances, although supervisors often do help counsellors to look at the overall effect which their current – or past – life experience is having on their work. The supervisor is not directly involved in the counsellor's training either, but one point of similarity between counselling and supervision is that of confidentiality. Both counselling and supervision are confidential in nature, and any professional discussions which take place outside the supervisory relationship should only be undertaken when issues of discipline or training for the counsellor require such discussion.

HOW MUCH SUPERVISION?

According to current British Association for Counselling recommendations 'the volume of supervision should be in proportion to the volume of counselling work undertaken and the experience of the counsellor' (*BAC Code of Ethics and Practice for Counsellors,* B.3.4, 1993). In other words, the amount of supervision which counsellors need depends on their experience and the amount of work they are doing. This obviously makes a great deal of sense, although it is not specific about the number of hours involved. At present, however, the minimum requirement for BAC accreditation of counsellors is one and a half hours of supervision per month. To a large extent, this has been taken up and used as a guide by training organizations for all counsellors who work with clients. This one and a half hour rule applies in one-to-one supervision situations, but supervision is also carried out in groups, and by peers; in these instances, time allocated will depend on the number of participants, and the experience which they have. Student counsellors should make a point of reading the BAC Code of Ethics and Practice for Counsellors, in particular the section which deals with supervision and issues relating to it. However, it is fair to say that students will need quite extensive supervision during their counsellor training.

THE SUPERVISORY RELATIONSHIP

The relationship between supervisor and counsellor needs to be positive if real benefit is to be gained from it. Respect and mutual trust are obviously important; so too are similarities of approach and background training. It goes without saying that a counselling supervisor should be well qualified in both theory and practice, and all aspects of the supervisory contract should be discussed with the counsellor before sessions begin. Apart from practical arrangements, supervisors should also be clear about their training, qualifications, theoretical approach, the methods they use and any other details which are relevant to their work with counsellors. See Figure 9.1 for methods of supervision.

EXERCISES

EXERCISE 1   CONFIDENTIALITY
Working in groups of two or three, discuss the various relationships in which confidentiality is a key factor – for example, between doctor and patient. Make a list of all these relationships, and say why you think confidentiality is an important component of them.

EXERCISE 2   LIMITS OF CONFIDENTIALITY
Working with a partner, make a list of all the situations in which absolute

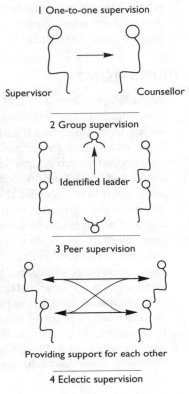

Fig. 9.1 *Methods of supervision.*

confidentiality might not be possible in counselling. Discuss your ideas with other members of the training group, highlighting any problematic areas of confidentiality which could be reviewed with a supervisor.

EXERCISE 3   STEREOTYPES

Working individually, look at the following list of occupations:

- lawyer
- tennis player
- priest
- chef
- sailor
- lorry driver
- care worker

- farmer
- policeman
- waitress
- nurse
- car salesman
- nun
- social worker

- teacher
- hairdresser
- tax inspector
- supermodel
- builder
- doctor

- What are your immediate responses to each of these occupations?

- Are there any which elicit really strong responses from you? If so, can you identify the origins of these reactions?

- Discuss your ideas with members of the training group, saying how you think stereotyping affects any relationships with other people.

EXERCISE 4   TRANSFERENCE

Transference plays a major part in the formation of important relationships. Working with a partner, discuss the problems which can arise in everyday relationships as a result of transferred responses. Some of the relationships you might look at include the following:

a) Husband–Wife
b) Employee–Employer
c) Teacher–Student
d) Patient–Doctor
e) Nurse–Patient

Consider the dynamics of each of these relationships, and say how you think the transference might work in more specific cases, for example male employer–female employee.

EXERCISE 5   POSITIVE RESPONSES

Working in groups of three or four, discuss individual experiences of positive responses to other people. Can anyone in the group recall a situation in which their immediate response to another person was totally positive? Then try to answer the following questions.

- What were the circumstances of the meeting?

- Why was the response positive?

- How did the other person react?

- Did the other person remind you of anyone else?

- Were there any similarities in both your backgrounds?

EXERCISE 6   COUNTERTRANSFERENCE

Working in groups of two or three, make a list of all those feelings which clients might elicit from counsellors during sessions. Identify those feelings which you think might work against client progress, and say how you think counsellors can deal with them.

EXERCISE 7   SUPERVISION

Working in pairs, look at the following questions and try to answer as many as possible. When you have finished, discuss your answers with members of the training group.

- What is supervision?

- How does supervision help counsellors?

- How does supervision differ from counselling?

- How often does supervision take place?

- How much does supervision cost?

- Who is qualified to supervise?

- Why are issues of confidentiality, privacy and trust important in relation to supervision?

- Why is it important for counsellors to be clear about what they want from supervision?

- What is the benefit of a contract between counsellor and supervisor?

- What should clients be told about the practice of supervision?

EXERCISE 8   METHODS OF SUPERVISION

Look at the following methods of supervision. With a partner, discuss the relative merits of each and any disadvantages which you think they might have.

a) individual supervision
b) group supervision
c) peer supervision
d) combination of methods

FURTHER READING

1 Dryden, Windy (ed.), *Key Issues for Counselling in Action*, Sage, London, 1993.
2 Nelson-Jones, Richard, *Practical Counselling and Helping Skills*, Cassell, London, 1988.
3 Ellin, Jeanne, *Listening Helpfully*, Souvenir Press, London, 1994.
4 Bond, Tim, *Standards and Ethics for Counselling in Action*, Sage, London, 1994.
5 Page, Steve and Wosket, Val, *Supervising the Counsellor*, Routledge, London, 1994.
6 Gray, Anne, *An Introduction to the Therapeutic Frame*, Routledge, London, 1994.
7 Hawkins, Peter and Shohet, Robin, *Supervision in the Helping Professions*, Open University Press, Milton Keynes, 1989.

REFERENCE LIST

1 *Code of Ethics and Practice for Counsellors*, B. 3.1 and B. 3.4, British Association for Counselling, London, 1993.
2 *Counselling Psychology Review*, Vol. 10, No. 1, The British Psychological Society, Leicester, March 1995.

3 *Training and Supervision for Counselling in Action* edited by Windy Dryden and Brian Thorne, Sage, London, 1991.

4 *Standards and Ethics for Counselling in Action* by Tim Bond, Sage, London, 1994.

5 *Supervising the Counsellor* by Steve Page and Val Wosket, Routledge, London, 1994.

6 *An Introduction to the Therapeutic Frame* by Anne Gray, Routledge, London, 1994.

7 *The Analytical Encounter – Transference and Human Relationships* by Mario Jacoby, Inner City Books, Toronto, 1984.

8 'A Study of Counsellors' Negative Past Experiences and Their Effect on Present Counselling Practice' by James Farrell (dissertation submitted in 1995 to the University of Manchester).

Relevant Names and Addresses

Association of Humanistic Psychology Practitioners
14 Hornington Grove, London E3 4NS (0181 983 1492)

British Association for Counselling
1 Regent Place, Rugby, Warwickshire CV21 1PJ (01788 550899)

British Association of Psychotherapists
37 Maplesbury Road, London NW2 4HJ (0181 452 9823)

British Psychological Society (BPS)
48 Princess Road East, Leicester LE1 7DR (0116 2549568)

Catholic Marriage Advisory Council
1 Blythe Mews, Blythe Road, London W14 ONW (0171 37 1341)

Central School of Counselling and Therapy
118–120 Charing Cross Road, London WC2H OJR (0171 836 1711)

Centre for Stress Management
156 Westcombe Hill, London SE3 7DH (0181 293 4114)

Cruse Bereavement Care
Cruse House, 126 Sheen Road, Richmond TW9 1UR (0181 940 4818)

European Association for Counselling
PO Box 82, Rugby, Warwickshire CV21 2AD (01788 546731)

Metanoia – Training in Counselling and Psychotherapy
13 North Common Road, Ealing, London W5 2QB (0181 579 2503)

MIND – National Association for Mental Health
Granta House, 15–19 Broadway, Stratford, London E15 4BQ (0181 519 2122)

Nafsiyat (Therapists and Counsellors from different ethnic and cultural backgrounds) 278 Seven Sisters Road, London N4 2HY (0171 263 4130)

POPAN – Prevention of Professional Abuse Network
Flat, 1, 20 Daleham Gardens, London NW3 5 DA (0171 749 3177)

Relate Marriage Guidance
Herbert Gray Cottage, Little Church Street, Rugby, Warwickshire (01788 573241)

Samaritans
17 Uxbridge Road, Slough SLI 1PQ (01753 32713)

Travistock Clinic – Adult Department
120 Belsize Lane, London NW3 5BA (0171 435 7111)

United Kingdom Council for Pyschotherapy
Regent's College, Inner Circle, Regent's Park, London NW1 4NS (0171 487 7554)

Victim Support
Cranmer House, 39 Brixton Road, Londcon SW9 6DZ (0171 735 9166)

Westminster Pastoral Foundation
23 Kensington Square, London W8 5HN (0171 937 6956)

Women's Therapy Centre
6 Manor Gardens, London N7 6LA (0171 263 6200)

Bibliography

ARGYLE, M, *Bodily Communication*, Methuen, London, 1975.

ARGYLE, M & COOK, M, *Gaze and Mutual Gaze*, Cambridge University Press, 1976.

ARGYLE, M, *The Psychology of Interpersonal Behaviour*, Penguin, London, 1983.

AVELINE, MARK, & WINDY DRYDEN, *Group Therapy in Britain*, Open University Press, Milton Keynes, 1988.

BENSON, JARLATH F, *Working More Creatively With Groups*, Tavistock, London, 1987.

BERNSTEIN, DOUGLAS, EDWARD ROY, THOMAS SRULL & CHRISTOPHER WICKER, *Psychology*, Houghton Mifflin & Co., Boston USA, 1988.

BOND, TIM, *Standards and Ethics for Counselling in Action*, Sage Publications, London, 1994.

BOWLBY, JOHN, *The Making and Breaking of Affectional Bonds*, Routledge, London, 1993.

BOWLBY, JOHN, *Loss, Sadness and Depression*, Hogarth Press, London, 1994.

BROOKFIELD, STEPHEN D, *Developing Critical Thinkers*, Open University Press, Milton Keynes, 1987.

BURKE, JOSEPH F, *Contemporary Approaches to Psychotherapy and Counselling*, Brookes/Cole, Monterey, USA, 1989.

BURNARD, PHILIP, *Counselling Skills for Health Professionals*, Chapman and Hall, London, 1989.

BURNARD, PHILIP, *Teaching Interpersonal Skills*, Chapman and Hall, London, 1991.

CLARKSON, PETRUSKA & MICHAEL POKORNY (eds.), *The Handbook of Psychotherapy*, Routledge, London, 1994.

CONYNE, ROBERTS K, *How Personal Growth and Task Groups Work*, Sage Publications, London, 1989.

COREY, GERALD, *Theory and Practice of Counselling and Psychotherapy*, Brookes/Cole, Monterey, USA, 1991.

DILLON, J T, *The Practice of Questioning*, Routledge, London, 1990.

DRYDEN, WINDY & BRIAN THORNE (eds.), *Training & Supervision for Counselling in Action*, Sage Publications, London, 1991.

DRYDEN, WINDY (ed.), *Individual Therapy – A Handbook*, Open University Press, Milton Keynes, 1991.

DRYDEN, WINDY (ed.), *Key Issues for Counselling in Action*, Sage Publications, London, 1993.

DRYDEN, WINDY (ed.), *Questions and Answers on Counselling in Action*, Sage Publications, London, 1993.

DRYDEN, WINDY (ed.), *Hard Earned Lessons From Counselling in Action*, Sage Publications, London, 1992.

DRYDEN, WINDY, & COLIN FELTHAM, *Counselling and Psychotherapy – A Consumer's Guide*, Sheldon Press, London, 1995.

EGAN, GERARD, *The Skilled Helper*, Brookes/Cole, Monterey, USA, 1990.

ELLIN, JEANNE, *Listening Helpfully*, Souvenir Press, London, 1994.

ELLIS, ALBERT, *Reason and Emotion in Psychotherpay*, Citadel Press Carol Publishing, New York, 1991.

ERIKSON, ERIK, *Childhood and Society* (2nd ed.), Norton, New York, 1963.

EVANS, PETER & GEOFF DEEHAN, *The Keys To Creativity*, Grafton Books, London, 1990.

FONTANA, DAVID, *Social Skills at Work*, The British Psychological Society & Routledge, London, 1992.

GRAY, ANNE, *An Introduction to the Therapeutic Frame*, Routledge, London, 1994.

HARGIE, OWEN, CHRISTINE SAUNDERS & DAVID DICKSON, *Social Skills in Interpersonal Communication*, Routledge, London, 1995.

HAWKINS, PETER, & ROBIN SHOHET, *Supervision in the Helping Professions*, Open University Press, Milton Keynes, 1989.

HAYES, NICKY, *Principles of Social Psychology*, Laurence Erlbaum Associates Ltd, Sussex, 1993.

HOBSON, ROBERT F, *Forms of Feeling*, Tavistock/Routledge, London, 1987.

HORNEY, KAREN, *Our Inner Conflicts*, W W Norton & Co., London, 1972.

HOUGH, MARGARET, *A Practical Approach to Counselling*, Pitman, London, 1994.

HURDING, ROGER F, *Roots and Shoots*, Hodder & Stoughton, London, 1985.

JACOBS, MICHAEL, *Insight and Experience*, Open University Press, Milton Keynes, 1991.

JACOBY, MARIO, *The Analytical Encounter – Transference and Human Relationships*, Inner City Books, Toronto, Canada, 1984.

KEANE, COLM, *Nervous Breakdown*, Mercier Press, Dublin, 1995.

KEANE, COLM, *Death and Dying*, Mercier Press, Dublin, 1995.

KENNEDY, EUGENE, *On Becoming A Counsellor*, Gill & MacMillan, New York, 1977.

KNIGHT, LINDSAY, *Talking to a Stranger*, Hodder & Stoughton, London, 1995.

LAKE, TONY, & FRAN ACHESON, *Room to Listen, Room to Talk*, Bedford Square Press (in association with BBC Radio 4), London, 1988.

LEICK, NINI, & MARIANNE DAVIDSEN-NIELSEN, *Healing Pain*, Routledge, London, 1991.

LONG, PARADISE & LONG, *Questioning Skills for the Helping Process*, Brookes/Cole, Monterey, USA, 1981.

MCKAY, MATTHEW & PATRICK FANNING, *Self-Esteem*, New Harbinger Publications, Oakland, Cal, USA, 1988.

MCLEOD, JOHN, *An Introduction to Counselling*, Open University Press, Milton Keynes, 1993.

MARSH, DR PETER, *Eye To Eye*, Guild, London, 1988.

MASLOW, ABRAHAM, *Motivation and Personality*, Harper & Row, New York, 1970.

MASSON, JEFFRY, *Against Therapy*, Fontana/Collins, London, 1989.

MASSON, JEFFRY, *Final Analysis*, Fontana, London, 1992.

MAY, ROLLO, *The Art of Counselling*, Souvenir Press, London, 1992.

MUNRO, ANNE, BOB MANTHEI & JOHN SMALL, *Counselling: The Skills of Problem Solving*, Routledge, London, 1989.

MURTGATROYD, STEPHEN, *Counselling and Helping*, The British Psychological Society & Methuen, London, 1985.

MURPHY, PM & GA KUPSHIK, *Loneliness, Stress and Well-Being*, Routledge, London, 1992.

MYERS, GAIL, & MICHELE TOHELA MYERS, *The Dynamics of Human Communication*, McGraw-Hill Book Company, USA, 1973.

NELSON-JONES, RICHARD, *Lifeskills – A Handbook*, Cassell, London, 1992.

NELSON-JONES, RICHARD, *You Can Help*, Cassell, London, 1993.

NELSON-JONES, RICHARD, *Training Manual for Counselling and Helping Skills*, Cassell, London, 1993.

O'FARRELL, URSULA, *First Steps in Counselling*, Veritas, Dublin, 1995.

OLDFIELD, SUSAN, *The Counselling Relationship*, Routledge & Kegan Paul, London, 1993.

OLIVER, ROBERT W, *Psychology and Health Care*, Bailliere Tindall, London, 1993.

PAGE, STEVE, & VAL WOSKET, *Supervising the Counsellor*, Routledge, London, 1994.

PARKS, COLIN MURRAY, JOAN STEVENSON-HINDE & PETER MARRIS (eds.), *Attachment Across the Life Cycle*, Routledge, London, 1993.

PINES, MALCOLM (ed.), *Bion and Group Therapy*, Tavistock Routledge, London, 1992.

PEASE, ALLAN, *Body Language*, Sheldon Press, London, 1989.

READER, A (edited by Oswold Hanlfing), *Life and Meaning*, Blackwell, Oxford, 1987.

RICHTER, HORST E, *The Family as Patient*, Souvenir Press, London, 1993.

ROGERS, CARL, *On Becoming a Person*, Constable, London, 1991.

ROGERS, CARL, *Client-Centred Therapy*, Constable, London, 1991.

SKYNNER, AC ROBIN, *Explorations With Families, Group Analysis & Family Therapy*, Tavistock Routledge, London, 1990.

SKYNNER, AC ROBIN, *One Flesh: Separate Persons*, Constable, London, 1990.

SPURLING, ROBERT (ed.), *From the Words of My Mouth*, Tavistock/Routledge, London, 1993.

STOCK-WHITACKER, DOROTHY, *Using Groups to Help People*, Routledge, London, 1992.

TATELBAUM, JUDY, *The Courage to Grieve*, Cedar Press (Heinemann Ltd), London, 1988.

WICKS, ROBERT J, *Helping Others*, Souvenir Press, London, 1994.

YALOM, IRWIN D, *Existence Psychotherapy*, HarperCollins, USA, 1980.

Index